Reproducible Pastoral Training

Church Planting Guidelines from the Teachings of George Patterson

Reproducible Pastoral Training

Church Planting Guidelines from the Teachings of George Patterson

Patrick O'Connor

William Carey Library
Pasadena, California
www.WCLBooks.com

Reproducible Pastoral Training: Church Planting Guidelines from the Teachings of George Patterson

Cover design: Amanda Valloza

Drawings: Justin Long

Typesetting: Galen Currah

Published by William Carey Library

1605 E. Elizabeth Street, Pasadena, California 91104

www.WCLBooks.com

William Carey Library is a ministry of the U.S. Center for World Mission, Pasadena, California.

Printed in the United States of America

Library of Congress Cataloging-in-Publication Data

O'Connor, John Patrick.
 Reproducible pastoral training : church-planting guidelines from the teachings of George Patterson / John Patrick O'Connor.
     p. cm.
 Includes bibliographical references and index.
 ISBN 0-87808-367-7 (alk. paper)
 1. Church development, New. 2. Missions--Cross-cultural studies.

3. Intercultural communication--Religious aspects--Christianity.
4. Christianity and culture. 5. Missions--Study and teaching.
6. Church growth. 7. Evangelistic work. 8. Patterson, George, 1932- I. Patterson, George, 1932- II. Title.

BV652.24.O26 2006

254'.1--dc22

2006002108

Endorsements

"Patrick O'Connor has accomplished the missiological version of crossing Niagara Falls on a tightrope while blindfolded; he has written an organized presentation of the principles for building up indigenous churches, without turning it into another fad system. Bravo!"

Gene Daniels, Author
In Search of the Indigenous Church: A Missionary Pilgrimage

"O'Connor has provided us with a great tool that will help guide thousands of church planters in launching healthy, growing congregations.

Geoff Tunnicliffe, International Director
World Evangelical Alliance

"The cost of missions is rising. The numbers of international workers from North America are shrinking. If there was ever a day when stewardship demanded that we leverage our resources, it is today. The principles of *Reproducible Pastoral Training* will make that happen."

Paul Seger, General Director
Biblical Ministries Worldwide

"The biblical principles I learned from Patterson directly affected the seventy-two Buddhist background house churches that we have seen established in Myanmar and Burma during the past three years."

A Strategy Coordinator, Burma

"It's been said that Christianity is always one generation from extinction. The proliferation of spiritual leaders is a crying need worldwide. *Reproducible Pastoral Training* shows churches in any culture how to leave a legacy of equipped spiritual leaders."

Jerry Rueb, Pastor
Cornerstone Church, Long Beach, California

"*Reproducible Pastoral Training* is an impressive, up-to-date manual on church planting that should be studied by all who are involved in church planting movements. The principles laid are universal and scriptural."

Victor Choudhrie, MD,
Nagpur, India

"Combining years of experience in the area of training leaders to multiply churches with a broad knowledge of scholarship in the field, O'Connor has given us an excellent reference for all who seek to increase their skill and knowledge in the crucial area. As a practitioner and as a teacher, I look forward to using *Reproducible Pastoral Training* to mentor, coach, and teach others."

Mikel Neumann, Professor
Western Seminary

"This reader-friendly book is a goldmine of information on effective church planting from two men who have been doing it for years. Whether you're a church planter or church leader with a passion for reaching the lost, you can't get any more practical than this!"

Rad Zdero, Author
The Global House Church Movement

"O'Connor has provided church planters around the globe a must-have resource. This material is dynamite. We used these principles to start Mongolia's first indigenous church planting movement. Don't leave home without it!"

Brian Hogan, Church Planting Coach
Youth with a Mission

"In 1974, I wandered into the Honduran home of George and Denny Patterson. They took a raw, inexperienced and untrained young man and taught me biblical, common sense ways of being a discipler and church planter. I've applied those principles everywhere the Lord has led me and they have not failed me. Nor will they fail you."

Jonathan Lewis,
International Missionary Training Network,
Mission Commission, and World Evangelical Alliance

Contents

Figures and Tables

Table

Guidelines

Foreword

I appreciate Patrick O'Connor's compilation of these church planting and training guidelines. He has shown painstaking perseverance while wading through piles of boring stuff, gleaning and organizing it. In compiling the topics in a useful order, he recovered many lost gems that I had forgotten. He also brings a fresh view from the field where he is currently immersed in church planting while training Christian leaders.

One of many missionaries whom I have mentored through the years, he has applied well what I taught him, but not blindly. For years he has adapted these guidelines to a neglected area of rural western Honduras where the Lord has birthed healthy church planting movements in a number of regions.

When Patrick first sent me his compilation of my writings and musings, I feared I would find in it some theories that I once taught but no longer affirm. To my relief, I found that he had weeded wisely. The guidelines that he retained should apply anywhere people are reasonably receptive to the gospel.

Some readers might seek more specific methods, but years of mentoring have convinced me that detailed methods that work well in one field seldom apply precisely and specifically to another. Mission strategists sometimes impair church planters' effectiveness by enticing them into importing rigid rules from other cultures.

I also want to recognize the editing and coaching of my friend and colleague, Galen Currah, who has assisted me with much of what I have written over the past several years, wisely tweaking many of my hastily-stated views. Thank you, Galen.

I pray that the Almighty will enable many of you to apply these biblical guidelines to multiplying flocks and leaders in neglected fields, as you extend the Kingdom of our Lord and Savior, Jesus Christ.

George Patterson
Sebring, Florida

A Daughter's Testimony

Years ago, when my father, George Patterson, went to Honduras, the country was ripe for spiritual harvest, especially in the rural areas. Although people considered themselves to be Catholic, the Catholic Church did not have the resources to put priests in most villages, and most villagers rarely saw a priest more than once or twice a year. They had neither the animist beliefs of the Indian population nor the Mass of the Catholic Church to channel their spiritual hunger, so when they heard the gospel presented plainly and honestly, they responded by the thousands.

My father began to visit homes in the rural villages of the Olancho and Colon regions, concentrating on heads of households. When people responded to the gospel, he baptized them and recognized them as flocks—real flocks—that served the sacraments and ordained leaders. The first man he baptized was killed with a machete in his own home, his faith a cause of violence. At his funeral, many of his family members turned to Christ, and a church was born. I remember when my father came back from that village with machete slashes in the seat of his motorcycle. The gospel was resisted, but could not be withstood.

To make disciples of new church leaders, my father introduced a reproducible system of equipping the saints. He had been turning over in his mind the difficulty in getting semi-literate men to study Scripture. One day, while sitting on a train and looking around, he noticed passengers reading the photo-novels and comic books that are popular in less-educated societies around the world. The light came on. He started extension classes in the leaders' homes, using pocket-sized, comic-illustrated study booklets that elders-in-training could immediately apply and disseminate to their own disciples. My father wrote the studies and found cartoonists to bring them to life.

Occasionally, leaders added to the curriculum by writing their own booklets. Flocks multiplying under this reproducible style of training quickly outnumbered older, more traditional flocks, and the movement could not be stopped.

On a personal note, I was privileged to grow up in a great movement of people turning to God all around me on the north coast of Honduras. I was fortunate to know great Honduran Christian servant-leaders and watch ordinary believers freed up to plant church after church within their own culture and beyond. It was a privilege for me to see the Spirit poured out among those new flocks of northern Honduras, and to this day, that vision helps shape my hope of what the church can be.

The Western church has seen phenomenal growth in the past and may see it again. But currently it is obvious that the Spirit's time has come to multiply the church in the non-Western world in ways seldom seen in the West. This should humble us Western church planters and prod us to see that we do not have all the answers; we risk hindering the Spirit's work by trying to keep control over pioneer fields. We should look to young flocks, fresh with the zeal and fire of the Spirit's outpouring, for hope and renewed faith, gleaning from them both vision and encouragement!

The New Testament church grew wildly, unexpectedly and uncontrollably, reproducing itself throughout the then-known world, turning it upside down. The same startling work of God is happening in many pioneer fields today where the Holy Spirit is reminding believers what the church can be and do. This was my experience in Honduras, and it is my prayer that this compilation of my father's writings will serve you well as you take part in the Lord's harvest.

Annie Patterson Thiessen
Oaxaca, Mexico

Preface

My wife, Deborah, and I are grateful to have been mentored by George and Denny Patterson since the 1980s. We shall never forget their love and friendship. I am especially indebted to George who coached me as the Lord raised up an authentic church planting movement in rural Honduras.

The Pattersons worked for some twenty years until the mid-1980s in northern Honduras where they were instrumental in birthing a movement of new churches. Since then, George has consulted around the globe. When my wife, young daughter, and I moved to Honduras during the early 1990s, our mission board's challenge to us was to replicate the "Patterson model" in another region. So we moved to western Honduras where the Lord has graciously brought forth a vibrant movement of new churches.

The idea for this book occurred to me during an informal chat with George in which we were interacting on some tough field issues. As I furiously scribbled notes on what he was saying, I could not shake the question forming in the back of my mind, "Why is this not written down in book form?" Now, after more than a decade of applying George's counsel here in western Honduras, I am finally able to bring much of his advice to light through the present work. Thus, this book is not so much an attempt to present one person's missiology as an attempt to elaborate a radically-biblical approach to reproducible pastoral training.

I enjoyed compiling this book! It proved wonderfully stimu-lating, refining my approach to the missionary task. I offer these guidelines not as theory for study but as practical guidelines for cross-cultural service. These action-oriented guidelines were not contrived in an academic greenhouse, but were hammered out in the field by Patterson and others. Much of this material has been proved not only in Honduras but around the globe by hundreds of workers.

While the layout of the book approximates a start-to-finish order for sparking church planting movements into existence, one should not try to follow the precise order. Wise church planters respond to local circumstances while seeking the guidance of the Holy Spirit. Guidelines are, admittedly, ideal generalizations that must be applied by imperfect people under vastly differing field conditions. Also less than ideal is my choice to employ the English generic pronouns, he, him and his.

Many thanks to George for spending scores of hours fine-tuning the text for publication. Also, deep appreciation to Galen Currah, who provided invaluable editing and typesetting. Finally, those who have read George's *Church Multiplication Guide* are familiar with his "talking birds" that have again been pressed into service.

My heart's prayer is that you will find encouragement, help and timely insight as you apply biblical truth to gathering the rapidly ripening harvest. May the Lord of the harvest Himself raise up and empower the workers whom you will train for the task!

Patrick O'Connor
Siguatepeque, Honduras

I heard a human say there is only one way to start new flocks—his way!

Isn't the Almighty a bit more creative than that?

Chapter 1

Gather New Flocks

Guideline 1
Permit the setting to shape your methods.

I have read "New Flocks in Twelve Easy Flaps" by Dr. Simplicity. I will follow his neat, flap-by-flap recipe!

Wait! It is not as logically consistent as you would like! No such formula fits all flocks. Let us learn about the dynamic, spiritual nature of a new flock's birth...

Building congregations that reproduce within a culture is a dynamic process with unpredictable factors, including the mystical work of the Holy Spirit. No single working formula fits all field conditions. A church body is not an organization put together by applying certain proven steps. Rather it originates through church planters who apply what they have learned by experience where the Lord is at work in the lives of new believers, drawing them together and connecting them as a spiritual organism. Patterson observed:

When I first went to the mission field, I followed a list of steps that others had prepared for church planers. Church planting manuals proliferated offering linear approaches such as "seven phases of church planting." I gleaned valuable insights from such manuals, but found it impossible to stick to rigidly-ordered steps, because local needs did not permit doing so. Eventually I found true what a friend shared with me: "Church planting depends more on the love and faithfulness of Christ's servants than on following a list of principles."

Let the Holy Spirit guide the process of gathering the Lord's flock, for spiritual dynamics transcend human definitions and pre-conceived steps. Each embryonic church follows a different path to maturity. A congregation filled with God's Spirit will practice the vibrant church body life described in the New Testament. That life comes through the grace and power of the Lord of the harvest, and it soon reproduces. It is more than a gathering of sincere believers. The Holy Spirit breathes life into such groups, creating a living, dynamic organism, a body whose members follow a harmonious design.

Guideline 2
Let the right people do the work.

Who should gather a new flock? Who should lead it?	That depends on field conditions. Let us consider some examples from God's Word...

At least five types of people gather new congregations and lead them: These include swarms of believers, founding pastors, mother churches, apostolic bands, and missionaries from outside.

1. *A swarm* (see Figure 1). Like those who fled Jerusalem following Stephen's martyrdom, a number of believers may separate from a mother church to start a daughter church nearby in their same

culture. Some have called this hiving or swarming, because it resembles a new queen bee leaving an overcrowded hive with a swarm of bees. Many of the persecuted believers from the first flock in Jerusalem fled and reproduced as new flocks in surrounding cities, and as far away as Antioch of Syria.

Figure 1
Swarm Method

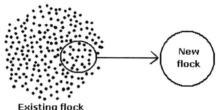

Existing flock

Normally, church planters from an urban mother church take with them a swarm of members, enough to form a critical mass. This should include enough people to begin worshipping and doing from the start all the activities that their mother church does, avoiding an embryonic phase of their development.

Occasionally people leave a church in frustration and start a new flock. Perhaps some believers feel that a leader has limited what they think that the Lord wants them to do, so they leave. Wise leaders can avoid such a painful divorce by recognizing potential leaders and encouraging them to start daughter churches or cells with the blessing and aid of the parent flock.

We're tired of being pushed around,
so let's form our own flock!

2. *Founding Pastors* (see Figure 2). Christian workers, such as Aquila and Priscilla, move into a neglected community, start a flock and shepherd it. Sometimes, helpers accompany them. Aquila and Priscilla started, helped to start, and hosted new flocks in their home in Rome, Corinth and Ephesus, where they went with Paul (Rom 16:3-5; Acts 18:1-5; 18-19; 1 Cor 16:19). They set the biblical pattern of tentmakers, a business approach to church planting.

Figure 2
Founding-Pastor Method

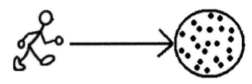

3. *Mother churches* (see Figure 3). Church planters from a nearby parent flock, like the church at Joppa, start a new flock. Six believers from the congregation in Joppa accompanied Peter to Caesarea (Acts 11:5-12). The workers normally train local leaders to shepherd the new flock while they themselves remain as members of their parent flock and visit the new work. Often an experienced worker leads or encourages volunteers who do the work, as Peter did with the workers from Joppa.

Figure 3
Mother-Church Method

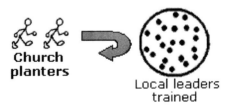

Church planters

Local leaders trained

Such mother churches are common in church planting movements in pioneer fields. The most effective church planting teams normally consist of members of a nearby mother church of the same culture. Workers from a parent flock evangelize, make disciples, and mentor the new flock's leaders. These church planters remain members of their mother congregation and return to it. They seldom stay on in the new flock.

4. *Apostolic bands* (see Figure 4). Experienced workers may form a church planting team or task group. They may belong to several cooperating flocks that seek to reproduce as new flocks in neglected communities. Some, like Paul, Barnabas and Silas, traveled far. Such apostolic works came to be called "missionaries" in Latin-speaking lands. Apostles can be described as "having itchy feet," always eager to move on to new areas. Apostles start the first few flocks in a region, leaving those flocks to carry on the process of multiplication to reach their entire region. Like the mother-church method, this approach normally mobilizes workers from nearby flocks to help plant new ones.

Figure 4
Traveling-Apostles Method

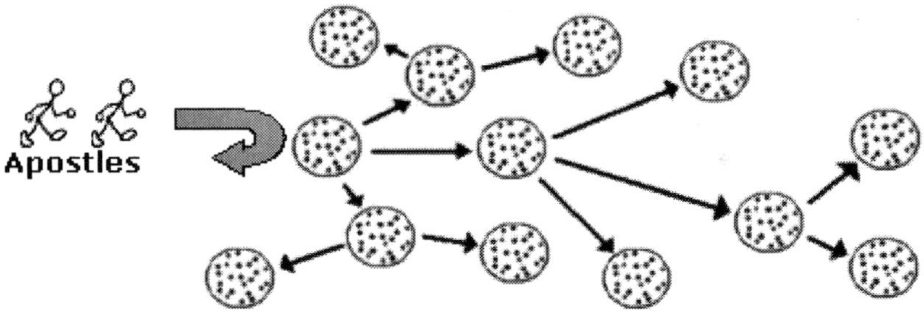

Apostles

In the New Testament era, apostles started only the first few flocks in a region. These flocks completed the task by continuing to multiply daughter churches nearby after the apostles had left. Wherever the apostles made disciples in the way Jesus said, flocks multiplied. The same happens today where a population proves reasonably receptive and missionaries teach disciples from the beginning to obey Jesus' commands, just as He ordered in his Great Commission (Matt 28:18-20). This method is also common in church planting movements where workers are involved with people of the same culture.

In a sense, those sent out as apostles carry their sending church's genetic code, its spiritual DNA, to a neglected people group. They sow that DNA as seed among receptive people, those whom Jesus called "good soil." The living Body of Christ exercises her God-given power to reproduce after her own kind. Strictly speaking, it is the church itself, the living Body of Christ that reproduces; neither the workers nor a mission agency begets churches. Church planters from outside a community or culture serve merely as spiritual "midwives," helping flocks to give birth to new flocks. As Paul expressed to a new flock in Corinth, "So I will very gladly spend for you everything I have and expend myself as well" (2 Cor 12:15).

Church planters from outside the community should consider themselves expendable servants, like temporary scaffolding. Phil Parshall wrote: "The missionary must move on as soon as possible after worshipping groups have been established. ... The missionary must keep before him constantly the imperative of pressing on to new frontiers."[1] Thus, the Kingdom of Heaven grows and multiplies, just as Jesus said it would in some of his parables, in a way similar to that of grain.

5. *Outsiders* (see Figure 5). Professional church planters and pastors may be called in from the outside to plant a church. A traveling church planter often starts a flock that will later call a pastor from outside of the community. Although Scripture does not depict this model, it has proven successful where believers are accustomed to the tradition of calling professional pastors from outside their local church body.

Church planters may combine two or more of the above models, like Peter did. He was a traveling apostle (see Figure 4) who mobilized workers from the nearby parent church at Joppa to help start a new flock in Caesarea (see Figure 3).

---

[1] Ralph D. Winter and Steven C. Hawthorne, eds., *Perspectives on the World Christian Movement—A Reader* (Pasadena: William Carey Library, 1981), 480-81.

Figure 5
Outsider Method

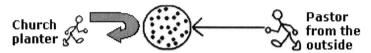

Church
planter   Pastor
                                                from the
                                                outside

Any of the five church-planting models
might give good results in a particular
project. None of them fits all projects.

Guideline 3
Follow proven guidelines to gather flocks.

What must we do first?   Let us see what
What spiritual gifts do we need   guidelines the New
to gather a flock?   Testament offers...

The Apostle Peter finally got it right. In Acts 10, the birth of a
new flock in Caesarea recounts the activities of Peter and his helpers
from Joppa. Some of those activities include the following:

- *Pray.* Peter and Cornelius were both praying when the Lord
  began to work.

- *Embrace the culture of the people you serve.* Emilio Nuñez in
  Guatemala City counsels new missionaries, "Live at an adequate
  level, neither too high above us nor too low below us. Adapt
  your lifestyle to the people with whom you work."[2] The Holy

---

[2] Emilio A. Nuñez C. and William D. Taylor, *Crisis in Latin America—An Evangelical Perspective* (Chicago: Moody Press, 1989), 416-18.

One of Israel prepared Peter to eat unclean food in a non-Jewish home. Such adaptation can be fun or it can be painful. Like Peter, cross-cultural church planters need Heaven's help to filter out their own cultural prejudice. One who thinks he has no cultural prejudice will trigger grim misunderstanding. A South Asian leader years ago pleaded to Westerners that new congregations "must be indigenous from the beginning. Care must be taken to plant indigenous churches. Everyone knows that the church in every land must be a church *of* that land and that culture."[3]

- *Form a temporary task group.* Peter took co-workers from Joppa with him, a standard apostolic practice.

- *Work through a man of peace.* Peter and his helpers found Cornelius who, although an army captain, was a God-fearing man of peace who received God's messengers and put them in touch with others of his social circle. Jesus told His disciples to seek out such hospitable people when they visited other communities (Lk 10:5-7). When starting a new church or cell group in the home of a man of peace or a new believer, do not let Satan make you flee, at the first bit of opposition, into a rented building or the home of a missionary. James 4:7 teaches sharply, "Resist the devil and he will flee from you." Stick with it. Deal with paganism's counterattacks within the homes and within the culture, lest you start a culturally irrelevant work that fails to attract entire families.

- *Present Jesus first to the family and friends of those who receive you.* Peter's team met only with Cornelius' family and intimate friends. Had Peter gone about the town inviting everybody, he would have missed meeting with the receptive circle of people that the Almighty had prepared. Evangelism through such exclusive meetings has proven most effective in many church planting movements.

---

[3] B. V. Subbamma, *New Patterns for Discipling Hindus* (Pasadena: William Carey Library, 1970), 92.

- *Relate the news of the death and resurrection of Jesus.* Peter told the simple gospel story and left it to the Holy Spirit to apply those historical and redemptive events to convince sinners. The apostles always told the story of Jesus' death and resurrection. Many Westerners neglect proclaiming Jesus' resurrection when they present Jesus, whereas the apostles always made it the main point of their testimony. Missionaries today may first need to create understanding of redemptive concepts by telling stories from the Old Testament or by relating analogies from the local lore or way of life.

- *Confirm repentance with baptism.* Peter did not delay baptism when he saw that the seekers had received the Holy Spirit.

- *Continue making disciples of the believers and coaching their leaders* (see Figure 6). Peter and his helpers stayed for a few days to establish the new church. D. L. Moody remarked that he would rather set ten men into motion than to attempt to do the work of ten men, as some often do.[4] Discipleship multiplies the labor force.

---

[4] Andrew T. LePeau, *Paths of Leadership* (Downers Grove: Inter-Varsity Press, 1983), 49.

Figure 6
Training Leaders to Serve Churches

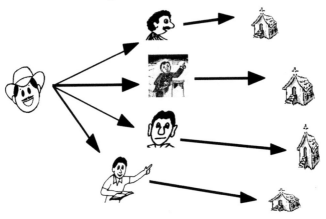

Oh, no!

Church is not a place. It is a body of believers who do what Jesus Christ commands, because they love Him.

Listening passively to prayers and sermons is nowhere commanded.

How should we define "church"?

My cousin said that it is where you go to hear inspiring hymns, prayers and sermons.

Rely on God's power and gifting. Wise church planting team leaders do not enforce detailed lists of activities required to gather a flock. Let workers use their various God-given gifts to start a church. Patterson observed:

Each Honduran worker had his own emphasis that he used to plant churches. All of the men presented Jesus, but their evangelism was part of their other ministries and was not an isolated effort.

Armando was a first-rate mentor who had a gift of exhortation. He and his co-workers used our pastoral training program, tied as it was to evangelism, to start flocks.

Gerardo loved to tell others about the Lord. He used personal witnessing as his main church planting tool, while he sold clothing from door to door.

Ricardo loved to help poor people find better employment. He and his co-workers taught woodworking and developed small businesses to gather flocks.

Pablo had gigantic faith. He and his helpers gathered seekers by praying for their healing.

Moncho loved God's Word. He and his helpers started flocks by teaching the Bible in depth.

Humberto was musical. He and his helpers gathered flocks by leading worship with heart-touching songs in seekers' homes.

Effective cross-cultural work requires help from the Lord. Had He not prepared Peter, for example, to work in another culture, Peter would have brought his Jewish practices into Caesarea as an unworkable model of discipleship.

What steps must we follow to gather a flock?

What must we do first?

The order to follow depends on local conditions.

Let us look at more guidelines...

Study different models, but not to import them in their exact form. Rather, glean from them underlying principles that are consistent with New Testament teaching. Ask the Most High to help you adapt these guidelines to the local culture. Incorporate procedures from other workers' models that use the spiritual gifts that he and his co-workers have.

Let church organization develop not from a preconceived ideology or structure, but from relationships as they grow with God's help. Patterson commented:

> At first I followed traditional practices because they were popular and logical, and because they would have set me up as leader in control of a movement, with power and prestige. I prayed for success in this venture, but failed—many times. I then prayed a very different prayer, "Lord, I no longer care about my own ministry, my success or my position. I ask only that You make my pastoral students successful in their ministry, and let me serve them." The Almighty answered this prayer and has done so ever since.

Start daughter churches from mother churches. In pioneer fields, church planters should aim at fostering a church planting movement. Although a team of outsiders may start the first few congregations, it is these young mother churches that reproduce daughter and granddaughter churches, birthing chains of new churches. It is the Lord who makes it happen, not the church planter. The church planter's part includes the following general guidelines:

- *Show your disciples what to do.* Let them observe and imitate you (1 Cor 11:1; Phil. 3:7).

- *Tell about the Lord first to heads of households.* Reach entire families. Go first where you or your co-workers have friends or relatives. Visit them in their homes. Do not simply hold public meetings. Do not overuse the word "personal" to describe faith in the sense of its being something private. While it requires an individual decision, an overemphasis on privacy can destroy your ability to work through families and networks of friends. The Lord does not view seekers as isolated individuals. Jesus let Zacchaeus and Levi gather their friends at once, in order to let the gospel flow to many. Likewise, the apostles always went at once to seekers' families.

- *Avoid preaching points or missions that are not real churches.* Sometimes outside workers merely preach weekly without forming a congregation that obeys Jesus' commands, including those about the sacraments, and without developing local leaders. Start obedient churches instead of mere *preaching points* by doing the following:

  Baptize repentant believers without delaying because of man-made requirements, and celebrate communion.

  Avoid having a new student or novice shepherd preach publicly. Let him first learn to witness in homes and to make disciples of newly-believing families. Have him witness to heads of families and disciple them. Have him baptize men with their families when possible, as soon as they repent and believe in the Lord. Have him teach believers from the beginning to obey Jesus' commands in love (Jn 14:15).

  Train local leaders from the beginning to gather and shepherd their family and their own flock. Training local leaders in their context should be the goal of every church planter (Ti 1:5, Acts 14:23). Missionary to the Philippines, David White, said, "A key to rapid church growth is to disciple new believers in a context in which *they* are comfortable, rather than bringing them into a context where *we* are comfortable."[5]

  Avoid weekly worship meetings for people who do not yet know Jesus, for unbelievers cannot yet worship in spirit and in truth (Jn 4:24).

- *Name mature adults as leaders, with more than one elder in each flock if possible* (Acts. 14.23). Give these men the responsibility for further growth and edification of the group. If they are new and unproven, designate them as provisional elders, because they do not yet meet biblical requirements for perman-

---

[5] David A. White, *Your Church Can Multiply* (Mandaluyong City: Philippine Challenge, 2000).

ent overseers. Let them begin at once to shepherd their own families.

- *Mentor new leaders for as long as they or their flocks need it.* Train them in a way that they can imitate, so that they can train others immediately. Show them what they must do. Let them take on more responsibility as they study and practice shepherding. If a number of potential leaders need mentoring, then spend time with one or two of the best ones first and let them mentor the others in turn.

- *Hold regular public worship meetings only when local leaders can lead them.* Seeing an outsider leading the meetings can brand the new church as a foreign religion. Inexperienced leaders should not practice pulpit oratory at first. Instead, they should serve the Lord's Supper, have testimonies, read Scripture, tell stories from the Bible, ask questions, exhort, sing, pray and direct the flock's other activities. If they have the gift of leadership, they will lead well, provided that someone mentors them until they gain more experience. Let new workers lead without interference. Outside workers should not step in and lead the flocks that new leaders have been commissioned to lead. At this stage, an outsider should instruct a flock indirectly by teaching its novice leaders and letting them pass the Word on to their own flock. To let an outsider lead or teach a new shepherd's flock in his place would weaken his ministry, for it draws attention to the outsider. By letting the novice leaders lead daughter churches, a mother church does not lose its own experienced leaders to the daughter church, and both flocks grow faster. Patterson recalled:

  > We commissioned a new shepherd in a village to oversee, baptize and serve communion. I returned later to mentor him and found that a missionary who had worked there previously had returned for a brief visit. Some believers asked him to baptize them, stating publicly that they preferred the missionary do it instead of their novice pastor. When the missionary baptized them, it devastated the new leader who resigned in frustration and disappointment. I have seen the same kind of thing happen in a number of fields with equally damaging effects.

Don't we need to budget lots of money? Don't we need to get the right equipment, first?	Keep it simple! Let us simply go where Jesus said to go and do what He said to do!

- *Cheer on new flocks to establish daughter churches without undue delay.* As soon as a flock is born, church planters should help it to reproduce new flocks nearby. So doing can soon bring about the birth of granddaughters of the mother church. Here are some hints that can help to reproduce daughter and granddaughter churches or cell groups:

Do not let their enthusiasm cool. Encourage new flocks to start at once to reproduce cells or other flocks. Have them begin by visiting their friends and relatives in other communities. In western Honduras, new churches were encouraged that the best time to launch a daughter church was within a mother church's first year. Instruct each new pastoral trainee as part of his regular assignments to imitate his mentor, repeating the same steps. Then he, too, will soon have trainees who form new flocks.

Enable your disciples to mentor others when they have won men to Christ who are potential elders.

Give pastoral trainees a checklist of vital church activities. Such tools can help novice shepherds to chart the progress of their flocks and of their trainees' flocks.

Provide for each new shepherd studies that fit the immediate needs of his flock. Do not force every pastoral student to study the same subject at the same time. Each new flock has urgent needs that their shepherds must deal with at once.

Start a cluster of new flocks or cells instead of just one at a time. The apostles in Jerusalem had their flocks meet in homes to celebrate the Lord's Supper and to embrace the apostles' teaching (Acts 2:42, 46). Such clusters can also be seen in Acts 13–14 and in Galatians 1:2. In Galatia, the apostles started several flocks at once. Isolated flocks can become ingrown and defensive, lacking identity with a larger body. New churches in pioneer fields are like glowing embers; when one ember becomes isolated from the rest, it grows cold and dims.

Guideline 4
Spy out the land.

Practical research means finding out facts about the community!

When you touch down in a new field, keep your beak shut and your eyes peeled! Be ready to face its harshest realities with faith...

Early research leads to more effective ministry. Jesus said, "Open your eyes and look at the fields! They are ripe for harvest" (Jn 4:35). Caleb and Joshua scouted out the Promised Land with a faith that enabled them to face its harsh realities with valor (Num 13). Faith moves church planters to investigate facts about the people and their culture where they plan to work. Making plans based on vague or dreamy wishes contradicts faith, because so doing overlooks truth. Faith welcomes objective, tough-minded investigation. Practical researchers seek relevant facts about the people's life and lore. They listen with a sympathetic heart, enjoy their stories of the past, laugh at their jokes and weep with them in their heartaches. Consider these examples of practical field research:

- In Kazakhstan, Muslims had long rejected the Bible as a Russian religious book. Missionaries did careful research to find words in the Russian Bible that offended Muslims and replaced them with

Islamic-sounding words. The result is a faithful, Russian version of the New Testament that many Muslims and seekers are glad to read.

- In Liberia, believers noticed that citizens did not listen to the international Christian radio station located there. Careful research into the kinds of programs that common people liked allowed the station to design programming that people willingly listened to and provided gospel truth at the same time. The number of listeners increased sharply.

- In India, some zealous, pious, expatriate-led church planting efforts have failed by ignorantly offending the people's history and culture.[6]

- In North America, community surveys revealed reasons why most people do not visit Christian churches. Offending practices included outdated music that hurts their ears, pleas for money, and Christian jargon that some did not understand. Churches that made adjustments found that visitors usually returned and many found faith.

- Researchers in the 1990s described activities that usually help churches to multiply. Now many missionaries practice such activities. These insights have helped them in hundreds of cases to remove obstacles so that churches are now reproducing more rapidly and are penetrating formerly resistant people groups, especially in South Asia and Southeast Asia.

Practical research enables believers to pray for real needs. Jesus said, "Ask the Lord of the harvest to send out workers" (Lk 10:2). One purpose of examining a field is to better pray for harvesters, making opportunities for harvesters to report to sending churches, supporters, and organizations accurate information about progress and setbacks. A praying congregation—or several flocks working together—can adopt a neglected people group, pray, and form task groups to harvest it. This calls for investigating particular fields.

---

[6] Roger E. Hedlund, "Christians and Missionaries in India: Cross-Cultural Communication Since 1500" in *Evangelical Missions Quarterly*, April 2004, 262.

When entering a new field, workers should seek answers to these kinds of questions:

Checklist of Questions to Ask about Potential Mission Fields

☐ What is the Lord already doing? What methods of ministry are working well? How receptive are the people?[7]

☐ What kind of missionary or team can work more effectively? Should the team include nationals or culturally-proximate workers? What specialized training will some workers need? Will workers need to adopt a certain doctrinal emphasis?

☐ What aspects of the local culture can I joyfully embrace? What is unique about their social life, cultural practices, history, lore and ethnic characteristics?

☐ What practical needs do they have that create opportunities for loving ministry?

☐ What kind of people make up the most receptive segment of the population? How can we avoid casting pearls before swine?

☐ What are their legal, economic, religious, and organizational structures?

☐ What symbols, gestures and other forms of communication do they use?

☐ What are their worldviews, heartfelt values, and beliefs?

☐ What are the real needs of the people and corresponding opportunities for ministry? What organizations are already dealing with those needs?

---

[7] World statistics are summarized in Patrick Johnstone, Operation World: When We Pray God Works (Waynesboro: Gabriel Resources, 2001); David B. Barrett, George T. Kurian and Todd M. Johnson, eds. World Christian Encyclopedia, Vol. 1 and 2. Oxford: University Press, 2001; A. Scott Moreau and others, eds., Evangelical Dictionary of World Missions, (Grand Rapids: Baker, 2000); Adopt-A-People Clearinghouse <www.adopt-a-people.org>.

Later, workers should evaluate strategies and plans not only in terms of their efforts, but also in terms of results. They should seek answers to such questions as these:

Checklist of Questions to Ask in Evaluating Outcomes

☐ How receptive has the community proved? Should we continue working with them or "shake off their dust"? What kind of evangelism has been effective?

☐ What kind of church will flourish easily in the culture? House churches? Small family-oriented cell groups? Underground or secret flocks? Small or large flocks?

☐ What kind of church organization fits the culture? What liturgical forms do the people readily embrace?

☐ What type of interchurch relationships and organization work well in the culture?

☐ What kind of pastoral training fits their present stage of development?

☐ What types of self-support lend to evangelism and church multiplication?

Research?!

It would bog me down in meaningless details!

Then do practical research!

How can you make wise decisions based on facts that you do not know?

Guideline 5
Bond with the people and their culture.

A missionary might be an expert anthropologist, but if he fails to bond with his host culture, he will probably fail to start flocks that reproduce. Reflecting on this, Patterson pointed out:

> During my first year on the mission field, I had no concept of bonding. I traveled some distance to attend monthly prayer meetings with missionaries in northern Honduras. Some of them would voice a critical, outsider's view of their Honduran co-workers. I felt stress, because by God's grace I had bonded with my Honduran co-workers, and they with me. Perhaps I was able to do so because, at that time, there were no other foreign missionaries in our small city. So I quit attending the missionary prayer meetings, because I could not in my heart reconcile their condescending attitudes with my relationship with Hondurans.

I do not like the color of those birds' feathers!

And their nests are not shaped like ours.

If you loved them like Jesus says to, then you would respect their culture.

Let us find how to bond with birds of other cultures...

Live among the people. Effective ministry begins with a personal relationship. "As your people get to know and like you, their desire to follow your direction and learn from you will increase. If they don't like you, they will not want to learn from you, and the equipping process slows down and even stops."[8] Ruth, the Moabitess, bonded with the Israelites and their culture because of her loving relationships, first with Naomi, her mother-in-law (Ruth 1:15-18), and later with her husband-to-be, Boaz. One's deepest social needs should be met by the people of the community, not by fellow expatriates, except one's immediate family.

Bonding with people of another culture is similar to the way a newborn child bonds with its mother. To study a culture anthropologically is helpful but it can also become a trap, if that is all a newly-arrived worker does. Some scholarly types see the people from a detached, professional point of view, rather than bonding with them emotionally as a child would do. They fail to become an integral part of the community. Workers who fail to learn from the locals and to bond with them in significant, loving relationships remain detached from them, analyzing them from the outside, often critically.

Some missionaries protect themselves from the people around them by a host of devices. They may never participate socially either in the local culture or through inviting people into their homes. They may not learn the language really well. They may be contemptuous of the uneducated and revolted by the unclean. They are not interested in the things that interest people. They are therefore remote, distant, and terribly cold."[9]

Leadership requires relationships, relationships require time, and time requires a slow-paced presence.

When missionaries do not allow worship with the music of the people, for example, or they import Western methods of teaching, organizing, and worshipping, then it usually takes at least one generation for flocks to break loose from these impositions and begin to multiply spontaneously. It often takes a generation for the children of the first believers to cast off, or become inured to, foreign

---

[8] John C. Maxwell, *Developing the Leaders around You* (Nashville: Thomas Nelson, 1995), 28.

[9] "Proximity or Neighborliness" in *Readings in Missionary Anthropology* (Tarrytown: Practical Anthropology, 1967).

influences. With this in mind, make connecting and bonding with the people and their culture a fundamental practice. Patterson recalled:

> The first Honduran congregation that I worked with had been started by foreigners and had many problems. A common musical instrument at that time was the guitar, but the church, because of our American influence, had an electric organ— totally irrelevant to the local culture. Fortunately, somebody stole it.

Recognize your own prejudice. Learn from the local people. A cross-cultural worker who thinks he has no cultural prejudice is like a person who never bathes or uses deodorant, becoming so used to his own odor that he thinks he has none. Such blindness is dangerous. No matter how learned one may be, one needs the Sovereign Lord's help to overcome prejudice and bond with the host people, like Peter did in Acts 10. Like the apostle Paul, he should become "all things to all men" (1 Cor 9:22). A prominent national leader in India took aim at missionaries with this regard, "In my many years of involvement in Indian missions I have never seen in even a single field *learning* ... among the strategies to reach the people...."[10]

Be slow to condemn others. Some Western missionaries, in their zeal for a pure church, overreact to what appears to them to be idolatry in another culture, while practicing the paganism of their own culture without realizing it. Jesus warned His disciples not to try to root out weeds among the wheat. Wise missionaries proclaim the Lord Jesus Christ and His Word, and then trust converts—who are filled with the Holy Spirit and know their own culture from the inside—to remove practices that they know to be demonic. A foreign missionary should not try to change another culture, but to appreciate it and bring Christ into it, trusting the Holy Spirit and local believers to transform it from within.[11] Patterson commented:

---

[10] Dayanand Bharati, *Living Water and Indian Bowl* (Delhi: Indian Society for Promoting Christian Knowledge, 1997), 16.
[11] Sherwood Lingenfelter, *Transforming Culture* (Grand Rapids: Baker, 1992) and Sherwood Lingenfelter, *Agents of Transformation* (Grand Rapids: Baker, 1996).

At first the villagers' idolatry shocked me. Some argued about which village's statue of the Virgin Mary had more power to heal diseases than did another's. I saw a man making the sign of the cross before attempting to steal from our house. A converted prostitute confessed that she had prayed to the Virgin Mary to get more clients. At first, I became overly critical. I wrote harsh study materials for our workers, condemning prayers to Mary, and I crusaded against all forms of idolatry. However, this brought a backlash from some uneducated peasants who countered with violence and some evangelicals were injured. My attacks did more harm than good towards both evangelicals and Catholics. Realizing this, in the presence of my co-workers I gathered up the negative studies that I had prepared—a big stack of them—and threw them into the trash. Our workers agreed to present Jesus in a positive way, using their critical facilities to examine our own errors instead of those of others. Persecution lessened and it became easier to win people to Christ. Thereafter, everyone felt more positive.

Love the people enough to respect their culture. Perhaps more than 95% of the elements of any culture—even of the most pagan ones—are neutral concerning morals and faith. So do not focus too much on the bad aspects lest you become judgmental and critical.

Let a flock be born within the people's own culture and community. When the Holy Spirit dwells in their hearts and they know the Word of God, they will remove many evils from their culture better than outsiders can.

Revelation 7:9 reveals that the unique features of different cultures will endure like facets on a diamond throughout all eternity, adorning and beautifying the eternal bride of Christ. The Almighty loves the different ways people express themselves. He brings out the best of a culture through His people within it. Remember, the Spirit of Him who raised Jesus from the dead lives in them (Rom 8:11), and they become "salt of the earth" (Matt 5:13). Thousands of cultures still await this divine salt to spill from Christ's church.

Missionaries who came some time after the apostle Paul into Galatia forced Jewish holidays and circumcision on Gentile flocks

(Gal 4:8-10; 5:2-6). Under grace, circumcision was no longer a biblical requirement (Acts 15), yet certain legalistic missionaries insisted on it! This was a cultural issue. Paul wrote a furious letter to the Galatians when they fell into this temptation. Yet, in another culture among Jews, he had Timothy, his co-worker, circumcised (Acts 16:1-3). Customs that fit one culture can cancel God's grace in another.

Focus on a specific culture and people group and plant culturally-sensitive churches within it. A people group is, by definition, the largest possible number of people among whom the good news can flow freely from one person or family to another, without being hindered by barriers of any kind. In pioneer fields, the most common barriers to the flow of the gospel are cultural issues.

Two cultures seldom integrate in a congregation; a dominant culture usually cancels out a minority one. Church planters who force two cultures to mix within a flock normally do so by introducing a paralyzing legalism. Some ministers force people of two cultures to worship as one in order to show their unity in Christ, as though unity meant physical proximity. A closer look will reveal that, although the people meet together physically, their cultures do not blend; one of the cultures will annul or suppress the other. Death of a culture is sad and painful.

Do not force seekers to embrace your culture. Such restraint requires discipline. Even the apostle Peter, after many years of faith, was unable to respect another culture willingly (Gal 2:11-14). In the West we exalt the Most High for churches where believers from different cultural and economic backgrounds worship together by their own choice. Forced heterogeneity is not their issue. By way of contrast, in church planting movements flocks multiply spontaneously usually within culturally homogeneous flocks, as the gospel spreads freely from family to family, friend to friend and flock to flock. The gospel does not spread as easily from one culture to another. Taking the good news into another culture entails a fresh, intentional effort. Patterson commented:

> Throughout my first term on the field in Honduras, I unwisely pastored a traditional church made up of devout believers of

three subcultures. Some members were white descendants of British pirates. These were the economic backbone and, although a tiny minority, it was they who controlled the hybrid flock. Others were black descendants of escaped slaves from Jamaica, and others were very poor Mestizos, a mixture of Mayan Indians, of Spanish colonists and of black Africans. Although all spoke Spanish, the church did not grow, in spite of much evangelism. Newcomers could not find where they fit into the amalgamated cultural mix. Although I urged them to form separate congregations, they refused, saying that to mix different cultures showed Christian unity. Years later a wiser pastor coaxed the groups to separate. New growth was immediate, especially among the poorer Mestizos who, for the first time, had a church that respected their culture.

Show patience. Church planters arrive on the field eager to serve. They have strained their leash during years of preparation and now yearn to serve their Lord and the people. These zealous new reapers need all their fresh vigor, but without patient guidance from more experienced workers, their eagerness makes them rush into detailed planning, sidetracking them into ineffective exertion and despair. Patience will help them to avoid ulcers during the long race ahead of them. The ministry is a marathon, not a sprint!

Learn the language well. The Lord confounded the languages of the builders of the Tower of Babel (Gn 11). Now, He sends His servants to learn those tongues and the many dialects that have evolved from them, in order to communicate His gospel to all peoples.

Long-term workers should not rely on interpreters, for those who do so rarely are able to establish culturally-relevant flocks. The few flocks they do start are often made up of students learning English and others who are drawn to Western culture. Such flocks can hardly spark a movement of the people within the local culture, because they are moving away from it.

Language learning is most effective when viewed as a ministry and not simply something that leads to future ministry. The community is the language learner's best classroom. Let him live out the Lord's love while practicing new verbs with the people.

Prepare families for the field and care for them there. Heads of families must so shepherd their households with loving, godly discipline that they can all bond with the host culture together. Westerners often embrace individualism so ardently that they neglect their own families. They glorify the private dimension of one's relationship with the Lord, emphasizing to excess its personal aspect. Thus, while they bond with locals, their spouses and children might not. The New Testament emphasizes love and solidarity within the family in whatever context they find themselves.

Guideline 6
Form and train the right kind of task group.

I am so well educated that I can do the work by myself without a team!

Really? Have you all the spiritual gifts needed to lead a healthy flock?

Can you stand alone against Satan and a pagan society?

Let us see how the apostles worked as teams...

If possible, form a temporary task group of volunteers to plant each new church. Both Peter and Paul gathered workers who joined them temporarily to announce the good news and begin new flocks. Peter took believers with him from Joppa to start another flock in Caesarea (Acts 10). Paul worked with Barnabas, Silas, Timothy, Luke and many others. The makeup of his team continually changed.

A task group may include workers from different flocks. Peter, who had come from the flock in Jerusalem, took six others from the church in Joppa, forming a temporary task force to labor in Caesarea

(Acts 11:11-12). Similarly, wise church planters work with others, not as individuals. Jesus never traveled alone, nor did the apostles (except as prisoners). Some churches commission missionaries on an individual basis and some mission agencies also appoint ministers only as individuals, but the New Testament provides no example of such an individualistic approach. Patterson recalled:

> A Honduran worker and I sometimes rode horses into a mountainous area of northern Honduras, but were unable to gather enough believers there to form a congregation. Neither of us had friends there. Then two believers who had lived there years before and had since come to Christ joined us to form a temporary team. They were neither gifted evangelists nor church planters, but with their knowledge of the area and contacts with past acquaintances, they fleshed out a temporary task group that the Lord used to set up a small string of churches. This same scenario worked for us in various different areas, with different helpers.

Include in a task group workers who are culturally near to the population in a field. Teams of American church planters had worked in North African fields for years with meager success, gaining only a few new believers here and there. Later some Latin Americans joined their team. Their background was similar to that of Muslim Berbers in that they had known poverty, came from large, poorly educated, rural families, and shared the same skin color. African Moors had occupied Spain for hundreds of years before Columbus and left much of their blood, architectural style and way of life there which were transported to Latin America. These Latin Americans made a welcome addition to the team, making it easier to form friendships and to gather congregations of believers.

The apostle Paul included Titus, a Greek, in his apostolic band as they traveled where Greek culture prevailed (2 Cor 7:5-6; Ti 1:5). Having culturally-similar workers assures communication that is more relevant during the initial penetration, when pioneering outsiders must do all the work. Church planters do not bridge the gap between themselves and people of a different culture simply by studying anthropological information about it. A better bridge is to enlist co-workers who are already of that culture or of a culture similar enough to be received as insiders. At first, if workers from outside of the culture do the evangelism alone, they can delay the birth of a culturally-relevant, reproductive church.

The compiler of this book made a blunder by trying his best to reach out alone to the Chortí Indians. He later learned from Patterson's experience who once mentioned:

> I do not have the gift of evangelism, but found that when I worked closely with someone who did have it, his anointing rubbed off on me. I could tell people in a natural way about Christ and the Holy Spirit seemed to use my words to convict them to repent and believe. However, when I tried to do it alone, I felt powerless and was not very effective. Often I would show new believers how to evangelize. We would travel together to a village and I would talk about Jesus in a home or two. Then I would tell my apprentice, "Now, you are to do so with the next family." They normally did it better than I could, but had needed me to help get them started.

Failing to prove relevant in a culture may not be a missionary's fault; he may do an excellent job adapting. The problem may simply be how the people perceive the new flock. If a foreigner starts it, the people may perceive it as foreign, no matter how well the foreigner has adapted. It is wiser to bring in culturally-proximate workers, even temporarily, to do evangelism at first. They will more readily reach serious, adult men. Once some heads of families receive Christ, locals will normally accept being mentored in the background by foreigners who sincerely respect them and their culture.

Guideline 7
Find the receptive vein within a society.

I have been telling those buzzards for months to repent but they only look for dead meat to eat...

Come back! Jesus has the answer. He said, "Do not give what is holy to dogs, and do not throw your pearls before swine!" You need not waste time with non-receptive people. Let us consider ways to find sincere seekers...

Find souls whom the Holy Spirit has already prepared to respond to the good news. When church planters enter a community, they should look for these people. Some are known for their good character, like Cornelius in the book of Acts. Although not yet a Christian, he had a reputation of being devout and of doing works of mercy. Others whom God has prepared have a reputation of bad character, like Zacchaeus. Yet, where sin abounds, grace abounds more.

The Lord begins His work in the hearts of people long before missionaries arrive in a community. If missionaries build on what the Lord has already begun there—letting a flock emerge as an integral part of the community's culture and life—then churches can more readily reproduce in daughter and granddaughter churches. With protection from local, God-fearing men like Cornelius, there will be less persecution. Church planters should proclaim Christ first to those whom these God-fearing men recommend, rather than inviting everyone possible to a meeting. In addition, fewer individuals will feign conversion seeking material gain from rich outsiders.

Persecution is inevitable when flocks begin multiplying where Satan has had a monopoly on people's spiritual thinking for centuries, and missionaries often cannot avoid hostility. However, they can avoid much of the persecution that they bring upon themselves needlessly because of their Western, individualistic approach to evangelism. For example, failing to work within existing networks of family and friends of persons of peace will surely provoke justifiable resentment.

That old buzzard has no friends and his family flew away, so he finally turned to Jesus.

I'm going now to tell him to be the catalyst to start another new flock.

Wait! To start a new flock, do not look for an isolated gold nugget like him. Look for the mother lode, for a receptive social network. Let us find out how...

A subtle danger lies in simply seeking people who appear at first to be anxious to listen to the gospel. Sometimes they are eager to please an outsider, and have wrong motives. Rather, look for someone who is a respected community member with a network of friends and relatives who relate well to each other, among whom the gospel can spread freely.

When entering a new region, seek out receptive communities as Jesus did. After Herod jailed John the Baptist, Jesus withdrew from Judea to work among the more receptive population of Galilee (Mk 1:14-20; Lk 4:16-30). In a pioneer or neglected field, the most receptive inhabitants are normally the working class or an oppressed minority. Had Jesus begun His public ministry among the more affluent and influential of Jerusalem, where they tried to kill Him every time He taught there, He would have been crucified prematurely. Widespread movements for Christ do not begin among those who are satisfied with the *status quo*. Such movements do occur among the middle classes normally after second or third generation Christians have arisen among them.

With exceptions like traditional tribes and societies long exposed to Christianity, evangelists who aim first at the rich and powerful, hoping that these natural leaders will win their own people, have almost all failed to spark a people movement. From the New Testament, we know that the Lord often chooses the lowly things of this world to show His power (1 Cor 1:18–2:16).

A spontaneous flow of the gospel through ties of kinship and friendship results in people movements in which thousands turn to Christ and national flocks multiply with little or no outside help. Like gossip and confidential information, the good news spreads from one household to another, from one set of friends to another, until stopped by barriers of difference in culture, language, or socio-economic class. Persecution, volatile political situations and physical barriers like mountain ranges can also prevent the flow. These factors can be used by the Most High for quality control among the sent ones and the new believers.

Since our Supreme Commander commissioned His followers to make disciples of all people groups, prudent missionaries carefully and prayerfully seek His will—with or without persecution—regarding which neglected people group they should penetrate. They should define their area of responsibility in terms of a people group or a subculture within a people group, rather than a geo-political region.

Guideline 8
Find a hospitable "person of peace."

Go where Heaven's King has prepared
someone to receive you.

If you do not find such people, then shake
the dust from your feathers!

Let us discover how to do so...

Discern what Jesus meant by "person of peace."[12] When penetrating an area that has had no witness for Christ, try to avoid simply
going from door to door. When Jesus sent His disciples to evangelize
new communities, He instructed them to find and stay with a person
of peace (Lk 10:3-9). A person of peace receives the Lord's workers
and helps them get along in the community. Examples include Levi
(Lk 5:27-31), Zacchaeus (Lk 19:1-10), Cornelius (Acts 10), Lydia
(Acts 16:11-15), the Philippian jailer (Acts 16:29-34), Aquila and
Priscilla (Acts 18:1-3, 24-26) and Justus (Acts 18:7). Lydia was a
person of peace who invited the apostles to stay at her home where
they witnessed to her family. Cornelius gathered his relatives and
intimate friends to hear Peter tell the good news. Patterson recalled:

Sometimes we entered Honduran villages where we knew no
one. At first, we simply started preaching in the public plaza, but
with little success. Then we learned to frequent the local *pul-
perias*—those small stores that made up the front part of many
homes facing the plaza. Following our long trek down dirty,
dusty and hot Honduran roads, we would drink semi-cold soda
pops and explain briefly that we were there to talk with others

---

[12] Literally, "son of peace" (Lk 10:6); in Matthew 10:11, "one who is worthy". Such
persons may be men and women, youth and aged.

about the gospel of Jesus Christ. We would ask "Who in this town might receive us?" For whatever reason, they would often mention the local schoolteacher, and in every instance that I remember, the teacher did in fact receive us, feed us, house us, and help us to establish valuable contacts with people who later came to Christ. I wish it were that easy in all cultures to locate a man of peace.

A man of peace normally offers hospitality to the Lord's messengers before conversion. Communicating the gospel with the approval of a respected person, even if that person is not a believer, allows the message to flow freely along the lines of natural relationships. In people movements the Word spreads like a chain reaction from family to family and friend to friend. Church planters stifle this spontaneity by going only where they can control the work, which causes the community to see the new movement as something controlled by unknown outsiders.

Reaching women (see Figure 7) can be easier than reaching men, but firm leadership roots into the community are harder to achieve. Working under the wing of a man of peace makes it easy to win entire families and assures that the new flock will be more relevant to the culture. A worker who tries to be self-sufficient may isolate himself from the community and evangelize only where he is in control. He may start churches by extracting individuals, mainly children and women, from their families and friends. Flocks that lack mature family men seldom take root deep enough in the culture to reproduce spontaneously through daughter and granddaughter churches.

A man of peace does not always convert to Christ. He may serve only as a doorway to his community. Church planters are widely welcomed because of their relationship to him. He introduces them to others who are seeking the Lord and he orients them to the life of the local community. A man of peace also might be peaceful only with his guests. He might be a military man or brutal in other contexts, as Cornelius and the jailer were.

Figure 7
Reaching Women Only

Persons of Peace in the New Testament

If you mentor workers who establish churches or cells, then they will carry out plans that you help them to make. You should prepare them to recognize the man of peace that Jesus told His disciples to seek in towns where they proclaimed the good news. Jesus commanded, "When you enter a house, first say, "Peace to this house." If a man of peace is there, your peace will rest on him; if not, it will return to you (Lk 10:5-6). You can review with your trainees the examples of such "children of peace" found in the book of Acts and draw guidelines from them. A few examples include:

Cornelius (Acts 10:25, 48). This Roman centurion was instructed by a holy angel to send for Peter. Cornelius welcomed Peter and his co-workers into his house where he had gathered family members and close friends. Later, he invited them to stay for a few days. Although Cornelius was willing to hear the gospel, without the Lord's special preparation of Peter he would have been unwilling to enter Cornelius' house. Because Peter was a Jew, he would have refused to eat food in a non-Jewish home. Despite Jesus' instructions to eat what a person of peace offered (Lk 10:7-8), Peter still had to learn to accept other races, their customs and their food.

Lydia *(Acts 16:13-15, 40)*. Lydia was a person of peace in the city of Philippi. When she believed and invited the church planters to stay at her house, they readily accepted.

The Philippian Jailer (Acts 16:29-34). This prison warden learned that his prisoners had not escaped following an earth tremor, and humbly begged the apostles to tell him how he could be saved. They offered salvation by faith to him and to his whole household. He brought them into his house and cared for them. They spoke the Word of the Lord to the household and baptized them.

Aquila and Priscilla (Acts 18:1-3). This married couple operated a small business. They received Paul into their home where he worked with them making tents until he received outside support. Later, this couple privately tutored Apollos, a popular public debater, and hosted Gentile churches in their home.

Justus (Acts 18:7). Justus, a devout man, whose house was located next door to a synagogue, hosted Paul for a time at Corinth.

The following are some guidelines about persons of peace derived from the above texts (perhaps you will find more):

- Persons of peace are often devout in their non-Christian religion, and are often heads of families.

- Persons of peace might not be types that you would expect. Cornelius, for example, was a professional soldier, trained to lead troops in battle against enemies of Rome. The Philippian jailer, prior to the earthquake, had tormented Paul and Silas, putting their feet in stocks. Be prepared for surprises!

- Persons of peace may appear somewhat unpolished in their dress and manner, and may lack theological sophistication. However, others listen to them, and they influence their households and friends.

- The Almighty arranges for praying believers to meet persons of peace whom He has prepared. Christians must be prepared to speak about the Lord Jesus and the gospel. Such persons will often invite Christians to explain the gospel to them.

- The Lord's servants must be willing to overcome cultural barriers to share the gospel with men of peace on their turf, as Paul did with the jailer. For Peter, it took a special revelation from the Almighty for him to accept his God-given assignment to share the gospel with Gentiles within their cultural surroundings.

- When invited to eat or stay a few days in the home of a man of peace, do so. Be willing to receive hospitality from such seekers, and not to feel that you have to offer payment, which in some cultures would be an offense. Church planters in pioneer fields should remain for a time in the home of a man of peace *following* the baptism of the family, like Peter and his helpers from Joppa did in Caesarea, in order to disciple the new believers and to mentor novice leaders. Often a man of peace, if mentored the way the apostles did it, will become a shepherding elder who serves the new flock. You, as his mentor, may have to make repeated visits and mentor one or more children of peace together.

- Men of peace can host a church in their home. In pioneer fields, most new flocks are born in the homes of men of peace. A man of peace and his family should not be brought into an older existing flock, unless for some reason it is impossible to start a new church in their home. Bringing them into an existing congregation can stop the process of church reproduction.

- New believers can be baptized in their own homes.

Guideline 9
Proclaim the good news with a power that keeps it flowing.

On Galilee's shore, Jesus told Peter and Andrew to fish for men (Matt 4:19). Jesus later summarized the gospel message as His death and resurrection, with forgiveness of sins for all who repent (Lk 24:46-49). Guidelines for the catch include the following:

Give to Christ's resurrection the emphasis that the apostles gave to it. Western believers often fail to mention Jesus' life-giving resurrection in their evangelistic messages and gospel tracts. This would have surprised Peter or Paul, for Jesus' resurrection was always the main thrust of their proclamation. Keep in mind:

- Neglecting Jesus' resurrection is not so problematic in the West, because it is common knowledge there that Christians believe that He rose from the dead. In most pioneer or neglected fields there is no such knowledge. To proclaim only that by His death believers have forgiveness of sins may still leave them without hope of Christ's eternal life.

- Scripture strongly emphasizes that our only hope of immortality lies in being united with Jesus in His resurrection (Jn 11:25-26; 1 Cor 15:17-26; Rom 6:3-11).

- Jesus' risen body is the "ark" by which all believers will be raised from "the waters" of death to glory (1 Pet 3:21).

- Jesus will raise both the saved and the condemned (Jn 5:25-29), the saved unto eternal life (Jn 3:36).

- Being raised in Jesus is already a reality in God's sight (Eph 2:6). This is easier to understand when a believer remembers that God is eternal. That is, He is not only everywhere but also everywhen.

- Witness to people telling what Jesus has done for you and your family.

Trying not to sound pious, speak in a natural way, not like some believers and preachers who, when talking about God, converse in a stilted, religious intonation that sounds weird and phony to unbelievers. Jesus and his Apostles spoke the language of the common people. They avoided big words and philosophical arguments when communicating the good news. The apostles related the historical, redemptive events of Jesus' suffering and resurrection simply as news. In the Gospels and the book of Acts believers witnessed for Jesus with the Holy Spirit's power, often under the sponsorship of a man of peace (Lk 10:5-7; Acts 1:8). They normally told the good news to the family and close friends of such hosts as Cornelius, Zacchaeus, Lydia, the Philippian jailer, and Crispus.

> Speak as friend to friend, calling sinners to repent.
>
> Let us consider how to tell the good news in a way that lets it flow to others, on and on...

Modern methods of evangelism often extract a new believer from his circle of friends and relatives and bring him into a group where the evangelist is secure and in control. This deliberate separation of a neophyte from his family and friends violates Jesus' command to love others and brings on needless persecution.

Call seekers to repentance. Believers who tell others about Jesus should ask them to repent, as John the Baptist did in Mark 1:4, Jesus in Mark 1:14-15, and Peter in Acts 2:38. Westerners often aim to elicit decisions for Christ, which is not a New Testament practice[13]. Mere decisions lead to superficial evangelism, overlooking the awesome holiness of the Most High. Prodding a person's conscience to manipulate him into making an emotional, crisis-driven decision often satisfies the evangelist without fully leading that person to submit to Christ as Lord. Many who merely make a decision for Christ fail to follow through, for a mental decision to accept teaching about Jesus, by itself, lacks repentance. Patterson said:

> An evangelistic team showed a popular gospel film in a number of Mexican tribal villages and reported 5,000 decisions for Christ. I helped local missionaries try and follow up these conversions. We were unable to find even one repentant believer. They had raised their hands, but there was no indication of a

---

[13] For a recent critique of unbiblical "decisions for Christ" see David Fitch, *The Great Giveaway: Reclaiming the mission of the church from big business, parachurch organizations, psychology, consumer capitalism, and other modern maladies* (Grand Rapids: Baker, 2005), 64-5.

heart change. Maybe their hands will go to Heaven! The closest we came to finding a positive response was the request of some to let them know when we showed another movie. Unfortunately, serious church planters have witnessed similarly sad scenarios in fields around the world.

While serving as an Anglican priest, John Wesley introduced the "altar call." He disliked giving the bread of the Eucharist to unregenerate church members, so he called them to the altar to pray first and to receive the Lord Jesus Christ spiritually. He then gave them the sacrament. This "altar call" soon evolved into a public invitation, which many modern evangelists calling individuals to "come forward" for salvation. Among some evangelicals, the altar call became a man-made sacrament that replaced biblical baptism as a means to confirm repentance. The original invitation of the apostles was to "repent and be baptized, every one of you, in the name of Jesus Christ for the forgiveness of your sins. And you will receive the gift of the Holy Spirit" (Acts 2:38).

Repentance has a positive and a negative side. The negative side is turning from sin, a kind of "dying to sin" in mystical union with Jesus through His atoning death. The positive side is a receiving of Jesus' resurrection life, being raised with Him to a new, holy, eternal life. Both sides are a supernatural touch of the Holy Spirit, as a person places his faith in Christ.

Repentance initiates an eternal process of transformation by which the Sovereign Lord brings believers into conformity with the image of His heir, Jesus Christ. Since without repentance there is no salvation, Jesus required His followers to call sinners to repent (Lk 24:46-48). Repentance is not a "work" that earns salvation, but is the human part in receiving the free gift by honoring the holy God.

Evangelism proves more effective when new believers are trained to reach out to their friends and relatives. New believers learn to witness best by observing and imitating a godly mentor, and they, in turn, can train others to do the same. Church planters should show new disciples how to testify for the Lord Jesus Christ.

As we have seen, the essential elements of Christian testimony concern Jesus' person, sacrificial death, life-giving resurrection and promise of forgiveness to all who repent (Lk 24:44-48). Even the newest believer can affirm these truths. The apostles always spoke these truths when they announced the good news. Patterson commented:

> A missionary friend refused to baptize a certain seeker, fearing that he was insincere, because his family members and friends had influenced him. What a sad mistake! He assumed that the Holy Spirit could use only the testimony of a professional minister like himself to convince sinners of their need. After he came to see that the Holy Spirit works most powerfully through the testimony of friends and relatives, he had better results.

Common Pitfalls in Pioneer Evangelism

A common pitfall in pioneer fields is to put evangelism under the control of an institution. Seldom does effective, church-planting evangelism result from an educational institution sending students out to evangelize, unless local church leaders provide specific support, accountability and follow-up. Workers should start new flocks working as an arm of a mother church. If there is no mother church, then establish one.

What does biblical repentance require, that a mere intellectual decision for Christ lacks?   **Let us find out...**

Another pitfall is evangelism that ends with superficial decisions. Western evangelistic messages and meetings often result in non-repentant "decisions for Christ". Foreign missionaries should let nationals develop their own methods of witnessing lest they adopt culturally-irrelevant methods that manipulate individuals into making mere decisions instead of urgently and lovingly calling their friends to repentance.

A third pitfall is that of church planters prematurely inviting the public to attend worship meetings. It is important to distinguish between worship meetings and evangelistic meetings in pioneer fields. Do not invite the outside public to a serious worship meeting until you have organized local believers to lead it, especially serious, mature men. Teach new leaders not to hold worship meetings for unbelievers, for these are unable to worship the God "in Spirit and in truth" (Jn 4:24).

A final pitfall consists of teachers who simply teach personal evangelism in a classroom. No one can make effective witnesses for Jesus in that way. Instead, go with your disciples and model evangelism as the Lord did. Leadership specialist John Maxwell described disciple making, "I model it—I do it; I mentor—I do it and you watch me; I monitor —you do it and I watch you. I motivate — you do it; I multiply—you do it and train someone else, too."[14] Show them how to proclaim Jesus' salvation to their friends and relatives. Weed out students who refuse to do practical field work, no matter how good they are with theory, lest they contaminate other students with an academic mentality that dwells on abstract theology while neither gathering nor edifying congregations.

[14] John C. Maxwell, *Developing the Leaders around You* (Nashville: Thomas Nelson, 1995), 99-101.

Guideline 10
Pray for healing of body, heart and soul.

Where flocks multiply rapidly, evangelism
normally goes together with physical
healing through prayer in Jesus' name.

Avoid the glitzy, commercial approach of
some high-flying screechers.

Here are some guidelines...

Pray for the sick to be healed in Jesus' name. Healing in the Lord Jesus' name is common where conditions parallel the time of the apostles when culture was pagan, tyrants ruled, fear prevailed, and people held a worldview incompatible with Christianity. In many pioneer fields today, the Holy Spirit does what He did in the book of Acts, for the same reasons. Where the gospel message is incomprehensible to most people, the Lord Almighty confirms it with signs as he did in the book of Acts. Many individuals in pioneer fields who lack schooling find it easy to pray with childlike faith for healing.

A wise church planter prays in Jesus' name for healing of the sick, as Peter, John, and Paul did. The apostles neither held showy healing meetings nor healed as a source of income. They healed as quietly as conditions allowed, as Jesus did when he healed a leper as recounted in Luke 5:12-14.

Missionaries who come from churches that rarely practice healing find that they must adjust their theology a bit. When they arrive where disease is rampant and medical help is unavailable, they find that God often heals the sick. To pray for healing is a major ministry of the church, now as well as in New Testament times. Historically and contemporarily, in movements where thousands have received the Lord Jesus Christ and churches have multiplied spontaneously, healing in the name of Jesus has been a prominent part of evangelism.

Let new believers proclaim the good news of Jesus' saving death and His resurrection, along with His power to heal. Let them share their testimonials of being healed in Jesus' name. Patterson commented:

> There are enough cases of genuine healing in the name of Jesus that people with the true gift of healing have no need to make up stories or falsify accounts. A so-called "healer" held a showy campaign in the city where we resided. He called on people to receive healing and a friend's household maid approached on crutches. When he laid hands on her, she dropped the crutches and ran out shouting, "God healed me!" Our friend later asked her what had crippled her; she admitted then that the "healer" had hired her to fake it, to encourage others to come forward. After that noisy campaign, a believer who managed a local bank told us that the "healer" deposited a large sum of money in small coins in a personal account after the meeting. The New Testament does not teach this sort of feigned healing. The Lord normally does heal more quietly in church planting movements. Commercialized, sensational, dishonest publicity creates skepticism and discourages non-gullible seekers.

Guideline 11
Let seekers and new believers host harvesting meetings.

Visit the nests of seekers. Hold small
harvesting meetings there.
Let us consider ways to do so...

Church reproduction often occurs through harvesting meetings hosted or led by seekers or new believers. Jesus let Zacchaeus and Levi invite their unbelieving friends to their homes to hear the good news. Peter and his helpers from Joppa started a congregation in the home of a seeker, Cornelius, who had called and hosted the gathering.

One can gather temporary harvesting groups in many ways, to bring together seekers and believers. One might invite them to enjoy a party or a meal, an athletic event, a fishing trip, a Bible study for seekers only, a project to serve needy people in the community, or to discuss a topic of mutual interest. Such groups are usually short-lived, because participants receive Christ and form a church, join an existing church, or reject the gospel and stop attending. New believers and seekers with many contacts with non-believers are normally the most effective hosts of harvesting meetings, provided a caring believer mentors them in the background.

Lest such harvesting opportunities dwindle after a group starts nourishing new believers, disciple making leaders must encourage new believers to continue doing evangelism. Biblical examples of new believers who gathered others include:

- Cornelius who was made a disciple by Peter.

- The Jailer and his family who were made disciples by Paul and Silas.

- Apollos who was made a disciple by Aquila and Priscilla.

- Publius who was made a disciple by Paul and Silas.

Small groups form easily when new believers host them, as Levi (Mk 2:13-17) and Zacchaeus did, both of them tax collectors shunned by religious people. They invited friends of questionable character to come meet Jesus at their houses where sinners met comfortably. Jesus met with unconverted seekers who gathered in such groups.

Avoid letting small harvesting groups become mere preaching points, where outside workers simply preach to a passive audience. Some unwise church planters seek to work only at locations where they remain securely in control. By way of contrast, Jesus and his Apostles would go where they were vulnerable and were often exposed to threats of danger, to insults and even to death, in order to reach people on their turf.

Guideline 12
Use stories and the arts to teach with greater effect.

Many believers have a beautiful song to sing or a story to tell that presents Jesus and inspires others to worship Him in an artistic way. Use the music and creative arts of a local culture to express praise to God.[15] David, the sweet singer of Israel (1 Sam 23:1) composed psalms set to music. Israelites sang these poems to the accompaniment of stringed instruments (the meaning of the word psalm). David even danced before the Lord (2 Sam 6:14). Believers can praise God with singing, reading, chanting, silence, dramas, citing poetry, praying, even shouting in unison. The Lord does not care how believers praise Him, provide they do so from their heart (Jn 4:24).

Westerners who work in other cultures too often introduce a foreign music style. Although young people may readily embrace foreign music, churches with only youth seldom reproduce well. Without compromising truth, the music and the church itself must be a reflection of their host culture. Though not of the world, the church remains in it and must reflect the local color and context. Hwa Yung of Singapore declared, "Unless genuine efforts are made at contextualizing the proclamation of the gospel and the practice of faith, Christianity will continue to be widely perceived as a Western religion."[16]

Relate the grand redemptive events of history as the apostles did in the book of Acts. When evangelizing, they simply told the story of Jesus' redemptive work, trusting the Holy Spirit to use historical truths to convert people. We too should build factual foundations first and allow detailed theology to follow later. Notice the biblical order:

- First the Old Testament history, then the inspired comments and conclusions of the prophets.

---

[15] For more on dramatizing stories and doing role play see guideline 34.

[16] Hwa Yung, "Strategic Issues in Missions—An Asian Perspective," in *Evangelical Missions Quarterly*, January 2004, 32.

Can we examine some guidelines
for teaching with stories?

- First the New Testament story of our Lord Jesus Christ's birth, miracles, trial, death, resurrection, and ascension followed by the coming of the Holy Spirit, then the theology of the Epistles.

Paul wrote philosophically to the Romans, but he assumed they already knew the stories of Adam, Abraham, Jacob, Esau and Moses. Teach doctrinal passages along with the stories upon which they are based.

Whereas religions are founded upon the metaphysical assumptions of some mystic, Judaism and Christianity begin with the historical events and build theology on them. These events include the creation, fall, flood, covenants, Passover, taking of the Land, kingdom of Israel, and events of the New Testament.

To debate with a Muslim or Hindu on a philosophical level leads to an intellectual duel, anger and unneeded persecution. Whatever the local culture, wise missionaries tell Old Testament stories to lay a foundation for understanding the gospel, especially in societies with a worldview that has no room for an all-powerful Creator or the sin that entails punishment by a holy God. Prudent missionaries also use indigenous art forms, symbols, dramas, and music styles. Storytelling remains universally effective. Throughout history biblical stories, whether read, recited, sung or dramatized, have proven pivotal in spreading God's Word in large movements towards the Lord Jesus Christ. For many years after Pentecost, Christians passed on the good news orally. Common people easily pass on stories, like passing a light baton in a relay race. Storytelling is often a normal part of people movements in which the gospel spreads widely and flocks reproduce until the entire people group has heard.

People remember stories and find it easier to apply truths embodied in stories, especially if the stories come from Scripture. Stories and role-plays enter not only into the brain's abstract memory banks, but also where the brain stores visual and audio images. For example, workers arriving in a different culture seldom do what they have heard in lectures or have read. They do what they have done before and what they have seen modeled. Therefore, trainers who teach these concepts to others through workshops of more than a day in length might form the participants into a temporary training church that does everything that a congregation does, role-playing anticipated fieldwork that the participants are later to imitate on the field.

Useful Stories to Teach Vital Topics

Holiness

Events from Scripture which show God's perfect holiness, because of which He cannot look upon sin and must punish evil:

- The flood (Gn 6–9).

- Faithful Israelites slew those who persisted in idolatry (Exodus 32).

The One True God

Stories which confirm the Unity of God; He is One; there are no other good gods, only demons and false idols:

- The contest between Elijah and the prophets of Baal on Mt. Carmel (1 Kings 18).

- The Lord punished those who worshipped the golden calf (Exodus 32-33).

The Almighty's Unlimited Power

Events which display His omnipotence—that He is all-powerful:

- The creation (Gn 1-2).

- The ten plagues in Egypt and parting of the Red Sea for His people to cross (Ex 1-15).

Man's Sinful Nature

Stories which illustrate the reality and danger of all men's sin:

- Adam and Eve in Eden (Gn 3).

- The great King David fell for Bathsheba (2 Sam 11-12).

The Need for Sacrifice

Stories which teach that the Holy One demanded blood sacrifice for covering sin and His forgiveness:

- Cain and Abel (Gn 4).

- The Passover lamb in Exodus (Ex 11-13).

- The Holy One cremated Nadab and Abihu when they entered His presence without the blood (Lev 11).

- Jesus' sacrifice on the cross (Mt 26-27; Lk 2).

Jesus' Deity

Events which show Him as the eternal Son of God:

- He claimed to be the Son of God and later was raised by the Eternal One from the dead (Mk 14-16).

- The Father recognized Him as Son at His baptism (Matt 3).

- Jesus' Humanity. Bible stories which reveal His humanity:

- Birth (Lk 2; Mt 2; Isaiah 9:6-7).

- Suffering during trials and crucifixion (Mk 15-15; Lk 22-24; Jn 18-20).

Grace

Stories that show that sinners receive unmerited favor from God:

- John the Baptist proclaimed forgiveness to those who confessed their sins (Matt 3).

- Jesus forgave very bad people but warned the Pharisees who trusted in their good works that they had not entered the Kingdom of Heaven (Matt 9 and 21:28-45).

- Jesus forgave a paralytic who had done nothing on his own initiative to come to Jesus (Matt 2).

- Paul promised salvation to the entire family of the believing jailer, before they heard the gospel (Acts 16:31).

Angels

Events which demonstrate the role of angels as God's messengers:

- Angels visited Abraham (Exod 18).

- Angels announced Jesus' birth to shepherds (Lk 2).

- An angel told Mary she would give birth to the Messiah (Lk 1).

- Angels announced Jesus' resurrection to the women at His empty tomb (Lk 24).

People remember well stories drawn from their own locale. "Local stories, folklore and proverbs," declared Jay Moon, missionary in Ghana, western Africa, "open ears of the locals to understand the gospel, clear away the fog of theology-related communication and root the gospel into vernacular soil." He related, "I was learning that the proverbs were an open window into the Builsa's deep cultural values. The more I understood these, the better I was able to understand and communicate in this culture."[17]

---

[17] Jay Moon, "Sweet Talk in Africa," in Evangelical *Missions Quarterly*, April 2004, 166.

Guideline 13
Find pointers to Christ in pagan lore.

In Athens, the apostle Paul used a heathen custom as a bridge to introduce the gospel (Acts 17:22-23). An on-the-ball missionary to another culture seeks within its lore analogies to introduce the gospel. The Omniscient One has seeded in many cultures keys to men's hearts, also called "redemptive analogies."[18] The Buddha predicted that a leader would come some day to do what he could not do, deal with sin. Some Chinese pictorial characters have apparent redemptive significance.

Wrong! Romans 1 says that the Spirit of the Almighty convinces everyone of sin through their conscience, and His creation shows everybody His power.

There's nothing of value in pagan culture!

He also has sown signposts in pagan lore that point to truth.

Do not make finding redemptive analogies a requirement for pioneer work. In many fields, people come to the Lord Jesus Christ readily when workers only explain the treasure of analogies found in Scripture. Seeking analogies from paganism sometimes causes needless delay. Examples of pointers to Jesus Christ in non-Christian traditions include these:

In a certain South Asian country, many Muslims believe that Allah has 100 names of which humans know only 99 and that only the camel knows the 100th. However, the *Koran*, they say, discloses

---

[18] The concept of redemptive analogies is well illustrated in Don Richardson, *Peace Child.* Ventura: Regal Books, 1975.

the camel's secret, the 100th name being "Isaa" (Jesus). Many Muslims have come to faith in Jesus through this approach.

In West Africa, Islamic brotherhoods think that their religious clerics have power to intercede with Allah, in this life and at the final judgment. Christian preaching about the cross and resurrection did not interest them. When informed Christians shared Jesus as a powerful intercessor with God, many Muslims sought Him.

In South Asia, Hindu villagers call on different gods to help in the areas of life that each god is believed to have influence, such as health, weather, marriage, travel, and money. When Christians learn about a community's local gods, and how those gods fail—which they often do—they can show that Jesus has power over those things, and many have come to Christian faith.

In Taiwan, innumerable folktales have been passed down for centuries relating to the origin of the cosmos, the origin of human beings and creation.[19]

Guideline 14
Reach entire families for Christ.

When you visit a nest, deal first with the bird
who heads the pecking order, otherwise you
will break up the nest!

Let us look at ways to reach entire families...

---

[19] Ralph Covell, *Pentecost of the Hills in Taiwan* (Pasadena: Hope Publishing House, 1998), 33f.

Acknowledge and befriend the head of a household. Witness to that person about Jesus the Messiah, as Paul and Silas did with the Philippian jailer (Acts 16:22-34). Some evangelists aim first at young people or women who seem easier to reach. Doing so proves a trap. A flock made up mainly of youth and a few women leaves the outside church planter in control, which, in cross-cultural work, spells doom for a church plant. Congregations that fail to embrace entire families have little cultural relevance and fail to reproduce until a generation goes by and the outsiders are no longer leading.

In pioneer fields, it is normally much more strategic to gather a flock by winning the head of a family to Christ. Immediately teach him to shepherd his own family and friends. After he is baptized, he is free to begin celebrating the Lord's Supper in his home. This freedom permits the new congregation to grow under the new leader's sponsorship and not that of the church planter who mentors him. Peter did so with Cornelius in Acts 10. An outside worker continues to mentor the new leader and other new believers who show leadership ability. Their pastoral responsibilities grow and blossom as they learn more of the Bible.

Keep the new families together. Program-oriented flocks segregate age groups, especially for Christian education. They ought rather to build edifying relationships between people of all ages. Children yearn to be friends with older children, who in turn desire approval of adults. Wise disciple makers enable flocks to tap this natural dynamic by having people in each age group disciple younger Christians. To segregate by age provokes youth to distrust their parents by encouraging an excessively individualistic faith which divides families.

Joshua took time to read to the people the commands of Israel's Deliverer. He included the little ones, even during the rush of his military campaign to occupy the Promised Land (Josh. 8:35). A wise Christian worker on his busiest days will read the Word of God to his children and explain it while teaching new churches to do the same. The evil one tempts us in our busyness to neglect our children and wives. Many families have suffered misery as a result.

Families that pray and discuss the Word of God together daily are stronger, happier and healthier. Scripture directs parents to train their children in the faith (Deut 6:4-7; Eph 6:4). No one can take the place of a parent to build the foundations of a child's faith. One simple way is for parents, especially fathers, to tell Bible stories to their children. Also, let older children prepare and tell Bible stories in the new churches and in their families. Be sure to allow and guide the children toward making disciples of their own younger siblings and friends.

A child who is old enough to discern right from wrong needs to know and obey the basics truths of Scripture, such as the Ten Commandments, the commands of Jesus, foundational Bible stories, and the "one another" commands of the New Testament. A child whose parents love and disciple him will learn as well as an adult does to become an active Christian. He will not merely listen passively but will obey the Lord happily.

Guideline 15
Baptize without delaying for legalistic reasons.

	Careful? You are careless!
I wait to baptize people until I am absolutely certain that they have straightened out their entire lives. I am very, very careful!	Because you doubt that our Creator has begun His work in their hearts, you discourage them! Do not exclude newly-hatched chicks from the nest! They need the flock's warm, loving acceptance.

Follow the Apostles' practice of baptizing new believers. Missionaries sometimes delay baptism, because they want to be careful. Delays discourage many seekers. Delaying baptism because of missionaries' doubts can prove deadly. If one feels that he must be careful, let him first be careful to obey Christ's command to baptize and thereby to assure new believers.

Church planters should baptize sinners to confirm their repentance, faith and new life in Christ, as soon as is reasonably possible, as Philip did (Acts 8:26-40). In pioneer fields, where Christian influences come mostly from a missionary, many adult converts fall away, unless they are baptized within a reasonable time. A new believer does not feel that the Lord Almighty has accepted him until His people have done so by baptizing him. In the apostolic church, they baptized adult believers at once, then instructed them in the faith (Acts 2:41-42). Delaying baptism to follow men's rules discourages new believers and obstructs the grace of God. Church planters themselves disobey the Lord's command, if they refuse baptism to repentant sinners (Acts 10: 47-48). The apostles baptized them and served them the Lord's Supper without delay, then taught them to do everything else that Jesus commanded (Acts 2:37-47).

A new believer is to be baptized into a local Body of Christ as a corporate disciple, not as an isolated individual in God's sight. Satan, our adversary, whispers that it is spiritual to add stiff requirements for baptism, for he despises God's grace! Some leaders take high Christian standards from the Epistles for Christians and make them into requirements for baptism. However, those instructions were for church members who had already been baptized and under pastoral care. Adding unbiblical necessities for baptism breeds legalism, which the Lord hates. Unlike the older brother of the prodigal son, let shepherds prove lavish with God's grace!

An evangelist has not completed his work until a new believer is added to a flock by baptism.

The apostles wisely counted converts only after they were baptized, as seen in Acts 2:41.

Some use baptism as a kind of graduation ceremony following a long period of indoctrination or probation, to make sure a seeker will not fall into sin after baptism! Such doubt discourages newborn believers. Does a mother leave a newborn baby outside the door until the child stops soiling its nappies? So also let a babe in Christ go through a time of infancy. Open the door wide and give him the loving care he needs! The only ceremony that Scripture specifies for opening the door into God's Kingdom is baptism. Of course, there are some valid reasons to delay baptism, which do not stem from doubt or legalism. For example, one might wait for family members to convert or until there are enough converts to defend themselves in hostile fields.

Do not baptize new believers in public if others might ostracize or kill them. Many have died needlessly, because Western missionaries assumed erroneously that baptism must be a public testimony. Paul baptized the Philippian jailer and his family privately at midnight and Philip baptized the Ethiopian in a desert without a public audience.

Guideline 16
Make disciples in a New Testament way.

To make disciples, I teach them detailed doctrine about every vital theological issue!

Jesus said to make disciples by teaching them to obey Him above all.

Sometimes missionaries can become so enamored with starting new churches, that they forget the means, which is to love and to obey the Lord by making disciples. Recall and practice continually a few fundamentals about making disciples.

What disciple making is

- Disciple making results in transformation of believers' hearts and wills by receiving the Holy Spirit and obeying all of Jesus' commands (Matt 28:18-20). Obedience, as an expression of love, is a major theme throughout the New Testament.

- Obedience is not legalism, for believers are to obey out of love. Jesus said, "If you love me, you will obey what I command," (Jn 14:15) and "You are my friends if you do what I command you" (Jn 15:14).

- The Almighty's part in this transforming process is to change believers from within by the power of His indwelling Holy Spirit.

- The believer's part is to obey Jesus' commands in loving, childlike, submission (Jn 14:34-35).

What disciple making is not

- Disciple making is not normally done one-on-one. While doing so is not prohibited, do as Jesus did who normally worked with twelve, sometimes three and on rare occasions, one.

- Disciple making is not merely helping new believers in their spiritual life nor is it teaching biblical doctrines. Jesus and his apostles made disciples of strong leaders as well as seekers, new believers, and growing saints, both by teaching them and by modeling Kingdom life and skills.

New Testament disciple making must prove highly relational. A congregation or movement of new churches remains truly alive as long as its members serve each other as corporate disciples. United by the Holy Spirit, they use their various spiritual gifts to edify one another in love (Rom 12:3-16, 1 Cor 12-14, and Eph 4:11-16). To make corporate disciples, big congregations can form cell groups that remain small enough to practice a "one another" church body life. When believers minister one to another, they get help with the problems in their lives and seekers come to know the Lord. Trusting leaders can organize such interaction in different ways, by fostering interpersonal relationships. Prison Fellowship founder, Chuck Colson, commented:

> I have seen this simple practice (of body life) work wonders in my own life. In fact, I would never have developed real Christian maturity merely by staying home, reading religious books, and attending church once a week—no more than an athlete can develop by shooting baskets alone in the driveway. We are all part of a larger Body, and as parts we can't operate alone. Nor is the Body fully formed when some of its parts are not fully integrated.[20]

New Testament disciple making fosters loving submission to the Lord before all else. Just before ascending to glory our Supreme Commander said that He had all authority in Heaven and earth, and he ordered His followers to make disciples by teaching them to obey all His commands (Matt 28:18-20). The first 3,000 believers in Jerusalem began at once to obey those commands (Acts 2:36-47). Their obedience suggests these seven foundational commands of Jesus:

Checklist of Basic Commands of Jesus

☐ Repent and believe (Mk 1:15; Jn 3:16; 20:22).

☐ Baptize new believers, enabling them to lead the new, holy life that baptism initiates (Matt 28:18-20).

☐ Break bread together often (the Lord's Supper, Lk 22:14-20).

☐ Love God and others (Lk 10:25-37; Jn 13:34; Mt 6:44).

☐ Pray using Jesus' name (Matt 6:5-13; Jn 16:24).

☐ Give to meet needs (Matt 6:19-21; Lk 6:38).

☐ Make disciples (Matt 7:24-29; 28:18-20).

These basic orders for Jesus' followers undergird all Christian life and ministry. Jesus said that to obey His words is to build on rock (Matt 7:24-27). He is the Rock and our part is to obey His com-

---

[20] John Trent, *Go the Distance* (Colorado Springs: Focus on the Family Publishing, 1996), 109.

mands. His commands remain the foundation and are distinct from the apostles' commands which came later and were written to baptized believers under pastoral care. The apostles' commands build on Christ's. For example, Jesus commanded the breaking of bread to commemorate His death, and Paul later separated it from a common meal, because some Corinthians were more interested in eating food than in the sacramental purpose of communion (1 Cor 11:20-34).

Three Levels of Church Authority

To avoid arguments about what new believers should be allowed to do, leaders can distinguish three levels of authority for church activities:

- *Divine commands in the New Testament.* These are required of all disciples. Practice them under all circumstances and never prohibit them. These include the foundational commands of the Lord Jesus and those of His apostles that build upon His commands. Believers should obey these commands without argument and without voting on them. These do not include Old Testament laws, or a church would have to stone people to death if they gathered firewood on a Saturday morning.

- *Apostolic practices.* These include activities mentioned, but not commanded in the New Testament. Leaders have no biblical authority to require or to prohibit their practice. Examples include worship on Sundays, baptizing immediately, fasting, using one communion cup, and many others. Since such apostolic practices were not commanded, one may or may not follow them, depending on local circumstances. Likewise, one should not prohibit them, since the apostles approved them.

- *Human customs.* These are church practices that are not mentioned in the New Testament. Their only authority lies in voluntary agreement within a congregation, so do not force them upon other congregations. Leaders must prohibit customary practices that hinder obedience (Matt 15:1-20). Examples include church buildings, pulpits, choirs, non-biblical requirement for ordination, and many others. Such traditions do not appear in the New Testament and believers should not impose them upon others with doubled fist. Only the Lord Jesus Christ has the authority to make universal laws for His people. Now, most human traditions do prove useful, but they almost invariably turn bad when forced upon people of a different culture.

Leaders can avoid many needless arguments by carefully discerning these three levels, for nearly all church splits and quarrels arise when legalistic, power-hungry, though well-meaning but ill-taught, believers put apostolic practices or mere human customs in the place of divine commands.

True disciple making maintains balance in the body. Perfectly balanced harmony originates as the nature of the Trinity flows into the Body of Christ, starting when one is baptized in the name of the Father and of the Son and of the Holy Spirit. The three Persons of the Trinity remain One God, sharing the identical attributes of deity. They are also three distinct Persons in eternal relationship. This implies that they have distinct, united personalities, individually reflecting three roles: (1) the loving Father's authority; (2) the loving Son's submission, as revealed in his becoming human and living within time and space doing the Father's will; and (3) the Holy Spirit's glorifying of the Son by indwelling and empowering believers for fruitful expressions of love and service. Balanced discipleship (see Figure 8) embraces and reflects these three roles of the Trinity who dwell in believers.

Figure 8
Personality Roles within the Trinity

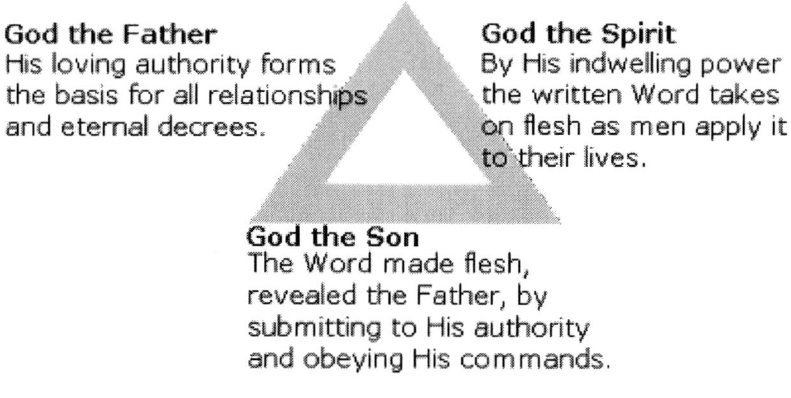

God the Father
His loving authority forms
the basis for all relationships
and eternal decrees.

God the Spirit
By His indwelling power
the written Word takes
on flesh as men apply it
to their lives.

God the Son
The Word made flesh,
revealed the Father, by
submitting to His authority
and obeying His commands.

Our relationships. God the Father eternally exercises loving authority in all His relationships. Thus, balanced disciples submit voluntarily to the loving authority of their Heavenly Father.

The Word. God the Son reveals and carries out the Father's will, in loving submission. He is the image of the invisible God, the eternal Word made human. Thus, balanced disciples learn and apply the Word to every aspect of their life. "His name is the Word of God" (Rev 19:13).

His work. God the Holy Spirit leads, empowers, comforts, convicts and bears spiritual fruit. Thus, balanced disciples let the Holy Spirit empower them for fruitful ministry.

Just as the persons of the Trinity work in perfect, balanced harmony, so believers should also keep in balance those three corresponding aspects of discipleship reflected from the Trinity. To separate them would weaken a congregation's ministry. One cannot receive one-third or two-thirds of God. Being one, the Persons of the Trinity remain eternally united and cannot be separated.

New Testament disciple making also proves highly reproductive. Disciples who are shepherds-in-training should begin at once to train others, passing on what they receive from their trainer. Help your trainees to begin doing so immediately. As a more effective means to gather new congregations, teach trainees to look for at least one mature family man who wants to study and pass on God's Word. Keep disciple making chains extending through your trainees and theirs as Paul did through Timothy, reliable people, and others also (2 Tm 2:2). Doing so reproduces shepherds and flocks at the same time. So ask trainees to do the practical work needed to establish and reproduce their flock. God prohibits the teaching of passive hearers (Jam 1:22).

Guideline 17
Worship and break bread in a way that fits small flocks.

Develop the skill of leading worship in very small groups. In pioneer fields, most new churches begin as tiny groups. Since many church planters have no experience with a small-group worship style, they force small groups to behave as though they were a big audience. Often the results prove grotesque. New, little flocks should not try to compete with big flocks by imitating big-group worship. Rather they should take advantage of the family atmosphere of a small group and practice an interactive church body life. So put the chairs (or mats) in a circular U-shape arrangement that promotes better interaction and helps everyone, including children, to participate in some way, without forcing shy people to speak before they are ready.

> Some unwise worship leaders strut like peacocks, confusing worship with performance and entertainment!
> Evangelism is different. Strut if you must—
> do what you have to do to communicate with non-believers!
> Let us look at guidelines for worshipping
> in a meaningful way...

True Worship

True worshippers enter the presence of the Most Holy One with the attitude that He requires—one of reverent awe (Heb 12:28).The Lord zapped with fire the sons of Aaron, the High Priest, when they waltzed into His presence in the Most Holy Place without blood (Ex 32; Lev 11). True worship is awesome, solemn and joyful (Psa 30). Serious worship discerns and respects the mystical Body of Christ in the Lord's Supper (1 Cor 10:16-17). Some careless believers in Corinth failed to do so, with harsh results; the Lord put them "to sleep," a euphemism for death (1 Cor 11:27-32).

When leaders fail to distinguish worship from evangelism, they push unconverted people into a form of worship for which they are spiritually unprepared. Careless worship leaders sometimes suffocate seekers with complex worship forms that they neither understand nor appreciate. Other shepherds try merely to entertain believers with an evangelistic style of meeting, when they ought to lead them into God-honoring worship. Some essential elements of worship include the following:

Checklist of Essential Elements of Worship

☐ Praise that may be sung, read, chanted, spoken spontaneously, danced, expressed with a variety of bodily postures, etc.

☐ Prayer which may be expressed in a variety of external forms.

☐ The Bible preached, read, discussed, dramatized, etc.

☐ Giving of money, time, food, etc.

☐ Confession of sins and assurance of forgiveness.

☐ The Lord's Supper.

☐ Loving fellowship between believers.

For small house churches, another element may prove useful: definite beginning and ending times that compensate for the informality of private homes.

Wise worship leaders do not try to entertain audiences or distract attention from the Most Holy One. Some worshipful churches, for example, have their musicians stay to one side or out of sight. However, some missionaries have introduced a style of worship that is inappropriate to the tiny groups that make up most new congregations in pioneer fields. Some import into other cultures an entertaining style of worship that appears frivolous and unfit for divine worship, especially in Muslim fields where believers have, consequently, suffered violent persecution. Lighthearted worship forms turn away serious men. In India, Christian leader, Dayanand Bharati, insisted, "We may worship the Lord in spirit and truth, but if it is in Western ways others in India will not understand it."[21]

---

[21] Bharati, 43.

Just as development workers recognize the need for appropriate technology to advance agricultural and micro-business effectiveness, there is just as great a need for appropriate worship. New leaders in pioneer fields only need equipment and methods that are available and commonly used among the people. Westerners, in their zeal for polished worship services, often thoughtlessly discourage those who lack expensive musical instruments and electronic equipment.

The Lord's Supper

Celebrate the Lord's Supper often as part of Christian worship. Believers affirm their membership in His Body when they share the Lord's Supper in faith (1 Cor 10:16-17; 12:12–13:3). Throughout history until the modern era, the Lord's Supper has been at the center of regular worship for evangelical, Orthodox and Catholic churches. Until about two centuries ago, most congregations located the pulpit to one side and kept the altar at the center with its symbols of the Presence of the Lord Jesus Christ. After the 19th century evangelical awakening, with its emphasis on biblical preaching, the pulpit began to take central place in many churches. Today in North America and in American dominated mission fields, contemporary worship often puts a "worship team" at the center in everyone's view, replacing or eliminating the pulpit. In a pioneer field, let new congregations have the liberty of developing their own liturgical forms just as older ones have done, without importing Western forms that have evolved in the West over the centuries. Let new churches glorify Jesus just as simply as the apostles did!

Remember the death of Jesus Christ regularly by celebrating communion. Jesus said of the bread, "This is my body," and of the cup, "This is my blood" (Matt 26:26-28; compare 1 Cor 10:16). Believers should be taught how to partake worthily by examining themselves in order to "discern the Body" of the Lord (1 Cor 11:23-34). Therefore, explain every time about the cup and the bread, and arrange for all the believers to participate without excluding one another.

Paul affirmed that eating the bread is a participation in Jesus' body and drinking from the cup is a participation in His blood (1 Cor

10:16-17). Protestants should not deny God's supernatural work in communion in reaction to the Roman dogma that the bread changes into the very substance of the body of Jesus. Should it surprise believers that the All Powerful One works as supernaturally in communion as he does through preaching and prayer? Transforming lifeless pieces of bread would edify no one; rather it is believers that need the transformation that God effects when they celebrate the Eucharist with sincere faith. The bread remains bread while the Almighty changes and sanctifies those who eat it in faith with a yielded spirit. "We who with unveiled faces all reflect the Lord's glory, are being transformed into his likeness with ever-increasing glory, which comes from the Lord, who is the Spirit" (2 Cor 3:18).

Why was the apostle Paul so adamant about "discerning the body" in the Lord's Supper? The Lord allowed some to be ill and to die because they failed to discern it (1 Cor 11:27-34). What "body" did Paul mean? The body of Jesus that hung on the cross? The universal Church? The body of believers that gathered in Corinth to break bread? Human reason clamors for a simple explanation, that the "body" be one or the other; but God's Word does not use language that way. The context of Paul's remarks about the bread and wine, including 1 Corinthians 10:16-17, shows that he was probably thinking about all three aspects of Jesus' body.

Some missionaries fail to show respect for Christ's body by neglecting the Lord's Supper, serving it seldom. Others refuse to let new leaders serve it out of fear that they might let it become dead ritual. Recent history shows that when it has become a dead ritual in a mission field, older leaders have usually been the ones who killed it! Some neglect it because their churches for generations have overreacted to excessive and superstitious emphasis on the sacraments. When they celebrate communion they almost apologize for it, and explain it in purely rationalistic terms. Their congregations lack discipline as a result. Their biased missionaries infect others with a damaging anti-ritual virus.

The adversary has tempted God's people to go to one of two extremes in their view of the Lord's Supper: either toward a magical view bordering on superstition or toward a rationalistic view that denies any mystery. Both are equally destructive. Many Protestants need to avoid being overly rationalistic. They should pray that the Lord will work just as miraculously through the Lord's Supper as they would ask Him to through their teaching. The bread remains bread, the wine is still wine but this does not annul the real presence of Christ. Faith brings to the symbols the power of the reality that they symbolize. The Lord's transforming, gracious power works in believers if they accept it with faith. Just as the bread and wine are digested and passed through the blood stream to every cell in one's body, so the Spirit of Christ permeates a communicant's entire being. The celebration becomes a true participation in the body and blood of the Lord (1 Cor 10:16-17).

To disobey Jesus by neglecting the sacred feast that He commanded in remembrance of His death denies His universal authority (Matt 28:18-20). If a congregation disobeys Him, then He is not its King or its Head.

Ordination

A problem always arises eventually when men impose non-biblical ordination requirements. Wise missionaries find that such requirements do not fit a local culture. Non-biblical ordination requirements from another culture sometimes force converts to disobey the Son of God, neglecting this command. Or some church traditions require that only ordained ministers serve communion. Some require education beyond what is reasonable for national pastors. Congregations—now discouraged—stop celebrating the Lord's Supper. Placing rules of men above Jesus' commands denies His deity and debases His Kingship. If your church requires ordination, then limit its requirements to those of Scripture. Any additional rules adapted to field conditions should facilitate rather than limit loving obedience to the Head of the Church.

Guideline 18
Train shepherding elders.

 To provide leaders for new flocks
in a pioneer field, show
newly-converted heads of families
how to tend their own nest,
shepherding their families and friends.

Let us consider how...

Appoint elders the way Jesus and his Apostles did. The apostles organized new congregations by naming spiritually mature men as elders and co-pastors to shepherd them. These were not traditional churches with buildings and professional, paid clergy. They met in homes and godly men shared leadership. Paul instructed Titus to appoint elders in Crete (Ti 1:5). Timothy was one of the elders in Ephesus, apparently the primary shepherd. Today many congregations designate such elders as "pastor," "vicar," "shepherd," "co-pastor" or "home group leader." Whatever the title, the job is to equip a small number of believers to serve and to shepherd.

Missionaries fail to let flocks multiply normally when they seek only full-time professional pastors. The elders in apostolic times did not overbearingly rule the church. They were co-pastors who shepherded home groups, taught the Bible, organized believers to serve in different ministries, and led worship (1 Pet 5:2-3).

In pioneer fields with no experienced leaders, congregations often multiply rapidly, and church planters name as leaders the most mature men that God gives them (compare Acts 14:23). Some missionaries call them provisional elders because they do not yet meet all the biblical requirements to be permanent, official elders. Without these inexperienced leaders, new flocks would have no leaders and Satan's wolves would soon tear the leaderless flocks to pieces (Acts 20:28-31). Missionaries and others confirm these provisional elders later as regular elders when they have proven their ability and as they meet the requirements for overseers stated in 1 Timothy 3:1-7.

Where churches are multiplying in pioneer fields and new leaders lack experience within a well-developed congregation, relational training is crucial. Show them how to do the basic ministries of a church. This desperate need is echoed through Nuñez and Taylor's analysis of Latin America in which they show that there is a "critical shortage of biblically trained leaders" and that "evangelicals love the Bible, but are biblically illiterate."[22] Without this training, congregations will lack essential elements of normal church body life. In pioneer fields, the biblical way to train new shepherds is to mentor them while they work with a flock, as Paul did. Do not wait until leaders have received extensive training in all areas before asking their congregations to do what Scripture requires of them! Teach the flocks what they need when they need it.

In an ideal scenario, missionary education becomes synonymous with Christian education. The local church embraces its role in bringing all nations to the worship of God by creating an environment out of which people minister, go, send, welcome those from other cultures, and mobilize for further involvement.[23]

Train elders relationally, that is, on the job, as the apostle Paul did. The book of Acts and the Epistles name various leaders-in-training who accompanied Paul at one time or another. In that way, Paul constantly reproduced himself. Jesus and Peter did the same, and church history affirms that the other original apostles did so as well. This relational apprenticing of new leaders lets churches and cells multiply spontaneously in pioneer fields. Leaders may supplement relational mentoring with seminars and other forms of training, but must not replace it as the backbone of training new leaders on the cutting edge of a church planting movement. Relational mentoring is a powerful, biblical tool for mobilizing many novice church leaders and holding them accountable.

Train elders to evangelize. Much has been written and applied through the years about Theological Education by Extension (TEE)

---

[22] Nuñez, 164-65.
[23] Paul McKaughan, Dellanna O'Brien and William O'Brien, *Choosing a Future for U.S. Missions* (Monrvia: MARC, 1998), 65.

as an effective on-the-field approach to training elders and pastors. Years ago, Patterson tweaked TEE to form Theological Education and Evangelism by Extension (TEEE), which combines pastoral training and evangelism in a church context, introducing the training "menu," a kind of checklist of vital doctrines and activities that novice leaders must learn.[24] The menu includes the same basic topics as does a traditional, biblical theological curriculum though not in the same prescribed order. The order of studies chosen from a menu follows the growth and development of each student's flock, enabling trainers and students to select studies that fit the current needs and opportunities of trainees' flocks.

Appropriate training curricula for new shepherds offer Bible, doctrine, and church history in bite-sized chunks. Trainer-mentors listen to their trainees like a waiter in a restaurant, in order to learn what their flocks are hungry for and what they lack. They then choose from the menu a study that will equip trainees to serve their flocks for a corresponding ministry. Mentors then help trainees to plan their church-related activities, practice needed skills, and assign readings that support their plan, so that trainees apply biblical doctrine immediately to the current life of their churches and to their role in the community. To train in this way, follow these steps in any order: in weekly, semimonthly, or monthly mentoring sessions with new leaders:

Checklist of Mentoring Session Activities

☐ Pray for guidance.

☐ Listen to each trainee report what his flock has done since the last session. Compare it with what he had planned in the previous session.

☐ Help each trainee to plan what his flock will do until the next mentoring session. Record plans and let both trainer and trainee keep a copy.

☐ Review studies that each has done since the last meeting.

---

[24] See more on TEEE under guideline 53.

☐ Assign studies that support each trainee's plans.

☐ Practice together any new skills the trainees need to learn.

☐ Intercede for the people that each trainee plans to serve.

The order in which these are done is not important as long as the mentor listens to discern needs before making plans. Pray with your disciples any time during the session that a need comes up. When traveling with Patterson, one quickly notices how often he stops to pray with his trainees.

Guideline 19
Teach the Bible biblically.

No. We must teach the Bible
biblically!

Isn't it enough
to teach the Bible in
any way we can?

Teach like Jesus and his Apostles did.
Teach in the way they told you to!
Let us find out how...

Christian congregations and house churches are multiplying by the thousands throughout the world, creating an urgent need to train many more shepherds. Traditional, expensive, institutional education programs and training materials prepared in a Western style cannot meet the need to train the millions of needed shepherds. Therefore non-formal training is needed as well, much like the training described in God's Word.

The Lord yearns for our obedience, and wise pastoral trainers lay a foundation of loving obedience towards Jesus. The first church in Jerusalem, empowered by the Holy Spirit, set a powerful example by obeying, from its first moments, several commands of the Lord Jesus Christ in their most basic form (Acts 2:37-47). Their motive to obey was not to escape the punishment that the Old Testament laws prescribed for law-breakers, but to show love for Jesus, enough to obey Him (Jn 14:15). The foundation of all life and ministry, according to Jesus' Sermon on the Mount, is to obey His words (Matt 7:24-29).

Continue training only those who obey what you have taught them. Jesus told His disciples to "shake the dust" from their feet and leave communities that failed to respond (Lk 9:5) and not to give pearls to pigs (Matt 7:6). Paul and Barnabas turned from people who rejected the good news to those who received it (Acts 13:45-46). Christian workers violate this pattern when they continue to proclaim divine truth to people who merely attend meetings without serving the Lord. Some teachers ought to shake the dust from their method of teaching. If they see no growth, it is usually because they failed to mobilize believers to serve one another, as the Bible requires teachers to do.

The Lord Jesus himself listened to learn about local needs. He described wise teachers in the Kingdom of Heaven in Matthew 13:52. Such teachers tap a variety of resources, "like the owner of a house who brings out of his storeroom new treasures as well as old." A skilled mentor adapts his instruction to current situations. Over time, he develops an assortment of studies that apply to various needs of flocks. He does not simply teach a systematic analysis of related topics. For example, Jesus brought forth old and new ideas when He taught:

> You have heard that it was said, 'Eye for eye, and tooth for tooth.' But I tell you, do not resist an evil person. If someone strikes you on the right cheek, turn to him the other also. And if someone wants to sue you and take your tunic, let him have your cloak as well (Matt 5:38-40).

Jesus and his Apostles prepared no systematic outline for the new leaders to follow. Rather they taught in response to questions, needs, criticisms and current events. New churches in pioneer fields need such an approach to training. Like newborn babies, they have various, urgent needs that require immediate attention.

As good mentors, like Jesus and Paul, listen to a new leader and learn what are his flock's needs, then use a "menu" to select studies that fit that need. Patterson recounted:

> We taught this kind of need-oriented training in India with a skit about a person who asked a storekeeper for a kilo of sugar. The retailer argued, "Sugar is bad for your teeth" and handed the person coffee instead. They argued about this for a while and the buyer left with his hands empty.

> I used to train elders of new churches in Honduras in the traditional way. I failed to listen to them explain what their flock was doing, what problems faced them, and what plans they had. I taught what I had arbitrarily decided that a shepherd might teach at some future time. Later, when I had learned to listen first and respond to each church's needs, trainees became highly motivated and applied immediately what they learned, by teaching or initiating action by their congregations.

Some teachers use a style of teaching that their flock cannot imitate, stifling the normal flow of God's Word from person to person and from family to family. By way of contrast, the Lord told simple stories to communicate biblical truth. "Jesus spoke all these things to the crowd in parables; he did not say anything to them without using a parable" (Matt 13:34). He used stories about everyday life that left sharp images in people's mind about the Eternal One and His Kingdom. Jesus' parables are still easy to remember and to pass on to others. The Holy Spirit uses Bible stories to convict and to illuminate both children and adults at all levels of society and with all educational backgrounds. The *Paul-Timothy* studies[25] that Patterson developed base most of their teaching on biblical stories. For example, teaching about faith focuses on the story of Abraham. These brief studies are written for new shepherds and combine Bible study with related activities to do during the week and also during the flock's weekly worship time. *Paul-Timothy* studies come in pairs; one study is for the new church leader while another is for the children's leader. Each study has three parts:

---

[25] Download *Paul-Timothy* studies freely from <www.Paul-Timothy.net>.

- A Bible study.

- Activities shepherds and their helpers can do during the week.

- Activity to do during an upcoming worship time.

Ezra included children in important teaching, as did Moses and other wise leaders of God's people. When "men, women and children gathered to him from Israel" (Ezra 10:1), Ezra instructed the Israelites to confess their sins and break relationships with idolaters. Their obedience led to nationwide renewal, which was too important to omit the children. Let children join with adults in serious spiritual endeavors. Traditional teachers are often too hasty in separating children from adults, preferring to tell children Bible stories during the adults' worship time. However, it is spiritually healthier to let children briefly act out Bible stories for adults and with them. Thus, the children know that they are an important part of the church body. It is imperative to include children in authentic church life.

Harmonize teaching with the other gift-based ministries. "The body is a unit, though it is made up of many parts; and though all its parts are many, they form one body. So it is with Christ" (1 Cor 12:12). Paul explained in 1 Corinthians 12-14 that just as the organs of the human body achieve harmony, so different gift-based ministries within the church are to be practiced together in love, coordinated by the Holy Spirit. Leaders must allow other believers to share in teaching others, freely practicing commands such as "teach one another," "correct one another," "confess faults one to another," "bear one another's burdens," "forgive one another," etc. In small cell groups, good teachers always avoid monologues and make it easy for everyone to take part.

Leaders must equip believers to instruct and serve one another. Ephesians 4:11-16 reveals the aim and means of teaching believers: the aim is to equip the believers for the work of service and to build up the Body of Christ. To achieve this aim, enable believers to instruct and serve one another in loving harmony according to the abilities of each one.

Speaking the truth in love, we will in all things grow up into him who is the Head, that is, Christ. From him the whole body, joined and held together by every supporting ligament, grows and builds itself up in love, as each part does its work (Eph 4:15-16).

Teach in a way that is easy to imitate. Paul wrote to Timothy, "The things you have heard me say in the presence of many witnesses, entrust to reliable men who will also be qualified to teach others" (2 Tm 2:2). Teach new leaders in a way that they can imitate at once, for your teaching style must be kept reproducible. When the apostles trained new leaders in the way Jesus said to do, churches multiplied. The same thing happens today in pioneer fields where missionaries and trainers pass on a "light baton." While training, avoid methods that are difficult to imitate, and leave out equipment that is unavailable to trainees.[26]

James taught for outcomes. James 1:22 pleads for believers to be "doers of the Word and not hearers only." Good teaching applies the Bible immediately in a practical way to people's lives. Before trying to instruct or to make plans, ask your disciples what their flock has done in response to previous teaching. Investigate the outcomes of trainees' teaching.

Help trainees to discover for themselves what the Word teaches. The Bereans searched the Scriptures to see if what Paul said was true (Acts 17:10-11). Give new leaders tools with which to mine gems from the Word. Let trainees discover for themselves the Almighty One's priceless truths. Good Bible studies enable students to find biblical truths easily and accurately. Instead of simply telling people what the Holy Spirit does for believers, ask them to make discoveries by examining for themselves passages like John 14-16; Acts 2; Romans 8; 1 Corinthians 12-14 and Galatians 5.

Jesus and his Apostles taught non-formally. They apprenticed new leaders by combining verbal instruction with fieldwork. Jesus taught the crowds by monologue, but also prepared novice leaders by walking and conversing with them (Matt 5:1-2). When Paul taught the Ephesian congregation, he interacted with his audience. The

---

[26] Appropriate technology is explained further in chapter 4.

context of Acts 20:7 is cordial and passionate, not a time for philosophical oratory. The idea is to maintain balance between classroom instruction and non-formal mentoring. Patterson and Scoggins wrote, "To meet in large groups saves time and encourages the participants—but we cannot do personal disciple making if we only teach large classes."[27] Teaching gives better results when done on the job, outside of a classroom. Paul wrote: "Follow my example, as I follow the example of Christ" (1 Cor 11:1).

Teach or write studies that would appeal to actual persons whom you know. Paul kept in mind those to whom he wrote his letters, sometimes naming them, dealing with specific situations in their flocks, and responding to questions and reported needs. Peter had shepherding elders in mind when he wrote 1 Peter. John wrote, "I write to you, dear children, because your sins have been forgiven... I write to you, fathers, because you have known him... I write to you, young men, because you have overcome the evil one" (1 Jn 2:12-14). Avoid abstract analysis of doctrine by preparing lessons with people and their needs in mind. Write as though the new study were a letter addressed to a specific person who is typical of those who need your instruction.

Find out what a congregation lacks and train its leaders to deal with it. Paul wrote to Titus: "The reason I left you in Crete was that you might straighten out what was left unfinished and appoint elders in every town, as I directed you" (Ti 1:5). A trainer must first listen and verify current needs of each flock, then supply at once through local leaders whom he trains what is lacking in each flock. Novice leaders can train newer leaders effectively, if they have a checklist of activities that the Lord and His apostles require of a congregation. The checklist enables trainers easily to chart a new congregation's progress. Church activities that the New Testament calls for within a congregation usually fall into one of several common categories.[28]

---

[27] George Patterson and Richard Scoggins, *Church Multiplication Guide* (Pasadena: William Carey Library, 1993), 100.

[28] A more detailed list of these fundamental church activities appears under guideline 20.

Checklist of New Testament Congregational Activities

- ☐ Assurance, counseling, visiting
- ☐ Bible, general studies about the Bible, interpretation
- ☐ Church planting
- ☐ Disciple making
- ☐ Evangelism, salvation from sin, death and hell, baptism
- ☐ Family life
- ☐ Giving, stewardship, self-support
- ☐ Growing in Christian character
- ☐ Historical events of importance
- ☐ Love, fellowship, helping the needy
- ☐ Missions
- ☐ Organizing, overseeing
- ☐ Prayer, healing, spiritual warfare
- ☐ Teaching in a biblical way
- ☐ Training leaders
- ☐ Worship, the Lord's Supper

Guideline 20
Promote dynamic interaction in small groups.

Teach new shepherds how to practice interactive church body life. When a group grows too large for its members to practice the interaction that the Bible requires, adjustments are needed. It may need to be reorganized. Believers should meet in cell groups small enough for people to relate to one another as the Almighty requires. How small does a group need to be? Shepherds that have had experience with small groups recommend from seven to fifteen adults. New leaders should begin with smaller groups.

Several churches in Portland, Oregon, formed groups small enough to instruct and serve one another. Here is what three of them did:

New Hope Community Church has formed more than 500 groups or cells that are small enough to deal with one another's unique needs, and they have won many hundreds to Christ.

City Bible Church has more than 150 shepherding groups. Members attend united worship every other Sunday and attend their home groups on alternate Sundays. The congregation's leaders train small group leaders in ministry skills.

Sunset Presbyterian Church tells all seekers and new members that they are to participate in home fellowships where they receive most of their teaching and spiritual fellowship. The pastors speak about this often to their congregations and interview people who have come to Christ or experienced other victories in the small groups, to keep interest white hot.

I am going to compartmentalize our programs to make them easier to administrate, by keeping them separate.

Come back! That is man's traditional way to organize.

The New Testament way gives better results. Its "one another" commands break down those isolated compartments.

The "one anothers" are listed below in four categories. A leader may want to print them for a small group. After interacting with one of the "one another" verses, agree as a group on how to put it into action in meetings, in relationships with each other, and with people who are not part of the group. A leader may want to write out this agreement as part of the group's covenant. It may require several meetings to work through these valuable "one another" verses.

Checklist of New Testament "One Another" Commands

To minister to each other:

☐ Teach and admonish one another: Colossians 3:16.

☐ Instruct one another: Romans 14:14.

☐ Exhort one another: Hebrews 3:13.

☐ Do good to one another: 1 Thessalonians 5:15.

☐ Care for one another: 1 Corinthians 12:25.

☐ Bear one another's burdens: Galatians 6:1.

☐ Speak the truth, as members of one another: Ephesians 4:25.

☐ Serve one another with whatever gift each has received: 1 Peter 4:10.

☐ Lay down your lives for one another: 1 John 3:16.

To encourage good fellowship:

☐ Have fellowship with one another: 1 John 1:7.

☐ Love one another: John 13:34-35; 5:12, 17; Romans 12:10; 1 Thessalonians 4:9; 1 John 3:11, 14, 23; 4:7, 11, 12; 2 John 1:5.

☐ Love one another to fulfill the law: Romans 13:8.

☐ Increase in love for one another: 2 Thessalonians 1:3.

☐ Abound in love for one another: 1 Thessalonians 3:12.

☐ Be kind to, bear with, and forgive one another: Ephesians 3:13; 4:32; Colossians 3:13.

☐ Have genuine mutual love from the heart for one another: 1 Peter 1:22.

☐ Maintain constant love for one another: 1 Peter 4:8.

To build spiritual unity:

☐ Show honor to one another: Romans 12:10.

☐ Agree with one another: 2 Corinthians 13:11.

☐ Live in harmony with one another: Romans 12:16 (see Romans 15:5).

☐ Wash one another's feet: John 13:14.

☐ Greet one another with a holy kiss (this corresponds to an embrace in some cultures): Romans 16:16; 1 Corinthians 16:20; 2 Corinthians 13:12; 1 Peter 5:14.

☐ Wait for one another to break bread: 1 Corinthians 11:33.

☐ Be at peace with one another: Matthew 9:50.

☐ No longer criticize one another: Romans 14:13.

☐ Do not speak badly against one another: James 4:11.

☐ Do not grumble against one another: James 5:9.

☐ Bear with (have patience with) one another: Ephesians 4:2.

☐ Be subject to one another: Ephesians 5:21.

☐ Through love, become slaves to one another: Galatians 5:13.

☐ Have unity, sympathy, and love for one another: 1 Peter 1:22.

☐ Clothe yourselves with humility in your dealings with one another: 1 Peter 5:5.

To build up the body:

☐ Encourage and build up one another: 1 Thessalonians 4:18 and 5:1, 11.

☐ Provoke one another to love and good deeds: Hebrews 10:24.

☐ Meet together, encourage one another: Hebrews 10:25.

☐ Glorify God together: Romans 15:6.

☐ Rejoice together: 1 Corinthians 12:26.

☐ Come together, each with a hymn, a lesson, a revelation, a tongue or an interpretation: 1 Corinthians 14:26.

☐ Welcome one another: Romans 15:7.

☐ Be hospitable to one another: 1 Peter 4:9.

☐ Confess your sins one to another and pray for one another: James 5:16.

☐ Suffer together: 1 Corinthians 12:26.

☐ Work together: 1 Corinthians 3:9; 2 Corinthians 6:1.

Guideline 21
Develop all the activities that God requires a flock to do.

Church planters finish their job when
local leaders are overseeing a flock that
carries out the ministries that Jesus and
his Apostles require.

Let us see what they are...

The New Testament calls all believers to serve the Lord, love one another, and show mercy to the needy of their communities in the ways listed below. These ministries are not to be separated into "departments" or "programs," nor are they to be implemented sequentially, but as needed. The New Testament provides for congregations to harmonize their ministries by having believers serve one another with various spiritual gifts operating within the same group. Thus, service groups maintain an interactive body life, even while performing specific services according to current needs.

Checklist of Ministries that the Lord Requires of All Congregations

Ministries that grow out of Jesus' command to repent, believe, and be born anew by the Holy Spirit

☐ Helping seekers to trust Jesus Christ and to follow Him, confessing their sins to God and turning from them in heartfelt repentance (Jn 3:16; Lk 9:23, Mk 1:15; 1 Jn 1 7-10).

☐ Showing believers what it means to open one's heart to the presence, power, and fruit of the Holy Spirit (Jn 20:22; Acts 1:8; Gal 5:22-23).

☐ Watching over the flock and counting only born-again believers as members of the Body of Christ. Confusion about this invites false doctrines and can result in a powerless body (Jn 3:3; 1 Jn 3:8-10).

Ministries that stem from Jesus' command to baptize

☐ Baptizing sinners who confess their sins, without delaying for legalistic reasons or man-made requirements (Matt 28:18-20; Acts 2:38; Rom 6:1-14).

☐ Assuring and embracing new believers with love and acceptance, assuring them of the Lord's grace and their position in Christ as sons of the Almighty and heirs of His riches (Matt 20:1-15; Eph 1).

☐ Encouraging all believers to live their new "resurrection" life of holiness that baptism initiates (Rom 6:1-14).

Ministries that stem from Jesus' command to break bread and worship

☐ Enabling all believers to participate actively in worship as a body, so that they do not worship by passively observing worship leaders as a form of entertainment (Jn 4:24; Heb. 10:25; 1 Cor 14:26).

☐ Asking the Lord to exalt Jesus and to strengthen believers and to unite them through the Lord's Supper (Matt 26:26-28; 1 Cor 10:16-17; 11:23-24).

Ministries that correspond to Jesus' command to love

(Note: Believers should do all ministries in love, but these ministries relate directly to love.)

☐ Cultivating fellowship and service among all members of the flock (Rom.12:3-21; Jn 13:34-35).

☐ Serving the needy, within the flock and outside of it (Matt 25:31-46; Lk 10:25-37; Acts 6:1-16; Gal 6:10).

☐ Showing disciples how to serve other flocks and to arrange edifying interaction between congregations (Acts 15:22, 27; 24:17; Rom 16).

☐ Strengthening family life and marriages (Eph 5:21- 6:4).

☐ Organizing in such a way that all believers use their spiritual gifts to serve each other in loving harmony, (Eph 4:11-16; 1 Cor 12–13; Rom.12).

☐ Forgiving enemies and seeking reconciliation (Matt 5:43-48).

Ministries that correspond to Jesus' command to pray

☐ Interceding (Col 4:3; 1 Tm 2:1-4).

☐ Praying for healing (Jas 5:14-15).

☐ Maintaining personal and family devotions (Jn 16:24; 1 Thes 5:17; Eph 6:4).

☐ Waging spiritual warfare (Eph 6:10-18; Rom.12:12).

Ministries that correspond to Jesus' command to give and to be good stewards

☐ Giving generously (Lk 6:38), investing in others' eternal future to receive a heavenly reward (Matt 6:19-21).

☐ Warning that materialism breeds selfishness and spiritual ruin (Lk 12:13-34).

☐ Instructing the flock that what they have belongs first to the Lord and that they are His stewards of what he has given them to administer (Matt 25:14-30).

☐ Using one's time wisely (Eph 5:15-17).

Ministries that correspond to Jesus' command to make disciples and to shepherd them

☐ Witnessing for the Lord Jesus Christ by the power of the Holy Spirit, telling others what He has done for them (Acts 1:8; 2 Tm 4:5).

☐ Proclaiming the message that Jesus spoke by telling others about the essential elements of the Gospel message, Jesus' sacrificial death, life-giving resurrection, and promise to forgive all who repent (Lk 24:46-48).

☐ Making disciples of all ethnic groups, by baptizing them and teaching them to obey Jesus (Matt 28:18-20).

☐ Equipping believers for the work of the ministry, applying the Word in the power of the Holy Spirit to their lives (Eph 4:11-16; 2 Tm 3:16-17).

☐ Watching over those under your care and warding off wolves who would lead them astray (Acts 20:28-32; Ti 3:9-11).

☐ Correcting the unruly and restoring the weak without condemning them (Matt 18: 12-14; 15-20; Gal 6:1).

☐ Mentoring leaders and modeling for them pastoral skills and holiness (2 Tm 2:2; 4:12; Ti 1:5).

☐ Sending missionaries to neglected fields (Matt 28:18-20; Acts 1:8; 13:1-3).

☐ Counseling those with problems, as Paul did in his letter to Philemon.

☐ Practicing servant-leadership (Matt 20:25-28; 1 Pet 5:1-4).

Guideline 22
Oversee work in a region in a liberating, reproducible way.

Field supervisors, do not try
to fly too high! Wise planners,
like those building the tower
in Luke 14:28-30,
plan backwards!

Let us see what backward
planning means...

Plan carefully and prayerfully, starting with your God-given, long-range objectives, as a first step toward coordinating regional activities. Wise supervisors discipline themselves to plan with their final goals in mind while considering intermediate steps to arrive at those goals, before defining specific policies and detailed plans. That is, they locate the stepping-stones all the way across a stream before sending people across it. They state goals in terms of results, not efforts, and they later examine the effects of the activities of those they lead. Sam Burton wrote, "Intermediate goals are the worst enemy of the real goals if you can't see beyond those intermediate goals."[29]

Keep in mind even the harshest of field realities as you reason back through the intermediate steps, until you have the complete picture of what your co-workers and trainees should do. For "Z" to happen, Y must be done. For Y to happen, X must be done, etc., all the way back to A.[30]

To plan strategically, forget for the moment who you are, your organization and resources, and think only about the people you are reaching and their circumstances. With these realities in mind, define

---

[29] Sam West man Burton, *Disciple Mentoring* (Pasadena: William Carey Library, 2000), 141.

[30] Backward planning is explained under the guideline *57*.

the field objectives, and then reason backward to where you are. Only then can you reason forward with an appropriate plan. [31]

For example, far-sighted planners envision mature churches multiplying in a field. What will the congregations look like? What type of regional leaders will they need? Will there be shepherds of shepherds? How will they become servant-leaders? Somebody first needs to model servant-leadership—who? This modeling requires an earlier step of training pastors, by making servant-leaders of them. This calls for an even earlier step of introducing biblical mentoring among new believers, which, in turn, defines the type of evangelism needed, and so forth. Liberating nationals in this manner requires planners to avoid certain pitfalls:

- *Avoid premature plans.* Before starting churches, define concisely your geographical and cultural area of responsibility and ministry. Know whom you are serving. Many missionaries cannot define their ministry and area of responsibility. If the Lord is using other workers or teams in the same area, verify where and with whom they are serving. Do not confuse the roles of pastor and missionary, or those you teach will reflect the same confusion and inefficiency.

- *Avoid dreaming while planning field strategy.* Some well-meaning field supervisors plan grand, expensive projects based on fantasies. Plan to do only what the Lord commanded—nothing more and nothing less. Make plans with short, easy steps so that no trainee or leader is frustrated. Do not ask the Eternal One to give you an empire. He will not, but Satan will. Instead, help your students to obey Jesus in humble faith, day by day.

- *Avoid sheep stealing.* Respect the flocks of other shepherds and mission organizations. Wolves abound and cause confusion and misery, especially among newborn lambs. Work where non-Christians live and/or where no effective outreach is taking place. Go where there are so many people that you will not draw

---

[31] On strategic planning see Edward R. Dayton and David A. Fraser, *Planning Strategies for World Evangelization* (Grand Rapids: Eerdmans, 1980).

away members of another flock. Do not let workers' areas of responsibility overlap, unless they are working as a team. Each worker should plant churches only in his area so that he does not confuse new believers in another worker's area. If one has a special reason to work in another area, arrange it first, with whoever is responsible for the other area. 2 Corinthians 10:14-16 comments decisively on this:

> We are not going too far in our boasting, as would be the case if we had not come to you, for we did get as far as you with the gospel of Christ. Neither do we go beyond our limits by boasting of work done by others. Our hope is that, as your faith continues to grow, our area of activity among you will greatly expand, so that we can preach the gospel in the regions beyond you. For we do not want to boast about work already done in another man's territory.

- *Avoid being aimless.* Discuss goals with all workers, so as to keep the overall direction sharp and in focus. Some missionaries keep their disciples in the dark as to the final aim of their work. Such weak, insecure missionaries—like weak pastors—dominate and overly control new works. They plan everything alone, stifling localized initiatives and frustrating workers.

Help each new leader to know where his flock should be heading, so he can take initiative to lead them there. New leaders in pioneer mission fields sometimes lack a concept of a well-organized church. Thus, they may appear to lack initiative, but that may not be the case. They simply do not know where they are going.

Help new believers to visualize a healthy, growing, obedient Body. Ephesians 4:11-16 paints a portrait of a well-organized congregation, edified by the ministry of every member of the local Body of Christ.

- *Avoid errors in leadership placement.* It is essential to authorize mature, respected men to lead new churches. Normally in most cultures, effective church planting starts with calling men first to faith and repentance. Then, help them win their families. Patterson remarked:

When women or single young men occasionally led Honduran churches, they seldom attracted entire families. In these cases, almost all church members were women and children; mature family men had little respect for the problem-ridden churches. I have seen the same situation in dozens of other fields. In two Asian fields, missionaries told me that it was hard to win mature men to Christ, and so they worked mainly with women and children instead. Investigating this I found that the missionaries and national leaders had not really tried to reach the men. They had accepted as fact the rumor that men were hard.

The Holy Spirit does not check out a person's gender before He convinces them of their sin and their need for salvation. In many fields when missionaries began working with men—giving them the respect they deserve as heads of families—they found them to be just as easy to reach as the women.

In most cultures, churches that began mainly with local women as church leaders do not grow and reproduce well, and local male leadership remains weak. Such flocks too often stagnate and fail to command the respect of "macho" men in the area. In most cultures, congregations are normally stronger and more respected by the community when led publicly by mature men. The apostles, following their Lord's example, established congregations with adult male leaders. With this having been said, the Lord has nonetheless blessed the endeavors of thousands of expatriate women church planting missionaries throughout the world. Most have prepared male leaders to take over as soon as possible. Many of them, like Priscilla in Acts 18:24-28, have effectively helped teach men to lead. In some societies, government restrictions and other cultural factors have made it hard for men to lead and the Lord has blessed the leadership of godly women in new churches.

- *Avoid unnecessary delays.* Do not accept the argument, "We cannot start a daughter church yet. Our church is too weak. We must wait until we have a strong home base first. We have no money and no firm leadership." No congregation is too young to obey the Lord Jesus Christ. As soon as a worker is available, send him out. The most effective evangelist is the new believer. Far more people come to Jesus through the testimony of new believers than through the efforts of professional evangelists.

New churches birth daughter churches more readily than old ones. If you wait for your flock to grow strong, it will also become inflexible. The longer a flock waits to reproduce, the harder it will be; its members will have become accustomed to neglecting Jesus' command to evangelize. It is very hard to mobilize an old, sterile flock to birth daughter churches.

- *Avoid communication breakdown.* Instead, maintain communication between mother and daughter churches and all key leaders. Ideally, one flock begets another, which begets another, which begets another and so forth. This requires much care and clear communication by the mother churches. As this takes place, the best church reproduction often occurs one or two links removed from any foreign missionary. As communication by local leaders occurs, national workers generally depend less on outside help, relying more on the Holy Spirit. This spontaneous multiplication of new indigenous flocks tends to avoid much of the damaging effects originating from the missionary's foreign background.

  Beyond four or five links from the first mentor in a training chain, communication among national congregations can break down. Leaders need to reorganize the chains of relationships and occasionally restructure relational connections between congregations and trainers.

- *Avoid detailed bylaws.* Do not saddle a new flock with bylaws from an older mother church. A new congregation should start simply by doing what Jesus says to do. When they are submitting to Him and need to develop their organization, have them add their own policies as needed. Do not let a legalistic-minded believer write bylaws.

I help my flock to be more spiritual by forcing everybody to follow many very harsh rules!

Oh, no! Rules that go beyond what the Lord requires will hinder progress and stifle the flow of Heaven's grace.

There are better ways to oversee...

Paul left Titus in Crete to coordinate the new church work by appointing elders in each town and instructing them in faith, conduct, and responsibilities. Paul did the same during earlier church planting trips (Acts 14:23). In both cases the flocks had been gathered before elders were appointed and were functioning as the Body of Christ, although immaturely. His own comment was, "the reason I left you in Crete was that you might straighten out what was left unfinished and appoint elders in every town, as I directed you" (Ti 1:5).

A coordinator must think in terms of what the New Testament requires of a local church. His duties revolve around this mentality, as cited here:

Checklist of Coordinator's Duties for Overseeing a Very Large Region

☐ Investigate who and where the neglected people groups are in his region, and make plans for trainees to enter those areas.

☐ Build up new church leaders by mentoring them, until they understand and obey the instructions of the Lord and his apostles. He should demonstrate the skills and godly conduct that the new leaders must imitate. This mentoring is easier when a "menu" approach is employed. Use checklists!

☐ Arrange with trainees and leaders to introduce all the ministries required by the New Testament to the new churches.

☐ Plan with leaders at all levels specific activities that will enable their flocks to reproduce by winning people to Christ and preparing local shepherds to lead them.

☐ Help pastoral leaders to identify and mentor new apprentices who lead new flocks.

☐ Provide training materials that mobilize new leaders of new flocks. He needs to provide training materials for all participants in his region. Because of the rapidly growing number of churches in fields where workers follow these New Testament principles, it has been found that procuring, copying, stocking and distributing training materials to mentors is a huge challenge. He should recruit others to keep track of materials.

☐ Arrange seminars for leaders and elders, to supplement the mentoring and to build a sense of joyful unity among older and newer leaders. For example, in parts of northern India where new flocks are born daily, regional coordinators, in addition to mentoring new leaders, lead training seminars twice a month. Yet, "training church planters is not just a matter of seminars. Mentoring is [the] valuable and necessary supplement to seminars."[32]

☐ Train others to also be coordinators and do these same things. The key is to prepare others for their own success.

---

[32] Alliance for Saturation Church Planting, *Omega Course: Practical Church Planter Training,* Manual Five (Crete: The Bible League, 2000), 27.

Guideline 23
Evaluate results with ruthless honesty.

Over 100 individuals made decisions for Jesus during the last three months, but very few want to receive baptism and join our flock. I feel discouraged!

Your problem is that you counted your chicks before they hatched!

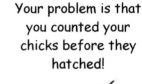

Continually evaluate honestly and accurately the results of evangelism. Some evangelists report huge numbers of converts, but when church planters try to follow up those converts, they cannot find any. Few or none of the so-called converts had been born again. Such reporting discourages workers, hinders church planting movements and weakens new congregations. Avoid foggy thinking, exaggeration, and confusion by following the apostles' practice of counting converts only after the Lord has added them to a church by baptism. Western evangelists also occasionally report exaggerated numbers of conversions and new churches. Perhaps they do so in order to impress their financial contributors. Such dishonesty perpetuates ineffective methods of evangelism.

If a community proves unresponsive to your evangelism, then move on elsewhere. Jesus said to leave towns that do not respond to his good news, even shaking the dust from your feet (Lk 10:10-11) and abandoning any project that the Lord does not specifically direct you to implement. Some workers will choose to stay there to do some sowing without seeing results, for it is God who gives the increase. If God has called you to endure the hardship of lifelong patience with little visible fruit, then keep your feet planted in your field, with eyes toward the Lord. Otherwise, prayerfully move on to fields that are "white and ready for harvest."

Evaluate your methods of evangelism prayerfully and object-ively. If the Lord does not use your efforts to produce obedient, loving disciples, then seek another, more receptive population. Patterson remembered:

> I have known several missionaries who "shook the dust" and shifted from one set of people to another. They then saw the gospel flow more freely. None had to change their place of residence. Rather they merely focused on a poorer, less educated segment of the same population. Even Jesus found greater acceptance among the working class people of Galilee than He did among the rich and powerful of Jerusalem.

The author recalls when he shook the dust and stopped holding "special meetings" as his main evangelistic tool. Instead, he trained local believers to witness in the power of the Holy Spirit to their relatives and friends, with much better results. Patterson observed:

> Years ago, I persisted too long in my first church planting project. Being a new missionary, I felt that my career depended upon success, as many new missionaries normally feel a bit insecure. However, I made so many mistakes with that first church plant that the project became a lost cause! My Honduran friends had to drag me away from it! Fortunately, Honduran workers later went to that same village and started a church properly. Many missionaries have discovered that the Spirit of God waters the seed that they have sown while they are away.

Do not assume that your work is effective simply because you have worked hard to apply some method that others have promoted. For example, some misapply the concept of friendship evangelism, believing that the Holy Spirit cannot work until they have spent months in building relationships. Neither the Lord Jesus Christ nor His apostles modeled such friendship, and workers should not wait so long to proclaim the gospel that they reveal distrust of the Lord's power to work as He did in the New Testament. In order to keep faithful flocks reproducing, do not keep on befriending and evangelizing those who reject Jesus. After a reasonable time, move on to receptive families.

Surely, our Creator will bless
our evangelism someday,
because we have worked for
months and spent much
money on it.

Evaluate the effectiveness
of evangelism not by your
efforts but by the results!
Let us learn how to do so...

Monitor your trainees' workloads. Avoid giving to your trainees too much work or assignments that others have failed to complete in the past. Do not continue a project if it overly discourages your trainees. If they get bogged down with a certain activity, then put it on ice and come back to it later. Perhaps you can find someone else who enjoys doing that activity, or can find an easier way to do it. Drop and avoid projects that have chronic problems and that use up too much time. Shake off the dust and move on, lifting up your eyes to see other fields that are "white unto harvest" (Jn 4:35).

While seeking to obey the Lord every way you can, remain willing to make adjustments without getting bogged down with doubts or with being overly pensive. Patterson said, "When one is busy doing what God's Word says, he has little time to worry about minor decisions and currently-controversial issues that in a few years will no longer seem so important. Even while evaluating your progress, avoid excess introspection." Satan is the accuser who wants us to condemn ourselves and others for every seeming failure.

Monitor how new congregations are doing. Church planters and pastoral trainers should refer to a list of vital ministries as a checklist to monitor progress. For example, Moses gave to the ancient nation of Israel, a list of ten basic commands (the Ten Commandments) that served as the foundation of their covenant with the Holy One (Exodus 20). Likewise, a church needs to know Christ's commands and the other ministries that God requires of them in the apostles' letters. Refer to a list of vital ministries each time trainees give their reports, to help them evaluate their flocks' progress and to expose neglected ministries. Refer to the same list as a curriculum guide for those who train leaders in essential pastoral skills, letting it serve as a kind of menu to choose the activities that each flock still needs to put into practice. Listen to trainees as they report on what the believers in their flocks are doing and on ministry opportunities that emerge. Only then can you teach appropriate biblical doctrines that apply to current flock life and development.

How can I be sure that my reports are accurate?

Keep careful, neat records of what your flock is doing and of what your trainees' flocks are doing.

Refer to your checklist in monitoring trainees' progress. If neither you nor trainees can recall the activities that the Lord expects of their flocks, then the believers will slip into a rut by simply maintaining a few old programs. Weak pastors lead merely by enforcing rules, while a true servant-leader inspires a congregation to move forward in their gift-based ministries. However, believers cannot move forward if their leader does not know where God wants them to go. Keep in mind the following recommendations:

Checklist of Recommended Mentoring Practices

☐ Keep track of what each trainee teaches and does with his flocks. A checklist that lists New Testament congregational activities may also include a number of personal objectives that certain trainees have agreed to pursue. Create your checklist from various guidelines in this book, or generate your own checklist from scripture and experience, ensuring that every activity enables believers to follow the commands of Christ.

Keep looking upwards.
Jesus said we would suffer for Him.
So do your paper work for His sake!

Lists frighten me.
I do not like to do
much paper work!

Record your flock's progress.
Mark items in a list of essential ministries
when the believers are doing them.

☐ Allow sufficient time for a trainee to complete specific field assignments. Two weeks is usually enough. If he keeps making excuses for not doing what he agreed to, then stop trying to train him lest he contaminate other trainees by his bad example. He has forgotten that it is not his trainer whom he serves but the Lord Jesus.

☐ Assess how trainees are performing their fieldwork, and help them when they try and fail by accompanying them as they work with people.

☐ Repeat studies and themes related to activities that a trainee or his flock have been neglecting. When you repeat a theme, assign different readings and verse references about it, if possible. For example, each time you review the activity of witnessing for Christ, assign new reading about Him and His salvation.

☐ Use the activity checklist like a menu to help each trainee choose practical work and readings that fit his flock's current needs. Of course, your checklist should always include the commands of the Lord Jesus Christ and of His apostles.[33]

---

[33] On detailed tips for training leaders see Chapter 4.

Chapter 2

Develop a Healthy, Joyful Body Life

Guideline 24
Let everyone in their flock serve in a vital ministry.

Paul tells all believers
—not just leaders—
to build up one another.
Can my flock ever do that?
They are mere chicks in the
faith, struggling with their
own problems.

To "build up" means
to add something new.
This requires loving
interaction between members.
Let us find how you can help
your young flock to do so...

Enable believers to serve one another and the community at large. Purposeful interaction between all members is scarce in big, traditional churches. However, it is easy for any member, including new ones, to form and lead small, interactive groups in which believers purposefully build up one another.

Assess the strengths and gifts of leaders and of all the believers in their flocks. One easy way to do so is to compare individuals with persons in the Bible, many of whom exhibited more than one gift. Have flock leaders read the following checklist to their flock members and ask each one, "With which of these gift-related activities do you most readily identify?" This assessment can help them to determine each one's gift mix.

I feel bad. My flock of chicks is satisfied to stay just as it is.

Maybe I need to examine my spiritual gifts again.

That will not help. Come here and listen. Look for the God-given abilities and interests of each member of your flock. Help them do what the Almighty wants them to do.

Let us find help in the Word...

Checklist of Biblical Characters and their Gifts

Help believers recognize their God-given gifts by having them choose Bible characters' activities with which they most readily identify.

David

☐ Led troops into battle—gift of leadership.

☐ Planned and prepared materials for building the temple—administration.

☐ Used the arts to praise the Holy One, sing or write Psalms of praise—prophecy.

☐ Dispensed justice—wisdom.

☐ Cultivated deep relationships, as with Jonathan—encouragement.

☐ Forgave his enemy Saul and showed mercy to crippled Mephibosheth—compassion.

Paul

- ☐ Traveled into other cultures experiencing many adventures—apostolic or missionary gift.
- ☐ Took offerings to the poor—giving.
- ☐ Explained theology in letters—teaching.
- ☐ Counseled Christian brothers—pastoral gift.
- ☐ Reached neglected people groups—apostle.
- ☐ Proclaimed the death and resurrection of Jesus—evangelist.
- ☐ Led a church planting task group and organized new congregations—leadership.
- ☐ Earned a living making tents—gift of service.
- ☐ Made disciples of Timothy and Titus—teaching.
- ☐ Prayed fervently for young churches—faith.
- ☐ Corrected false doctrines—discernment.
- ☐ Kept a healthy balance between all these areas of ministry—wisdom.

Priscilla

- ☐ Helped her husband make tents as together they planted churches in difficult fields—helps.
- ☐ Hosted assemblies in her home and cared for traveling missionaries—hospitality.
- ☐ Corrected Apollos' deficient doctrine—teaching.
- ☐ Cared for her husband and family—gift of service.

Peter

- ☐ Proclaimed Jesus' death and resurrection to many at Pentecost—evangelist.
- ☐ Baptized converts and made disciples of them—pastoral.

☐ Sat at Jesus' feet learning about the Kingdom—knowledge.

☐ Discussed church policy with the leaders who came from Antioch—discernment.

☐ Started a church in the Gentile household of Cornelius—apostle or missionary.

☐ Led the church planting group to Cornelius' household —leadership.

☐ Wrote letters to believers to encourage and comfort them—prophecy.

☐ Kept a healthy balance between all these areas of ministry—wisdom.

Nehemiah

☐ Interceded for his people with the Almighty—faith.

☐ Bore the cup for the emperor—gift of service.

☐ Used diplomacy with kings; helped Ezra communicate with an emperor—wisdom.

☐ Traveled far amid perils and adventures to do the Lord's work—apostle.

☐ Scouted Jerusalem's ruins to plan and manage reconstruction—administration.

☐ Inspired the people to work—encouragement.

☐ Put down opposition—leadership.

☐ Compiled names of the exiles that returned to the Promised Land—knowledge.

☐ Explained and applied the Law of the Lord—teacher.

☐ Carried out broad reforms—discernment.

Moses

☐ Led God's people through a perilous desert; supervised the elders of Israel—leadership.

☐ Interceded for his people when they committed idolatry—faith.

☐ Listened to and ruled on cases of injustice—wisdom.

☐ Recorded details of the law—knowledge.

☐ Monitored planning and building of the tabernacle—administration.

☐ Helped Aaron work out forms of worship and composed psalms—gift of prophecy.

Esther

☐ Acted as a "mole" within the royal palace to liberate her people—service.

☐ Exposed Haman's evil plot, following the advice of her mentor, Mordecai—wisdom

☐ Used tact and diplomacy to convince the emperor to enforce justice—exhortation.

☐ Planned important banquets—administration.

Solomon

☐ Dispensed justice—wisdom.

☐ Wrote proverbs—teaching.

☐ Wrote the drama of Song of Solomon with mystical types and symbols—gift of prophecy.

☐ Supervised construction of the temple—administration.

☐ Interceded for Israel in his prayer of dedication—faith.

Mobilize believers to fulfill the vital, five-fold ministries of Ephesians 4:11. The Lord promises to every church apostles, prophets, evangelists, pastors and teachers who equip all believers to do ministry that edifies His Body. The two demonstrations provided below can be acted out to show your flocks plainly how trainees can perform each of these five ministries.

Demonstration 1
Define the five vital ministries which the Lord gives to churches.

The presentation of each of these five ministries follows the same format. Participants need not memorize their words; let them simply keep in mind the general idea.[34] Coach each actor just enough for them to understand what to say.

Actors: *Mentor, Learner* and *Satan.* (Satan, form horns with your fingers as you tempt others.)

Introduction by the MC or main teacher: The MC explains that he will demonstrate what might have happened in Crete about 2,000 years ago, in response to Paul's instructions to Titus. He explains that helpers from the audience will act out the demonstration using the five ministries of apostle, prophet, evangelist, shepherd, and teacher.

Mentor speaking to Learner: A foreigner came. His name is Titus; he had a letter from the apostle Paul. He gave me a copy. It explains his mission here. (Hand to Learner a sheet of paper. It can have the verse written on it.)

Learner reads aloud Titus 1:5: "For this reason I left you in Crete, to straighten out what was left unfinished, and name elders in every town, as I directed you."

Mentor speaking: Titus is a regional coordinator. He told me to train you to start new churches. He said that God gives people to

---

[34] This presentation was made in several Indian states by Patterson, Currah and O'Connor with active audience participation. One pastor commented, "I have heard those whispers from Satan!" Ever the jokester, Patterson commented to O'Connor, "You make a very good Satan."

every congregation to do the five basic ministries. You can read about them in the letter that Paul wrote to the Ephesians (4:11-12).

Learner: I remember! God gives to a congregation apostles, prophets, evangelists, shepherds and teachers, to equip His people to do His work to build up the Body of Christ.

Ministry #1: The apostle

Mentor: "The first ministry is that of the apostle."

Learner: "I know what an apostle is... one who travels far to start churches and is supported with money."

Satan: (form horns with your fingers, sneak up behind Learner) "You would make lots of money!"

Learner "I want to be an apostle and make lots of money!"

Mentor: "Wait! There are two kinds of apostles. Both are "sent ones." You described the first kind. The second kind is normally self-supported and gathers new flocks nearby."

Learner: "I can do that."

Mentor: "For every one of the first kind of apostle, God wants hundreds of the second kind."

Ministry #2: The prophet

Mentor: "The second ministry is that of the prophet."

Learner: "I know what a prophet is... one who shouts and warns sinners of future judgment."

Satan: "You will have great power over people!"

Learner: (echo Satan's words) "I will control people!"

Mentor: "Wait! There are two kinds of prophets. 1 Corinthians 14:3 reveals a second kind who strengthens, encourages and comforts people, to build up the Body."

Learner: "I can do that."

Mentor: "For every one of the first kind of prophet, God wants hundreds of the second kind."

Ministry #3: The evangelist

Mentor: "The third ministry is that of the evangelist."

Learner: "I know what an evangelist is … one who preaches the gospel in big meetings."

Satan: "You will be admired by great crowds!"

Learner: (echo Satan's words) "All will admire me!"

Mentor: "Wait! There are two kinds of evangelists. The second kind is any believer who tells his family and friends about Jesus. It is simple: new believers win more people to Christ."

Learner: "I can do that…"

Mentor: "For every one of the first kind of evangelist, God wants hundreds of the second kind."

Ministry #4: The shepherd

Mentor: "The fourth ministry is that of the shepherd."

Learner: "I know what a shepherd is… one who leads congregations."

Satan: "Yours will be the biggest congregation. Many will leave their churches to go to yours!"

Learner: (echo Satan's words) "Many will follow me!"

Mentor: "Wait! There are two kinds of shepherds. The second kind shepherds cells and house churches, and they who are usually self-supporting."

Learner: "I can do that…"

Mentor: "For every one of the first kind of shepherd, God wants hundreds of the second kind."

Ministry #5: The teacher

Mentor: "The fifth ministry is that of the teacher."

Learner: "I know what a teacher is… one who explains God's Word in a classroom."

Satan: "Everyone will admire your great intelligence!"

Learner: (echo Satan's words) "All who seek truth will come to me!"

Mentor: "Wait! There are two kinds of teachers. The second kind mentors new leaders the way Jesus and the apostles did, usually not for pay."

Learner: "I can do that…"

Mentor: "For every one of the first kind of teacher, God wants hundreds of the second kind."

Conclusion by the MC or main teacher: Explain these ideas:

- All five ministries must be harmonized for best results.

- A leader who is weak in one of these ministries must work closely with another who is strong in it.

- A leader may do more than one of the five ministries.

- Leaders who are doing any of these ministries can best gather congregations by working together with others who have the other gifts.

Demonstration 2
Portray the Five Vital Ministries in Action

Participants include the apostle, prophet #1, prophet #2, evangelist, shepherd, and teacher.

Introduction by the MC or main teacher: The MC explains that he and a few helpers will demonstrate a small group using the five ministries of apostle, prophet, evangelist, shepherd, and teacher. The audience is to identify, after each demonstration, which of the ministries was portrayed.

Ministry #1: The apostle

Apostle: (say in your own words) "Now that you are baptized and are doing what Jesus commanded you to do, you are now a flock."

Anyone: Ask which of the five ministries this believer demonstrated. (Answer: *apostle*, who normally starts new churches in neglected areas.)

Ministry #2: The prophet

Prophet: (say in your own words) "We have all committed deeds of which we are ashamed, and we still fail in many ways. Even so, the Lord forgives us and can help us do better."

Anyone: Ask which ministry was demonstrated. (Answer: *prophet*, who speaks to comfort, strengthen and edify others, 1 Cor 14:3.)

Ministry #3: The evangelist

Evangelist: (say in your own words) "I would like you guests to know that we believe in Jesus Christ. He is the one who died for our sins and rose from the dead. Since I trusted Him to forgive my sins and give me eternal life, I have peace and joy in my heart. We are praying that you will do the same."

Anyone: Ask which ministry was demonstrated. (Answer: *evangelist*, who presents Jesus in a simple way.)

Ministry #4: The shepherd

Shepherd: (say in your own words) "Tomorrow, we are going to take help to some needy people. I have prepared a list of tasks for each of us, and set the time and place for us to go together."

Anyone: Ask which ministry was demonstrated. (Answer: *shepherd*, who provides direction for the whole flock.)

Ministry #5: The teacher

Teacher: (say in your own words) Jesus taught us to obey all of his commandments. Let us review those commands and then describe how to obey them together."

Anyone: Ask which ministry was demonstrated. (Answer: *teacher*, who applies God's Word to equip believers to serve the body.)

Guideline 25
Lead with the Spirit's power; do not simply enforce rules.

"'Not by might nor by power, but by My Spirit,' says the Lord Almighty" (Zech. 4:6).

My flock always has so many problems!

I will scold them more and make stricter rules!

No, no! Scolding focuses on negative ideas and your flock will follow your example. It may become ingrown and defensive, and retreat before Satan's attacks!

Wise leaders serve with power from the Spirit of the Lord, the energizing "olive oil" of Zechariah 4:1-6. Spiritual power comes through personal humility, while egotistical individuals fail to yield control to the Most High. Any weak leader can complain about problems, but it requires the Holy Spirit's help to transform the mentality of many in a widespread movement. Andrew Murray wrote a century ago in Africa, "Humility is not a posture for a time … but the very spirit of our life."[35] The Spirit illuminates ripe opportunities and healthy trends; like the seven-branched, oil lamp

---

[35] Andrew Murray, *Humility* (Minneapolis: Bethany House, 2001), 53.

of Zechariah's vision, He leaves no corner in shade. Spirit-empowered leaders force Satan to flee before them as they lead God's legions to expand Christ's Kingdom by exposing truth.

Wise leaders pursue their God-given goals like Joshua who led his people to occupy their promised land by relying on the Lord's help (Josh 1:1-9). Strong leaders believe that the Lord has given them to their flock to lead and holds them responsible to do so wisely.

As Joshua wisely delegated responsibility for the work to other leaders (Josh 1:10-18), so wise leaders help those whom they coach to define and follow their God-given objectives. The best leaders always delegate authority to other so that they may act on their objectives, and they let new leaders make mistakes. Patterson observed:

> At first, I found it hard to release less-educated Honduran leaders to take serious responsibility, fearing that they would make mistakes. Well, of course, they did. They made almost as many as I did! The biggest mistake I made was not to let them make their mistakes. Jesus often let his apostles err, and used each occasion as a positive teaching opportunity.

Satan seeks to lure well-meaning workers away from their God-given tasks, into fruitless but very spiritual-sounding ministries. For example, some pastors are quick to say, "Do not open a new church in this neighborhood of our city, for our church is already located here. Help us instead." This sounds correct at first, but often such a church fails to reach its neighborhood, because its members live elsewhere and feel little compassion for the people who live near their meeting place. It would be wiser to start a new congregation with those who reside nearby. Patterson recalled:

> On my way to a church planting workshop near Los Angeles, I observed the local neighborhood and saw a large number of Hispanics. However, among the members of the host church there were no Hispanics. When I told their head elder that I had seen many Hispanic families in the neighborhood, he replied, "Oh? I never noticed." It was no surprise to me to hear a year

later that the congregation had disbanded, because it was blind to the fields ready for harvest.

Wise leaders let adversity develop their integrity. When did Jesus most ardently demonstrate God's grace? When crowds admired Him and sought Him? No! It was when they were spitting on Him, jeering at Him, and pounding spikes into his hands and feet. Likewise, believers and their leaders can best show God's grace and develop their character precisely while suffering Satan's most painful attacks. Job endured tragedy, pain, and abandonment by those he loved, and suffered venomous criticism from his closest friends. Yet he maintained his integrity before the Almighty and grew in his understanding. For all eternity, Job will thank God for those misfortunes. We too must trust the Lord during adversity, knowing that it will produce precious, eternal fruit (1 Pet 4:12-19).

The most discouraging attacks of Satan often come through other Christians. Patterson commented:

> When unbelieving scoffers jeered at us, threw large stones, and, on three occasions, shot at us, I could sleep at night in peace because I expected that from non-believers. Then our Christian brothers whom we loved began criticizing us for following New Testament models instead of their cherished traditions. That was far more painful and hard to endure. Every missionary that I know, whom the Lord has used to spark a church planting movement, has endured severe, satanic opposition. The most painful attacks are often criticisms from traditionally-minded co-workers.

> Workers in a people movement often receive painful criticism from missionaries who have not bonded with the culture or from churches that are too legalistic to spread Heaven's grace. Recall how severely fellow believers criticized Paul!

Newly-arrived Christian workers sometimes cause misery by their impatient criticism of older peers. Likewise, some older ministers, hungry for power, refuse to release new workers to use their God-given abilities. Criticism may also arise from those who live in other countries and make occasional visits to the field, "know-it-alls" who want to dictate to field workers.

Jacob's son, Joseph, experienced envy and an aborted attempt on his life by his own brothers who sold him as a slave. Later his Egyptian master's wife unjustly accused him and had him imprisoned. The Lord brought Joseph to the depths before raising him to a position of powerful influence. The Lord's servants normally reach their potential through painful testing and heartbreak. Brokenness humbles believers (Psa 51:17), so that they can draw near to the Lord and enter the battlefield armed with deeper faith. Church reproduction has a price; the old dragon yields no territory without a fight.

Wise leaders form dedicated task groups. Establish ministry teams as Paul did. Mission organizations often commission Western missionaries individually instead of helping churches to prepare and send out cohesive task groups, which is the biblical model. Working alone too frequently leads to burnout, bad choices, an unbalanced ministry, and, sometimes, immorality. Patterson recalled:

> When we first went to northern Honduras, Denny and I were part of what our mission agency called a team. It met once a year and we argued about budgets and strategies. I did not learn to work as a genuine team until he Lord gave me Honduran co-workers who were accustomed to the culture. I soon learned to enjoy working closely with them and not as a loner.

Jesus never worked in the ministry alone, nor did His apostles. No single person has all the spiritual gifts needed to develop strong congregations. Healthy congregations practice loving, Spirit-empowered interaction as demonstrated in the New Testament and send out healthy task groups to start daughter churches.

To plant churches within a culture group, the most effective task groups consist entirely of national workers. To penetrate other cultures, effective task groups may temporarily bring together workers from two or three cultures, like the temporary team that went from Joppa to Caesarea with Peter who was from Jerusalem (Acts 11:12). The task group from the Antioch church included Paul, Barnabas, and Mark; all three were from the same flock, but workers with other nationalities joined them later (Acts 13:2-5; 15:32-34).

A task group should, if possible, include workers with the following spiritual gifts, keeping in mind that each task group member will normally have more than one:

Checklist of Task Group Member's Gifts

☐ Evangelism.

☐ Leadership.

☐ Teaching.

☐ Compassion, especially in fields with much poverty or painful circumstances.

☐ Healing, especially in pioneer fields where there are strange and diverse diseases and sparse medical help.

☐ Shepherding. Foreigners should not lead flocks but train local leaders.

☐ Other gifts that relate to the needs and opportunities that are specific to a field.

Wise leaders quickly correct a believer who commits an offense. They do so in the power of the Holy Spirit — firmly, yet with humility and gentleness.

One member of my flock stole from another.

As punishment I will exclude him from the Lord's Supper for six months.

That would be a mistake. You should discipline offenders to restore them, not to punish them.

The Bible does not say to bar them from communion for a specified length of time, but to restore them as soon as they repent.

To discipline, correct, and restore unruly sheep is a shepherd's most unpleasant task. Jesus laid out these steps to deal with offending believers (Matt 18:15-18):

Checklist of Steps for Restoration of Offending Brothers

☐ Pray for him and talk with him alone.

☐ If that fails, go with a humble spirit with two or three others who are spiritual, and clearly explain the offense.

☐ If that fails, then take the problem before the congregation.

☐ If that fails, shun the offender. Do not break bread with him until he repents.

Other relevant scriptures include Matthew 5:44; 1 Corinthians 5; Galatians 6:1 and Titus 3:10-11.

Wise leaders help co-workers to persevere. Jesus warned not to look back once you put your hand to the plow (Lk 9:62). Perseverance flows from commitment to goals and to one another. Help new leaders to define goals prayerfully, according to their gifts and those of their co-workers. Good goal-setting takes into account the situation, research findings, co-workers' vision, the aims of sending churches, and the Word of God.

Those lazy birds on my team quit. They lacked dedication to Jesus.

No! They quit because you did not let them do what God had gifted them to do. Trust your co-workers! Orient them to their God-given tasks until they are confident that they can do them.

Someone with an apostolic gift will seriously commit to making disciples in neglected people group, especially when he knows the facts about it. He may even take a short-term trip to gather information about it. Then, if the Eternal One has spoken to him, he will go there and keep working there until he and his co-workers have done what Jesus said to do, by teaching the disciples to obey all that Jesus commanded.

Wise leaders know and convey precisely what the Lord wants His flocks to do. A leader of God's people looks towards where God wants His people to go. Moses would often remind the people, "The Lord your God brings you into the land you are entering to possess" (Deut 7:1-2).

Teaching is not the same as leading. Of course, someone who does not know where the Lord wants His people to go cannot lead them there. One can lead only when he knows what the Lord wants His people to do at any time and in a situation; otherwise, he can only teach. He might teach well, enforce rules, furnish funds, and even attract others with his charismatic personality, but none of these actions makes one a leader, biblically speaking. Such a person would be wiser to encourage others to lead and stand ready to help them with his stronger spiritual gifts. Patterson recounted:

A missionary in Honduras headed a Bible institute supplying a fair number of churches with pastors. The institute produced many preachers but few shepherds. When churches needed shepherds to correct deficiencies left by departed pastors who preached without leading, the missionary would seek out from our churches shepherds whom we had mentored on the job, who had learned by experience to combine teaching with shepherding. Ironically, that missionary continued to criticize our training program, because, he said, it lacked his type of classroom-oriented, institutional teaching.

Pity flocks who call as a pastor
some big-beaked bird who
merely seeks a pulpit!

Those flocks never know
whether they are flying
north or south!

Guideline 26
Cultivate the Fruit of the Spirit.

Wrong! If that were all it
meant, then a toad or
a rotten egg would be holy!

Let us find out what holiness

Holiness means simply
that we are sinless.

really means, and lead our
flocks into it...

Cultivate the Fruit of the Spirit in yourself and in those whom you lead (Gal 5:22-23). The Holy Spirit produces virtues in believers who seek to walk with, imitate, and obey Jesus Christ. His ministry in us begins with an intimate connection to the Master. "Every surge of missionary activity in history has grown out of revitalized personal prayer and personal renewal."[36] While false holiness tries to sanctify one's self by merely obeying rules of men—and ultimately keeps people from Jesus—His holiness is marked by loving God with all of our heart, soul, mind, and strength (Mk 12:30).

---

[36] Steve Hake and Bill Taylor, *Send Me!* (Pasadena: William Carey Library, 1999), 34.

Checklist of Christian Growth Disciplines

☐ Crucify daily your old desires that grieve the Holy Spirit (Gal 5:24-25), asking Christ to live through you.

☐ Walk with the Lord each moment, submitting yourselves to Him and His Word (Jn 15:10-17).

☐ Cultivate the Spirit's virtues of love, joy, peace, patience, kindness, goodness, faithfulness, gentleness and self-control (Gal 5:22-23).

☐ Pray without ceasing, asking for the Holy Spirit's help (1 Thes 5:17).

☐ Work together as a body, harmonizing different gift-based ministries in freedom and love (1 Cor 12-13).

Let a new flock develop the virtues
that the Holy Spirit produces.
Let us look at some of them...

Love fervently. All mission work should begin and end with sacrificial love toward the Lord and toward others. Love is the Lord's Great Command. Galatians 5:22-23 lists love first among the virtues that are the Fruit of the Spirit. In the same chapter, Paul records, "The only thing that counts is faith expressing itself through love." Instruct your trainees to let love unite believers and motivate them for ministry, as it did Jesus and his Apostles (Jn 15:12-14; 1 Cor 13). Sacrificial love is born of God and based on truth, not feelings. True love unites believers without demanding blind submission to a human organization. It does not mean that we always get along with each other. Paul, like Jesus, often found himself at sharp odds with other people and angry with some Christian ministers.

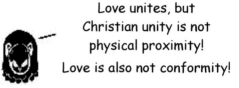

Love unites, but
Christian unity is not
physical proximity!
Love is also not conformity!

Remain one in the Spirit. Unity in the Spirit is the opposite of conformity, permitting different expressions of love through very diverse gifts, abilities, personalities and ministries. What we want to avoid is a phony and forged unity.

False unity forces seekers to change their culture to become Christians. Paul condemned this throughout his letter to the Galatians. False unity requires new believers of two cultures to worship together. While so doing may take place voluntarily, God allowed cultures to remain intact. He sent Peter to the Jews and Paul to the Gentiles to avoid conflict (Gal 2:7-9).

False unity calls for everyone to embrace the same practices and scruples. Romans 14 condemns conformity of scruples and practices.

Such errors are common and violate the freedom to which the Lord calls all believers. The New Testament passages that urge unity also distinguish it from conformity. The Holy Spirit manifests differences within a church body. He does not require all to look nor be alike (1 Cor 12-13). Love enables believers to practice different spiritual gifts in harmony (Rom 12:3-21, 1 Cor 12-13, Eph 4:11-16). In essentials, UNITY; in non-essentials, LIBERTY; in all things, CHARITY (love).

Unity in the Lord Jesus Christ is already a reality in Heaven's sight. The Holy Spirit baptizes all repentant believers into the eternal, invisible Body of Christ (1 Cor 12:13).

Pray with faith. Because of Abraham's faith, the Eternal One made promises to him that laid the foundation for both the Old and New Testament. Believers receive blessings as spiritual sons of Abraham when they trust the Lord as Abraham did, in childlike faith (Gn 12:1-3; 15:6; Gal 3:6-9). Faith is not correct belief. It is a correct relationship of trust. It is like a child who clings to the one Source of needed forgiveness, true holiness and everlasting life.

Teach new disciples to pray in faith, without presuming that they do so just because they know Christ. Patterson recalls:

> We had started a congregation in a remote area in Honduras and taught them how to pray. Anyway, we thought we had taught them to pray. My church back home in the USA held prayer meetings in which we rose from our chairs, turned and kneeled with our elbows resting on the chair. I showed the villagers this posture. A few weeks later, we returned and were astonished to find that they still were not praying. I asked why and their leader said, "We cannot pray. It is an insult to turn our rear ends toward God!" To them the front of the meeting place with the small table they used as an altar symbolized the presence of God. We quickly changed our instructions concerning prayer!

**What does the Almighty do when
we forget to pray? I always forget!**

An easy way for new believers to learn to pray is to repeat after you each brief phrase of a simple prayer, until they can talk to the Lord on their own, as a child would talk to his father. Thus, helping families to have a daily family devotional time is an important ministry of a church.

Serve with humility. Humility readily accepts accountability to God and to His leaders. Abraham trusted his steward Eliezer to oversee his household (Gn 15:2-3). Believers are God's stewards doing work for which He equips them. Good stewards give high priority to using funds and deploying workers to fulfill Jesus' Great Commission for His church. The Lord commands His churches to reach all peoples, including where authorities are hostile. Unfortunately, only a small percentage of career ministers go to such fields, which comprise a large amount of the world's population. Humility enables leaders to relinquish funds of their church to send workers where they are more urgently needed.

Humble workers seek God's will rather than their own selfish preferences for their careers. Short-term trips, for example, give believers exposure to other cultures, test their gifts, inform them about people groups, and they challenge participants to consider long-term mission work. Those whom the Lord does not call to foreign work normally return from short-term trips edified and enriched, eager to work as senders. Yet, short-term service alone cannot disciple all peoples. One gifted as an apostle, or a "sent one" (i.e. the missionary), will not limit his commitment to a short term. Because God's gifting defines what a believer is and because His gifts are permanent (Rom 11:29), one must think long-term. In many cases a short-term experience confirms the Lord's call as a career apostle and many discover their missionary gift and return gladly to the field. Committed to making disciples as Jesus commands, they will stay on the job for as long as it takes. Thus, short-term service has its place and God uses it for many purposes, but seldom for reproducing churches in a widespread church planting movement. Humility seeks His face to discern God's best desire for one's life.

Show kindness and compassion. Love people in need in a practical way, as the Good Samaritan did (Lk 10:30-37). As an expression of love, deal with poverty, loneliness, disease and ignorance. "If anyone has material possessions and sees his brother in need but has no pity on him, how can the love of God be in him? ... Let us not love with words or tongue but with actions..." (1 Jn 3:17-18).

Avoid merely giving money to the poor out of what you have left over. One's heart should cry out to improve their condition and meet their deepest needs. Go beyond merely helping in emergencies and deal with the root of their poverty.

You cannot buy loyalty...
You can only rent it!

Help poor people to visualize a better future. Give them voca-
tional training and other aid to help themselves and each other. If,
however, they merely seek material reward for becoming Christians,
then giving creates beggars and false converts and the flocks will
suffer. They will be more motivated if disciple makers walk beside
them, helping them to improve the skills they already have, rather
than simply giving new technologies which they must struggle with
to master. Patterson remarked:

> I knew of new believer who was a poor peasant and living by
> subsistence farming. He complained to me about his poverty,
> hinting for a handout. I asked him how much land he was
> cultivating and then suggested that he plant double the amount of
> land so that he could sell part of his crops. The land was public
> domain and free to use. His answer appalled me: 'Jorge, you do
> not understand. I was born to be poor!'

Help the poor deal with superstitions and "doctrines of demons"
(1 Tm 4:1) that perpetuate poverty, such as the idea of the peasant
who thought that he was born to be poor. Some Christian reformers
urge the poor to seek liberation by appealing to their envy of the
rich, but envy breeds hatred. Mercy ministries exemplify
compassion, but require wisdom. Simply giving to the poor out of
pity—except in life and death emergencies—robs them of their dignity and builds dependence that perpetuates their poverty.

Show new shepherds how to examine Scripture as the Bereans
did in Acts 17:11, mining its gold rather than simply listening to it or
reading it passively. Give believers the tools to mine its gold. Teach
shepherds to look at the details of a Bible passage before consulting
commentaries, Of course, they must first ask the Almighty for guidance to draw His truth from His Word.

Guideline 27
Listen as the Lord speaks through His Word.

My cousin said
only the clergy know how
to interpret Scripture.

Peter's second letter says anyone
can interpret it. Do not let men
force their opinions on you!
Let us look at ways to find out for
ourselves what a Bible text means...

Checklist of questions to ask about the background of a passage of Scripture

☐ What does it say before and after the passage?

☐ What was its historical occasion?

☐ Were the people addressed still under the Law of Moses, or had Jesus inaugurated the New Covenant of Grace?

☐ Who wrote it? When, where, why, and to whom?

☐ What do related Bible passages say about the same topic?

Avoid carrying the inductive method of Bible study too far and too fast with inexperienced shepherds-in-training. Do not simply tell them to analyze a text without providing help. Prepare a study for them and suggest to them what to look for. Patterson elaborated:

> When our churches in Honduras were still young, confusion prevailed concerning the Holy Spirit and many contradictory opinions prevailed. I voiced my view but only added another opinion to the jumble. One new leader was obnoxiously dogmatic as he asserted his views to the others. I asked him if he would settle the confusion at the next meeting. Surprised, he asked, "Do you trust my opinion?" "No," I replied, "but I trust

God's Word. Promise me that you will search the passages that explain the Holy Spirit's work in believers and tell the group only what you find there, without adding a single word beyond that." He agreed and kept his promise. I carefully assigned him only relevant passages: John 14-16; Romans 8; Galatians 5 and 1 Corinthians 12-14. At the next meeting, he summarized what God affirms about His Spirit and it settled the matter. The other workers searched the same passages and passed on the liberating truths to their flocks. We mined the Bible for its gold.

Guideline 28
Watch out! Here come wolves!

Do not rob chicks from
other birds' nests!
The Almighty hates proselytizing.
Let us learn ways to avoid it…

Watch Out! Jesus and his Apostles strongly warned shepherding elders to watch out for wolves and their divisive teaching. When flocks reproduce spontaneously, Satan sends predators to devour their lambs, as Jesus warned in Matthew 10:16. Paul warned that some wolves would come from within a church itself (Acts 20:28-31). Some frustrated Christians, unable to gather a flock of their own, seek to take over what others have built. If they cannot take it completely, then they divide it. If they cannot control it, then they try to destroy it. Their most common divisive tactic is to insist that new believers embrace a doctrine that is unique to a wolf's organization.

Titus 3:10 condemns such divisiveness. How can prudent leaders ward off wolves? Patterson related:

I found a "wolf" in the house of some new believers. He justified his presence by attacking our doctrine. I told him that he lacked the power of the Holy Spirit to win people to Christ, and the proof was what he was doing in that home—stealing sheep from another shepherd's flock. Furious, he called me names and left. But he did stop his unethical proselytizing in our area. Wolves are proud and cannot endure an honest public rebuke.

Sometimes the missionary who arrives first in a region thinks its population belongs to him, especially if he has experienced persecution. He resents other missionaries moving in on his turf, unless he can control their work. Such possessiveness causes setbacks in many fields, setting an example that may lead to wolf-like behavior in others.

Sometimes newly-arrived missionaries are surprised to find churches already there and Satan may shoot a fiery arrow of resentment into their minds. The poison from this arrow causes anatomical alterations. Soon they develop pointed ears, long noses, long teeth and the appetite of wolves. Such predators are widespread across every continent except Antarctica, with frequent sightings in pioneer fields. Their diet consists of weak lambs, especially when shepherds are not watching like Jesus and his Apostles warned them to do.

How to Spot Wolves

Sharp teeth. He or she (she-wolves can be especially clever at hiding true intentions) appears loving and very friendly, at first. He wears sheep's wool clothing and says "baa" sounding like a devout, well-intentioned believer. However, he will soon begin to bite with those sharp canine teeth, by criticizing and casting doubt upon a church, its teaching and its leaders.

Pointed ears. He is an excellent listener. He especially listens for criticism of a flock's legitimate leaders. He sets up private meetings and conversations about the leaders' faults, and he may urge others to pray for the leader's weaknesses, in order to sow doubts.

Padded paws. He sneaks up deftly. Like a thief, he enters by a window instead of the door, that is, without an invitation from the legitimate leader. He neither asks advice nor recognizes the authority of rightful leaders.

Big mouth. He will come to you with a flashy, painted smile. He must also have the last word in every conversation. Legalistic to the core, he will dwell on an issue that superficially sounds spiritual, in order to draw a following. He imposes rules to keep himself in power. He judges and condemns all who disagree with him. He is too proud to accept a rebuke. If confronted with his sin, he refuses to discuss it rationally. He will resort to name calling, bitter arguments or a vicious attack, often involving church politics.

Shifty eyes. He quickly spots weak lambs and unattended sheep. He befriends them and fills their minds with his criticisms and rules.

Slobber. Insatiably hungry, he moves on when he runs out of lambs to consume. If he gets a following by deceptive diplomacy, it is short-lived, for his motives are not pastoral and he fleeces the flock instead of feeding it. He leaves his stolen sheep bruised and bleeding, as he looks for greener pastures containing unsuspecting sheep with careless shepherds.

Paul warned that wolves would come from within and without (Acts 20:28-31). A wolf from within is a misguided believer. A group of shepherds may tame an "insider" wolf by confronting him in a spirit of humility, as Galatians 6:1 directs. Patterson recalled:

A newly-arrived missionary found it easier to start churches by criticizing and dividing ours than by starting new ones through evangelizing neglected communities. I suggested to some leaders in the region that they should go to his house and confront him. They went and signed an agreement in his presence, to deal with members of other shepherds' flocks only when the other shepherds invited them to do so, in the spirit of Romans 15:20-21. The predator refused to sign it, thereby openly declaring himself to be a wolf. Word of this meeting spread, and he lost most of his followers. Thankfully, he ceased his unethical proselytizing.

On another occasion, two wolves were dividing flocks in a remote, mountainous area. Since they represented a reputable denomination, I contacted their national headquarters and reported their activities. Their director wrote back to assure me that they would send in a respected, well-known pastor to investigate the case and, if what I reported was so, they would deal with it. A local pastor confirmed the unethical activity, so the leaders of that church association "defrocked" the wolves. However, they did not stop their divisive work; they simply renounced their denominational affiliation. Nevertheless, by resisting their church's discipline, they exposed to the public what they were and nobody heeded them any longer.

Wolves from without are non-believers who teach doctrines of unorthodox sects. They do not glorify Jesus Christ as the divine Son of God and only way of salvation. If you asked a deep-rooted Jehovah's Witness, for example, to bow his knee before Jesus with you, as Philippians 2:10 says to do, he will not. Most wolves from the outside deny either Jesus' deity or His humanity. They seldom affirm the Trinity. Their dealings invariably damage the spiritual life of churches.

Deal with a wolf swiftly and firmly. Usually, if rebuked publicly by someone stating the facts of his activity, a wolf will leave a flock; wolves are proud and cannot bear to be shamed publicly. Titus 3:10-11 requires believers to shun a divisive person.

Guideline 29
Resist demons in a biblical way.

I cast the demons
out of every room
before I enter it, and...

Wait! To voice such rebukes into the air makes untaught humans think that evil spirits are present everywhere and know everything. Demons, like their leader, Lucifer, crave that kind of attention. Only the Almighty, Omniscient God is everywhere and knows everything!

Overcome evil spirits in the way the Bible prescribes. In Senegal, West Africa, demons plague many rural people under the guise of ancestral spirits. Most sinners who become followers of Jesus experience deliverance by praying in His name as part of their conversion. In the rapid house church movements of north India, most new believers can recall a miracle as part of their submission to the Most High. Examples include freedom from harassing demons, a clear and evident physical healing, or provision for a vital need.

In Tanzania, east Africa, where fetish users and Islamic witch doctors call on spirits, people often complain that they can do nothing about it. However, as the Christians pray in Jesus' name, the counterfeit miracle workers have been known to leave town.

In Copan Ruins, Honduras—home of the ancient Mayan religions and gruesome rituals of old—missionaries report intense satanic opposition, especially with regard to evangelistic outreaches to the Chortí Indians.

When flocks multiply, the hungry old dragon counterattacks angrily. Congregations that bring many to Christ and give birth to daughter churches come under his fire. He yields no terrain without a fight. He provokes mature and immature believers alike—especially those who thrive on wielding power—to attack the Lord's most effective harvesters. He tempts us at every turn, seeking to dethrone the Lord.

Teach your trainees to don God's armor as it is described in terms of Roman soldiers (see Figure 9). Believers must resist Satan and his fallen spirits by using the armor listed in Ephesians 6:10-18. Some ministers do spiritual warfare only by verbally binding demons, but the struggle requires more than that. Ours is a daily discipline that requires the armor of the Spirit:

Checklist of Spiritual Armor

☐ Wearing truth as a belt. Jesus is our way, our truth and our life (Jn 14:6).

☐ Having righteousness as our breastplate. We wear nothing for one's back, for God provides no retreat. Jesus is our breastplate of righteousness: "But if Christ is in you, your body is dead because of sin, yet your spirit is alive because of righteousness" (Rom 8:10).

☐ Wearing our peace like boots can well take us anywhere, carrying the gospel of peace to others. Jesus himself "is our peace" (Eph 2:14).

☐ Wielding a shield of faith that wards off Satan's fiery arrows. "I am your shield, your very great reward" (Gn 15:1).

☐ Protecting our heads with the helmet of salvation that protects us into eternity. Jesus is our salvation: "Therefore He is able to save completely those who come to God through Him, because he always lives to intercede for them" (Heb 7:25).

☐ Brandishing the sword of the Spirit, which is the Word of God.

☐ Maintaining constant communication with our Commander-in-Chief, praying alertly and interceding. The Psalmist exclaimed, "In return for my friendship, they accuse me. But I am a man of prayer" (109:4).

Figure 9
Roman Soldier in Full Armor

Instruct new believers to don the armor of God, putting on the Lord Jesus Christ and making no provision for the flesh (Rom 13:14). Teach them to denounce and reject all involvement with the occult and anything which may compromise their exalted position in the heavenlies. Show them what it means to enthrone Jesus as Lord in every aspect of life. As Peter said, "In your hearts set apart Christ as Lord" (1 Pet 3:15). Teach them that every aspect of our armor relates to Jesus. Show them what it means to have Him living His crucified life through us. Satan loses his grip on seekers when believers live in the name of Jesus and proclaim truth with the Holy Spirit's power. Demons lose their oppressive influence when believers rebuke them using the authority they have by invoking Jesus' holy name. Replace demonic lies prayerfully, purposely, and faithfully with the sword of the Spirit, the Word of God. Show your trainees what it means to memorize it and to dwell on it. Teach them that the Lord uses His Word to preserve, to strengthen and to purify us. Show them that He uses His Word—written on hearts—to align our perspectives and inner core values to His heavenly ideals.

Instruct your trainees to deal with demonic oppression the way Jesus and his Apostles did. They spoke to demons only when they manifested themselves through the lips and bodies of victims that they oppressed. In societies where Satan has controlled the thought patterns of the people for centuries, cases of overt spirit activity are common. Workers had better go prepared to meet it. In such societies, Jesus frees repentant converts from idolatry and from the spirits that feed upon the worship that idolaters render to them.

Persons of any culture who practice the occult eventually suffer a deterioration of their personality. Only the Lord Jesus Christ can free them (Jn 8:32 and 37). Help them think and pray through all areas of demonic influence in their lives, past and present, so as to confess and repudiate them. Replace blurred thinking about the Almighty and about themselves with truth, especially promises made to believers about who they are and what they have in the Lord, as taught in Ephesians 1-3.

<table>
<tr><td>How can I avoid temptations? Satan and his messengers are much stronger than I am!</td><td>Martin Luther once quipped, "We cannot avoid birds flying over our heads, but we can keep them from nesting in our hair!"</td></tr>
</table>

Teach your trainees, "Resist the devil and he will flee from you" (Jas 4:7). Believers are vulnerable to attacks by Satan, and his evil spirits lie to believers moving them to dishonor their Lord. Believers deny their own sins in many ways; they make excuses, rationalize, blame others, and justify their faults, instead of admitting their guilt. When a believer fails to repent from an obvious sin, then those who are spiritual are to correct and restore him, so that the adversary cannot continue to torment and deceive him (Gal 6:1).

The adversary uses legalism as a weapon against devout believers. This virus of the Pharisees creeps in unnoticed, because it appears spiritual. Its insidious, deceptive infection opposes the grace of God, discourages new believers and weakens congregations. Jesus was gentle with repentant sinners, yet was angry with proud legalists. A person who is hungry for power enforces rules and beliefs that sound spiritual, while keeping others under his control. Such rules may come from the Bible, but he emphasizes them to excess without regard to other Scriptural teachings that balance them. For example, some teachers overemphasize repentance and doing good works to the point of denying God's grace, while other teachers overemphasize grace to the point of denying the need to repent.

Teach your trainees to pray fervently and persistently for deliverance of a demon-oppressed person by the all-powerful name of the Lord Jesus Christ. He revealed His power over demons when he cast out "Legion"—a horde of spirits—from a Gadarene (Mk 5:1-20). Confrontations with demons are never enjoyable. In educated societies, demons seldom show themselves openly, but they are present and foster a pall of skepticism about spiritual realities. To deal wisely with demonic spirits, discern three types of demonic activity[37]: 1) oppression, 2) obsession, and 3) possession.

Demon Oppression. Demons commonly oppress people who believe the enemy's lies, worship idols, or seek occult experiences. Jesus breaks such bondage when converts denounce past evil and occult practices, turning to the Lord, accepting forgiveness, and embracing the truth of the Lord Jesus Christ.

Jesus, by His death and resurrection, destroyed the power that demons once had (Col 2:15). If a Christian believer chooses to believe a doctrine of demons, then the Holy One will let him suffer the consequences in this world. Even though the serpent is powerless since the Son of God de-fanged him (1 Jn 3:8, Jn 16:11), he still hisses his lies into ears that are willing to be deceived.

Demon Obsession. Some people have a morbid preoccupation with evil spirits. They rebuke demons constantly, even when there is no evidence of their presence. As a result, congregations may suffer from increased demonic activity. Paying attention to demons serves as a lightning rod to attract them and the misery that they bring with them. Some deluded believers will not enter a room without casting demons out of it first, and others consider even common colds to be attacks by demons.

---

[37] On spiritual warfare see the bibliography for works by Neil T. Anderson, Mark Buyback and Francis Frangipane.

The Lord Jesus Christ and His disciples addressed and exorcised demons only when those demons made their presence known through the bodies and lips of individuals whom they possessed. They never sought out demons nor rebuked them when they had not shown themselves. Why not? If one rebukes them where they are not showing themselves, he is acting as though they were everywhere or knew everything. This can lead untaught persons to suppose that devils are omnipresent or omniscient, which is blasphemy, for the Almighty God alone has those attributes. Such indirect praise glorifies Satan who, in diabolical pride, boasted that he would be like the Most High (Isa 14:13-15).

Demon Possession. The term possession describes individuals whose mind and body are controlled by evil spirits. Ministers do great damage if they say someone is possessed when he is not. If one is really controlled—body and mind—by demons, he needs someone to cast them out who knows how, a person of faith with a gift to discern spirits who can bring Jesus' authority to bear. He also has to have God's Word retained in his mind, carved on his heart, and lived out in his life. Thus prepared, he can deal swiftly and effectively with the deceit that the person has embraced, while maintaining his own needed sense of peace. "The mind controlled by the Spirit is life and peace" (Rom 8:10).

Teach your trainees to endure both violent and social persecution, to stand firm with unwavering faith against hostile authorities and persecution, as Stephen did in Acts 6:5-8:3. Where conversion to Christ brings death, loss of jobs, rejection by family and friends, or imprisonment, believers must gather in secret, as has been the case in much of China.[38]

Congregations have freedom to baptize secretly to avoid hostilities, as in Acts 16:22-35. They also may delay baptism until enough people can defend themselves collectively. Some Westerners in Muslim fields have needlessly caused the death of many converts by making baptism a public testimony of their faith. Such a practice misses the purpose of baptism in Scripture. If one desires to make his

---

[38] Ralph R. Covell, *The Liberating Gospel in China* (Grand Rapids: Baker, 1995).

baptism public and suffer the consequences as a testimony for the Lord, let that be his own decision. He will have a privileged position in glory (Rev 20:4).

Westerners can also bring violence to national leaders by failing to use a safe mailing address, by publishing believers' names in missionary literature, and by bragging about them in churches. When hostile authorities detect references to unauthorized meetings or assemblies, they arrest the leaders and often torture, imprison, or kill them. Authorities seldom do so to Western workers that they find participating in unauthorized meetings; instead, they simply cancel their visas.

Most neglected fields have laws against starting churches. Only a criminal can plant churches there!

Unfortunately, most missionary candidates lack experience in underground, criminal activities!

Some Old Testament prophets of the Lord had to live in caves to escape Queen Jezebel's persecution (1 Kings 18:4). Likewise, hundreds of thousands of tiny flocks today meet underground to elude hostile authorities. Where authorities forbid the planting of churches—as in most of the world's remaining neglected fields—only an outlaw can do so. Therefore, missionary training must include experience with the following:

Checklist of Missionary Training Experiences

☐ Reaching networks of relatives and friends, through hospitable persons of peace.

☐ Providing worship that fits a very small group, with the Lord's Supper as a central part.

☐ Mentoring leaders in a way that others can repeat with other, newer leaders.

☐ Birthing daughter and granddaughter churches.

☐ Maintaining secrecy, using a safe e-mail address and withholding information from possible informers who pretend that they want to learn about Christianity and hint to be invited to a church. Programming your laptop computer to re-format itself automatically if started without a password.

☐ Discerning ministries that are essential to church life and avoiding unnecessary activities that merely attract attention without building up the Body of Christ.

Guideline 30
Let the poor give sacrificially.

Let all believers and their leaders share in God's blessing by giving to others. Here are ways to make giving easy, even for the poor...

Show your trainees what it means to give wisely and sacrificially to the Lord's work, including work in other regions, as the Macedonians did in their extreme poverty (2 Cor 8:1-5). Believers should give a portion of what the Lord has given them back to Him, as Abigail gave generously to David's men in need (1 Sam 25). Even the poorest disciples must be taught to give, for giving is a command of the Lord Jesus Christ (Lk 6:38). He also said, "It is more blessed to give than to receive" (Acts 20:35).

Some people live off the land and have little money, so they give rice or other goods that they produce. In the New Testament the Lord does not promise to give believers great material wealth. His blessings are firstly spiritual (Eph 1:3). Nevertheless, He will enrich sacrificial givers materially, so they can give more (2 Cor 9:11). Missionaries in pioneer fields often observe this: the poor who give generously live better after a few years, not in luxury but with adequate housing, steadier jobs and healthier children. On the other hand, those who give little and look to the church to receive something from it continue in their economic misery. Missionaries, who hesitate out of pity to ask the poor to give sacrificially, rob them of a blessing and perpetuate their poverty.

The poor widow's two small coins added up to more money before God than all that the rich people gave at the temple (Lk 21:1-4). The Lord works his mathematics by a different standard, using the small offerings of the very poor for His glory. Teach believers to give in loving obedience to Jesus who promises to bless givers (Lk 6:38). Do not rob poor believers of this blessing. When the Lord multiplies their bit in His mysterious way; they and their flocks will prosper spiritually (Lk 21:1-4).

If, out of pity, church planters fail to ask poor converts to support their own congregation's work, such misguided compassion erodes believers' dignity and sense of stewardship. Patterson recalled:

> During my first year on the field, I felt sorry for a pastor when he complained about the small salary that his congregation gave him. I began to subsidize his salary by a certain amount. The congregation, whose members earned even less than their shepherd did, promptly lowered their giving for him the precise amount of my dole! Instead of modeling good stewardship, I had weakened theirs.

> When I arrived on the field, most of the people were extremely poor. Their houses had dirt floors and disease was rampant. Many children died in infancy and good jobs were scarce. As they became believers, some of them gave sacrificially to the Lord's work, like the poor widow of Jesus' parable. If they had no money, they gave rice or other produce.

> Others, because of their poverty gave little. After a few years I noticed that the poor believers who had been giving sacrificially no longer lived in dire poverty. Their children wore shoes and ate better, their houses had cement floors and fathers acquired

better jobs. However, those who had not given generously remained miserable; their children still died in infancy, and fathers still earned little.

Church planters stifle a new congregation's stewardship by supporting it financially when the believers should support their own work. Such easy money often stifles church reproduction. When a few pastors receive financial aid from the West, they form an elitist class. The others resent it, which breeds division and stifles growth. Paying pastors with outside funds corrupts both the pastors and their congregations, especially in very poor communities. If a congregation is too poor to pay its ministers, then encourage its members to serve voluntarily, as is common in economically impoverished areas throughout the world. Train several men to work together. Never let a congregation become dependent on foreign aid, as it will quickly breed resentment, spiritual weakness and unhealthy control by foreigners.

New congregations of poor people should commission a treasurer publicly to pay out only what a simple budget authorizes. Instruct him publicly to give no loans. Name another person to help him count the money.

No loans, Mr. Treasurer!

Not even to your
cheerfully-chirping
brother-in-law!

Guideline 31
Equip lay workers.

Christian workers are fully
dedicated to ministry only
if they do it full-time.

Right?

Nonsense!
It requires more dedication
and greater sacrifice for a
worker to be self-supported.

To sustain church or cell group multiplication, a huge number of volunteer workers must participate. In his highly acclaimed book on launching house church movements, Rad Zdero wrote: "The weight of responsibility and leadership for emerging house church movements should be placed squarely on the shoulders of grass-roots volunteers."[39] Within the American scene, effective use of lay leaders is seen through Rick Warren's ministry with Saddleback Community Church, where the church is distinguished for growing at the seams by successfully mobilizing hundreds of lay persons for community expressions of love.[40]

Someone may ask how believers can help workers whom they do not pay to stay focused on coordinating pastoral training in a way that keeps churches and cell groups multiplying. The answer is to equip only bivocational, lay workers, not the unemployed and unemployable who would depend on others to finance them.

It is not sufficient that mission agencies send out paid, full-time missionaries who disguise themselves as tentmakers, pretending that they gain a living from a secular job. While doing so may reflect a

---

[39] Rad Zdero, "House Church Movements," *Mission Frontiers*. (March-April, 2005), 17.

[40] Jeffery L. Sheller, "Preacher with a Purpose" in *U.S. News & World Report*, 31 October, 2005, 52.

meaningful desire to mobilize workers, that strategy has very real shortcomings and cannot provide enough workers to finish the task that Jesus assigned His Church. The key is to mobilize many self-supported lay workers everywhere. The words part-time lay worker do not imply that a worker is not fully dedicated, for those who are experienced and gifted for spiritual work are often as effective and dedicated, sometimes more so, as their full-time counterparts.

In today's world most of the remaining, neglected fields have authorities that are hostile towards traditional missionary work. Neglected fields that can be evangelized effectively by traditionally trained missionaries are few and dwindling rapidly. Today's fields need self-supporting workers who are trained to run small businesses or other vocations that enable them to mix freely with the common people. They also need experience in leading small group worship, training leaders in the background, evangelizing through heads of families, and reproducing clusters of tiny house churches while maintaining secrecy.

Having a secular job can, of course, limit one's time. Workers can overcome this disadvantage by working as a team and quickly delegating pastoral responsibilities to new leaders whom they mentor. Many secular jobs offer superb opportunities for witnessing for the Lord and enable workers to launch churches more readily than can those who receive full-time support and lack contacts.

Although lay workers are eager to serve at first, later their zeal may subside, especially where traditionally-minded individuals coax lay workers back into familiar programs that depend on paid workers, causing church multiplication to decline. So let volunteer workers define their own job description and set their own goals, deciding on the amount of work that they will do.

Pastors and missionaries too often ask lay workers to do more and more, until they burn out. Rather than piling more on a few of them, leaders should delegate to them more responsibility to lead and mobilize others. Most volunteers want to see flocks multiply and empowering them facilitates church reproduction.

To keep lay persons working requires regular, caring communication. Constant motivation often depends on maintaining a heart-to-heart connection between area leaders, lay group leaders and the groups themselves.

Motivation also relates to workers' personalities. Patterson found that it helps to know what keeps a volunteer worker enthusiastic. Sanguine types, he says, are like playful puppies; they keep working when they are with people they like. Others are like bulls that butt obstacles aside to get the job done and seem to enjoy doing so. Still others are like cart horses that keep plodding along because they love the process and can see constant fruit from their labors. Some are like eagles that aim at long range objectives and often follow their vision to steer the process. The rest are like hybrids and act a bit like the other four.

Keeping volunteers on the job requires more than applying popular psychology. While being aware of personality types and knowing how to direct volunteers' energies is imperative, motivation must proceed from the Lord and the encouragement provided by close-knit co-workers. Being constrained by the love of Christ and possessing sensitivity to Him are superb motivators. Sincere believers yearn to obey Christ, because they love Him (Jn 14:15). Likewise, believers who work in the area of their spiritual gifts feel more satisfaction and motivation to remain faithful to their tasks.

Paul himself set the example of working with one's hands, not only to meet one's own needs, but to support one's co-workers and to set an example for lazy believers (Acts 20:31-36; 2 Thes 3:7-12). Fields with hostile authorities and those in which being a professional clergyman is impractical require self-supported workers. Like Aquila and Priscilla in Acts 18:1-3, workers can have two vocations, a secular one that is acceptable to the authorities and another one that is pastoral and often secret.

Aquila and his wife Priscilla were qualified in three ways to gather secret churches. Acts chapter 18 recounts their story.

1.   They were real tentmakers who did not raise support.[41]

---

[41] See Jonathan Lewis, *Working Your Way to the Nations—A Guide to Effective Tentmaking,* 2nd ed. (Downers Grove: Inter-Varsity Press, 1996).

Their secular vocation was genuine, not a cover. Tent making was their vocation.

They also provided needed employment for the apostle Paul.

Their small business allowed flexibility to move to cities that lacked churches.

Their business remained independent, with low capital investment and simple technology, which allowed time for ministry.

Their business did not isolate them from the common people.

2. As lay workers, they ministered in the background, mentoring men like Apollos (18:24-28).

3. They were hospitable, hosting house churches in Rome, Corinth and Ephesus (Rom 16:3-5; 1 Cor 16:19).

Self-Support Issues in India—A Case Study[42]

To the elders among you, I appeal as a fellow elder, a witness of Christ's sufferings and one who also will share in the glory to be revealed: Be shepherds of God's flock that is under your care, serving as overseers—not because you must, but because you are willing, as God wants you to be; not greedy for money, but eager to serve, not lording it over those entrusted to you, but being examples to the flock (1 Pt 5:1-3).

Six Christian Indian professional men, medical doctors and military officers from different states plan and direct a cooperative church planting movement. In the past four years they have seen more than fifty thousand verifiable house churches planted in the northern states called the "Hindi belt". They have established and currently maintain five levels of church planting workers:

- International, interstate directors.

---

[42] Patterson, Currah and O'Connor taught these and other concepts, by invitation, for nearly a month in seven states in India.

- Regional coordinators who train and supervise in states of 70 to 170 million.

- Full-time district church planters who train and supervise in regions of 2½ to 3 million.

- Block coordinators who train and supervise workers in a number of villages or a section of a city.

- Congregational shepherds who lead ten or so families and mentor novice shepherds.

In 2005 the directors informed all trainers that they have until the end of 2006 to become self-supported. Their reasons for their move to self-support include:

- Depleting resources (they gave all they had).

- Slowing of the current endeavor.

- A theology of "resources in the harvest."

- Sifting out those with mainly financial motives.

- Shift to self-supported, novice workers, keeping the movement indigenous and non-dependent.

During a workshop in Nagpur while interacting about self-support, trainers themselves voiced these questions, comments and objections:

- Other organizations pay salaries to those who defect to them.

- Could currently supported trainers keep their support while allowing trainees to remain self-supported?

- Directors who have access to foreign money are asking trainers to become self-supported.

- Part-time work that allows time for ministry is hard to find.

- Those who have moved back to self-support are able to witness on the job, but are less effective than full-time workers.

- Indian traditions disapprove of holy men doing secular work.

- Although normally only one spouse earns money, perhaps both could earn.

- The apostle Paul was single and could live on self-support, whereas Peter had a family and received support.

- Jesus chose many of his disciples from among self-supported workers.

- Old Testament Levites received tithes, so we should, too.

Several workshop participants reported these means of self-support:

- Teaching in government schools.

- Working as government agriculturalists.

- Sewing new clothing for the wholesale market.

- Keeping poultry and milk cows.

- Maintaining fish ponds.

- Tutoring students.

- Reselling used products in the streets and from door to door.

- Hiring themselves out as day laborers.

- Operating a rickshaw service.

- Working as a horticulturist.

- Operating a laundry service for hotels.

- Serving as a building contractor.

Most of the workshop participants were optimistic about self-support and voiced their approval. Some observed that the most effective, scriptural, church planters often supported themselves. The presenters also made some observations which the Indian directors confirmed. The first two related to self-support and the remaining related to reproducible training among lay persons in general.

First, pastoral trainers have begun to make adjustments as they move towards self-support. Most were self-supporting before being hired, and they were already planting churches or evangelizing. Most still received partial salaries from donors in India and overseas, allowing them to travel and train more freely, but since their salary was not enough to support a family, they had to find additional funding. Some trainers are already earning extra support by leading seminars while others were receiving income from their flocks.

Second, where there is a socio-economic difference between trainers and shepherds, the latter tend to become passive listeners, taking little or no initiative to reproduce themselves or their flocks. Thus, the move to self-support will prove a partial solution, reducing the economic divide between trainers and shepherds.

Third, regional trainers often fail to listen to shepherds report on their activities and the needs of their new congregations, so neither do they make plans with them about what they will do with their flocks until the next training session. Thus, training consists mostly in dispensing lessons and good, though untimely, advice. Mentoring has been difficult to introduce in India. Although the movement's trainers have done a superb job of spiritually-powerful and sacrificial evangelism and church planting, they report that their novice shepherds do not easily reproduce other, newer shepherds.

Where local shepherds do take initiative and reproduce themselves and their flocks, leaders should recruit those shepherds as mentors rather than from outside. This practice could eliminate the socio-economic differences that hinder progress at the grassroots level.

Guideline 32
Let children do serious ministry.

Have children take an active part in church life. Mentors often hear the question, "What should we do with children during worship?" They mostly hear this from leaders of new churches or small cell groups, but almost never from non-Westerners. The answer is fourfold and applies a biblical response to four Western practices: 1) children's participation, 2) Bible exposition, 3) method variation and 4) age harmonization.

What should we do with little chicks during worship?

You sound like a Westerner! Let us look at ways to let children do serious ministry together with adults!

Children's participation. Let children actively participate instead of simply listening passively to a children's sermon or story. Patterson's daughter, missionary Anne Thiessen, explained:

> We want the children to participate, so we meet with the children before the worship and practice acting out either the Old Testament or New Testament reading (whichever is more story-like). We learn a song together and a verse for them to share, which we practice over time until the children learn them well. During the worship time, the children act out the reading. Previously Bible readings often been poorly done and more poorly understood by the illiterate tribal people. The adults enjoy a visual aid and the children appreciate having a part that does not require much planning.

> The worshippers soon get used to allowing activities that are enjoyable, especially drama and music that are introduced in a non-threatening way. If adults also watch the children rehearse, then the impact is even stronger, because it means there are more prompters and better understanding. Including children can prove amusing, even fun. I let the older children take increasingly more responsibility for this. I help them to pick out from the Bible passages the dialogue for the younger children to speak or act out, and to summarize the story in child-sized words. Adults, young people, and children who have never helped lead in a flock before now jump in and put their whole heart into it, learning as they grow. The experience proves amazingly freeing.

Bible exposition. Teach the Word the way Paul did, for good Bible exposition lays a foundation for abstract doctrinal understanding. Many ask, "What can we do if the Bible text does not lend itself to dramatization, such as the book of Romans." The answer lies in Romans itself, for it builds on historical passages that illustrate or give the legal basis for an abstract doctrine. In writing Romans, Paul assumed that his readers knew the Old Testament stories of Adam, Abraham, Moses and the law, referring to them constantly. Both Christianity and biblical Judaism are unique among religions in that their doctrines grow out of great redemptive events of history. All other religions were founded upon some dreamer's philosophical musings on metaphysics, aestheticism and ethics, if not violence. Christian doctrines, however, flowed from inspired reflection on concrete, historical, redemptive events including creation, the fall, the flood, the pact with Abraham, slavery and deliverance from Egypt, the giving of the Law, etc.

As an example of an abstract doctrine, take the "trial by fire" before the Lord's judgment seat (1 Cor 3:11-15) which is to prevent believers "sneaking contraband" into Heaven. The legal and historical basis for this doctrine appears in the book of Numbers, chapter 31. Moses confronted victorious soldiers who were bringing illegal booty into the holy camp. He required them to build a fire and pass the objects through it. Only what they purified by fire could enter. Recounting an Old Testament story provides purely doctrinal New Testament text with a historical basis. So link New Testament texts with Old Testament passages or an earlier New Testament event that gives it a prophetic or legal basis which children and adults can act out. When they teach the Word, teachers and pastors too often rob believers of a great treasure, not to mention a lot of fun, by failing to act out or depict its foundations. Patterson commented, "I thought this all applied well to house churches and so shared it on a house church Internet site. Responses varied from mild skepticism to 'Them's good groceries!'"

When teachers fail to plan active participation, it may be due to laziness or ignorance of the need to build relationships while teaching. Anne Thiessen explained:

If the passages for the day lack drama, I simply find something related. Today, we studied prayer and how the Lord provides for us, so we acted out Elijah and the ravens. A small girl played a raven with a piece of tortilla in her beak. A boy was the prophet sitting next to the brook (a bowl of water found in the home). An adult spoke the Lord's words telling him to go find a widow. Last week we read Psalm 23, so we acted out the parable of the lost sheep. The poor lamb bleated loudly and pitifully in the next room during the first part of the service. Then the children went with the shepherd to find it. It was the high point of the service. Another time they pretended to slay a lamb on an altar before taking communion, which made all of us realize how dramatic the Lord's Supper is.

Method variation. Vary the ways in which you present a passage of Scripture. Jesus varied his methods between conversation, lecture, parables, object lessons, questions and even wielding a whip. You can illustrate the slaying of a lamb in Old Testament worship with no spoken lines. Someone enters the room pretending to pull on a rope, followed by someone on hands and knees, bleating like a sheep. Tell the worshipper to lay his hands on the sheep's head and to confess sins. Then have priests place it on the altar and pretend to slit its throat. An adult describes the blood spattering all over them, the noise, smell, flies and fire. As worship this act proves shocking and repugnant—because our sins are shocking and repugnant to the Most Holy One. Sometimes people simply act out a truth silently, other times they may read lines. Patterson commented:

> You might teach from Romans 5 about the grace that abounds to many through the obedience of the final Adam whom Paul contrasted with the first Adam. Act out Adam and Eve's fall without making it into an elaborate production. It needs not be long and is not supposed to entertain or to display anyone's acting skill. Participants simply read the words of Adam, Eve, the voice of the Lord, the serpent and the narrator while performing appropriate actions. Little children may portray animals as Adam names them. If you want a moment of amusement, then have the most mature and serious man in your congregation—the last person people would expect—play the serpent. When he

appears, have him hiss at the audience. Let young people teach the passage to younger ones and practice the reenactment well ahead of time. Help adults to disciple their families and younger friends by making it easy for them. And be sure to model by doing so first, and praise their efforts publicly.

Age harmonization. Mixing different ages, including adults, to dramatize sermons makes a greater impact. It edifies more people when the older children prepare the younger ones, making disciples of them in the process.

Children of all ages and cultures have a natural desire to receive attention from older children. It is a crime to segregate them by age at every meeting. Sometimes it is normal for them to gather with their peers, but not all the time. So doing would impair their ability to relate normally to other age groups.

Patterson recalled that a youth advisor wanted two boys to leave the group, because they made noise and distracted others. He felt that they were simply bursting with energy and creativity, so he asked them to start a new group and disciple younger children. He proceeded to help them plan and gave them tools for disciple making. They blossomed as young leaders and the younger children thrived under them as a result.

Patterson's apprentice, Galen Currah, observed from Africa and Asia that in most societies, children are considered members of society *in training* and are made a part of most social events. They hold cultural events to mark every child's transition towards adulthood with new behavioral expectations. Western secularization of education, he has pointed out, has imposed artificial grading and graduation, effectively tearing apart families and delaying adult behavior.

Rethinking Christian Education for Children

While traveling in Gujarat, India, late one night, Patterson recalled, with a reminiscent grin, a conversation he had had 50 years earlier. A seminary professor exclaimed to Patterson that Christian education at all levels needed to be drastically more relational and tied directly to students' fieldwork with churches. Patterson probed,

"Prof, if churches and schools practiced your educational philosophy, would it not replace most seminary programs and your job?" The elder Christian educator frowned, then smiled and whispered, "It would. But let us not say that too loudly here and now!"

This line of thinking has led many missionaries to design pastoral training in which experienced pastors mentor novice ones. This kind of practice facilitates the training of novice leaders in a movement of church reproduction in many countries, by providing a balance between classroom instruction and personalized mentoring. Patterson does both; he teaches formal contexts while mentoring students and missionaries outside of the classroom.

This kind of practical, relational approach to education can also apply to a church's Christian Education program, for three reasons. 1) A radical application of the New Testament approach to education would enable churches and parents to better train children and youth. 2) Fewer Christian youth would abandon church and faith during their teen years. 3) Churches provide an ideal situation to train with the following advantages:

- It can prove applicable to current circumstances, ministry opportunities and needs.

- It can be done relationally as teachers and disciples listen and respond to each other.

- It remains non-professional, relying more on the Holy Spirit than on academic preparation.

- It is already Church-based, that is, non-institutional.

- It draws mainly from the Bible, both for content and methodology.

- It employs a variety of methods, as the prophets and apostles did and parents still do (Matt 13:52).

Training must, of course, be adjusted for children, youth, adults and mixed groups:

Training little children. Christian parents, especially fathers, must do far more training of children, and churches should have more activities that include whole families. Lionel Mota, a pastor in Los Angeles, California, reported that he reorganizes his Sunday school to include teaching in family-oriented small groups meeting in homes, which has brought many to the Lord, restored family unity and revitalized the entire church body. Similar examples of brave Christian educators abound.

Training young people. Have you noticed the strong desire of children and teens for attention from older children and teens? Elementary school children crave attention from secondary school-aged children, but seldom receive it. Junior High children admire older teens, who in turn would love to receive more attention from college-aged youth. When Patterson experimented with this in various places by giving young people tools and opportunities to lead and to disciple younger ones, both grew as a result and it bore good fruit.

Training mixed ages. The practice of segregating age groups, if carried to an extreme, can cripple young people's social development, for many fail to learn to relate normally to older or younger persons, including their parents. It is normal for all to seek out peers of their same age, and churches must provide activities for children and young people of the same ages, though not all the time. Churches must deal more decisively with the modern breakdown of families and the oceans of misery it causes. Simply preaching against the evil tide has not stemmed it. Traditional Sunday Schools must supplement age-graded classrooms with more family activities and opportunities for young people to disciple younger people.

Training adults. Let adults serve and not just sit and fill their memory banks with biblical data. Educational psychologists warn that abstract lecturing is a weak expression of communication and results in little knowledge retention. Sermons and Bible teaching that include role-plays, skits, interaction—anything that helps the people avoid being passive hearers only—can communicate doctrine and help people more effectively to experience life changes than can an eloquently-presented monologue. Anthropologist-educator, Charles

Kraft, noted that education is more than simply an accumulating of information, for "true education is the process of total formation."[43]

Aim, therefore, for training in cell groups. Let willing Christian educators add something radically new—and radically New Testament—instead of another structure with recipe book steps to follow. Doing so may require reorganizing in a way that allows shepherding believers in groups small enough to practice the biblical "one another" commands. This will require the enlisting of conscientious and reliable instructors who listen to each person's report on what they are doing for Christ—listening for needs and opportunities. Doing so takes time, so if a group or class is too big, then its teacher should appoint helpers who will listen, in order that every person and family receives real shepherding.

Gear teaching to immediate opportunities for serving others and meeting their needs. A good portion of the teaching should focus on participants' immediate needs and ministry opportunities, requiring that their teacher become aware of these by listening to them. So listen to those whom you teach, to visitors and to those whom you visit in their homes. In relational cell groups, teaching edifies people better when several members of the group contribute insights. For example, teachers can ask individuals ahead of time to relate Bible stories that provide a background for doctrinal passages. Doing so greatly enhances doctrinal teaching and can attract to a small group believers who normally attend no church.

Picture a child saying, "Uncle, will you come watch me help teach the story of the Prodigal Son next Friday night? I'm going to be the rear end of the fatted calf!" Uncle and his family would prove very apt to go.

Train leaders the way Jesus and Paul did. The Bible calls shepherds themselves to apprentice novice leaders. They might delegate this training to fellow shepherds, but it is their responsibility to see that it happens, just as much as preaching and overseeing the sacraments. Jesus and his Apostles modeled such training while

---

[43] Charles H. Kraft, *Anthropology for Christian Witness* (Maryknoll, New York: Orbis Books, 1996), 275.

2 Timothy 2:2 and Titus 1:5 exemplify it. Doing so does not rule out institutional training, but does require supplementing lectures with mentoring for novice leaders. When pastors fulfill their duty in a receptive, pioneer field, they can normally provide enough new leaders to sustain rapid church reproduction.

Train relationally. Jesus said, "If you love me, obey my commands" (Jn 14:15). Relational Christian education requires that teachers supplement their linear curriculum with menu-driven training. A menu of options lets both teachers and students choose what will best edify them, their families, and their flocks. No two Christians or flocks follow identical paths to maturity or have the same needs. Some needs are common and a linear curriculum serves them well while other needs are peculiar to individuals, families and flocks. Therefore require that teachers listen and respond to such needs specifically. Two teachers who co-teach can more easily keep this balance. Teachers who name helpers to meet with students can also achieve this balance, and there are other ways, too. One key is to apply New Testament guidelines that assure this balance in whatever ways fit your people.

Help children to participate actively in the Lord's work. Before Jesus fed more than a thousand in the wilderness, He asked his disciples what resources they had. Andrew replied that a boy had brought along five loaves and two fish. Jesus took that boy's offering and fed the crowd with it (Jn 6:9-10). Early church writers reported that this boy later became a Christian leader. Children who take an active part in God's work develop spiritually more readily than those who merely listen passively to teachers.

Children often win younger children
to Christ easier than adults can. Let
young people disciple younger people!
Young adults can easily win teenagers,
and so forth on down the line.

Recognize what each child has to offer. If a leader lets children become bored and passive during worship and other weekly activities, then many of them will fail to grow up using the gifts and resources that the Master has given to them. Here are five more guidelines for mobilizing children:

Children benefit more from working and playing with adults and children of different ages. Children of every culture desire the friendship of older youths. To develop socially, children must have a balance of time spent with children of their age with time spent playing and working with persons of different ages. Traditional public schools and Sunday Schools often deny children such opportunities, segregating them abnormally by age. In our flocks, we should free up children from such a stifling, socially-damaging practice as consistently clustering children of the same age.

Children love to act out Bible stories for adults during worship time. Before the worship time, children can meet with a teacher to prepare a short, speedy and even humorous dramatization of a Bible story that relates to the adults' study topic. Such dramas need little preparation. A key is to keep the children's dramas brief and simple, by eschewing polished productions and elaborate costumes. Instead, have them use only simple props. Children enjoy looking around the meeting place to find props such as rocks, sticks, chairs, tables, papers and baskets. Here are some tips for effective dramas:

- Coach the children to speak loudly. To help them do so, have them direct their voice to listeners who are on the other side of the room.

- Dramas are more effective when children of different ages and adults do them together. Very young children can play the parts of spectators in crowds, other members of a family, animals, and even trees.

- Older children do better, if they do not memorize lines word for word, but rather the general ideas. Their teacher can give them ideas for short dialogues and can prompt them if they forget. For example, tell "Philistines" to laugh at little David and say in their own words how silly it is for him to fight a giant.

Children thrive on being creative. God has given to them spectacular imaginations. Let older, energetic children write poems, skits and short songs to present to the other children and, if they do it well, to adults, too. Such compositions should illustrate the topic that the adults are learning that week. Let musicians occasionally set the children's poems to music. Children like to draw symbols and pictures of Bible stories. Let them show their pictures during worship and explain how the pictures illustrate the teaching.

Children enjoy teaching and making disciples. Older children can very effectively help teach and disciple younger ones. Teachers can help children beforehand to prepare simple questions about details in a Bible story. When the congregation meets, the children can, after acting out the story, ask these questions. Children can also give the correct answers to their own questions, if the adults do not remember the details. Children take pleasure in memorizing Psalms and other Scriptures and enjoy reciting them for adults.

Children learn well from non-verbal teaching. Most church planting movements multiply family-oriented congregations. Flocks are small and have no separate nursery, so accepting the children as an authentic part of the church body remains a natural thing to do. When a child helps others understand the truths that he has just learned, then those truths take root in his heart. Children also recall better the truths they have learned and are more eager to participate in worship. They are more likely to grow up loving the church instead of finding it boring. Jesus Himself welcomed children and found ways for them to participate in His ministry, making use of their gifts and resources. Let us do the same.

So, if you lack experience in teaching little ones, remember that:

- Younger children are keen on singing songs to lively music while making hand motions. They should practice songs with hand motions and sing them for the whole congregation.

- Children love lessons presented with objects that they can see, touch and handle. An astute teacher uses physical objects to illustrate topics, allowing the children to handle them and explain what they mean.

- A wise teacher prepares object lessons beforehand, coaching the children in how to explain them during congregational worship.

Guideline 33
Organize women for significant ministry.

The Almighty has used many
courageous women,
like Deborah, to begin
His work in dangerous fields
where few men volunteered!
Shame on us guys!

Ladies, follow Priscilla's example. She played an important role in Ephesus where she helped to teach Apollos, a powerful leader, alongside of her husband Aquila (Acts 18:24-26). Scripture always mentions Priscilla and Aquila together, for they worked in harmony. Real tension results when a man and his wife have not agreed on her role in ministry.

Show sensitivity to the culture when considering women's roles. In many cultures, if a woman has a public leadership role, few men will serve as leaders under her, especially if she is not accountable to a male leader. In other cultures, women plant and lead strong flocks that include men. Patterson commented:

> During our first years on the field, our churches had no married men; mostly women, children and teenagers attended our meetings. While leading worship, young, single pastors would glance from time to time towards a woman missionary who would subtly smile or nod her approval, obviously in control. I saw men come to a meeting place, watch through a window from outside a few minutes, then walk away and never return. They were seeking God, but what they saw—a flock dominated by women and young people—disillusioned them. I came to realize that in their *macho* culture the churches could not gather entire families until they had strong male leaders. So my few, young co-workers and I resolved to work with mature men, especially heads of household, and within a few years the congregations we worked with all had a healthy balance of men and women.

For a time, I took an unbending, dogmatic position against women leaders—until Sonia appeared. Once, when I traveled to her remote village to mentor pastors of that area, she told me that for several evenings a man would shoot his gun at the pastor and his house. Fortunately, the rascal was always drunk and missed each time. After a few days of boarding up windows and huddling in the dark, the pastor fled from the village with his family. Sonia, determined to keep the church alive, began to lead the flock. She told me how people were calling her *pastora* and so she asked me if that was permissible. I said no, that our churches did not have women leaders. After I left the village, the Holy Spirit did not give me peace about that, for I was not honestly facing reality. So I went back and told Sonia to let the people call her *pastora*, because she was indeed shepherding the church and to deny the fact would have been a lie. She was greatly relieved. I then suggested that she let a man take over when it became safe to do so again, because in that *macho* culture the drunk would never shoot a lady. Sonia said that was her wish, too, and a male leader did take over a few months later.

Some congregations, after placing women in top leadership positions have found years later that few strong male elders remained in leadership and that fewer men attended church meetings. This may be why the apostle Paul cautioned Timothy against letting women take high profile positions of leadership over men (1 Tm 2:9-15).

Guideline 34
Dramatize biblical events.

My flock falls asleep when I preach! How can I keep their attention? Should I crow louder?	Please don't! Narrate or act out historical events in Scripture! Then ask questions about them! Let us look at some guidelines...

Role-plays and demonstrations can be effective teaching tools that can help us:

- Teach God's Word to believers.

- Train leaders.

- Practice needed skills.

Role-plays can simulate situations that require believers to practice new skills. Team-teaching with two or more instructors working together makes it easy to plan simulations. Choose role-plays wisely for use in leadership training workshops. Listen first to participants' questions, plans and goals before selecting role-plays.

Pastor Martinez ambled into the seminar room, sat and sighed. "Three boring days! Another foreigner will mumble about his abstract ideas and irrelevant methods! Oh well, the food is good! I shall go out and run errands between sessions."

The foreign speaker, however, immediately asked for three volunteers. To Martinez he said quietly, "Sir, will you role-play the part of Mr. Trainer? Simply listen to your trainee—this other volunteer here—report what his flock is doing." To another he said, "Will you play Mr. Moneybags, interrupt the others and offer this trainee a scholarship to study in a distant city? Martinez, you argue that you are already training him the way Jesus and Paul trained leaders and that he is beginning a new, growing congregation as a result. Mr. Moneybags, you keep insisting with arrogance and pomp that yours is the only way to get education, and ask the audience if they agree with you."

This initiated three days of intense, fun, lively and Bible-based interaction. At the end, Martinez exclaimed to his friends with chagrined bemusement, "I never learned so much in such a short time. And we students did most of the talking!"[44]

Since the best shepherds and mentors seek to train others through human relationships, rather than analytical classroom lectures, they often find that students learn more through stories, especially when they act them out. Fortunately, the Bible contains scores of good stories. Besides, acting comes naturally, since most people do some of that daily.

A skilled mentor and workshop leader will incorporate stories and skits into training sessions, both to enhance learning and to teach how to mentor others using a simple, easily-transferable method. Stories and skits are fun to do in every culture of the world. The Bible itself originated largely through the retelling of stories, historical accounts of God's dealing with men, not as a theology book. Some ways to teach a story to make an impact include:

- Reading it. (This is good.)

- Recounting it by memory. (This is better.)

- Having helpers read or say by memory the dialogue of different characters. (This is better still.)

- Act it out, adults together with children. (This is the best.)

Benefits of Teaching by Role-Play

Stories and role-plays are easy for hearers to pass on to others if presented in a simple way. Oral societies need to hear the Bible in

---

44 *MentorNet* is an electronic newsletter by George Patterson and Galen Currah in response to common questions <www. MentorNet.ws>.

story form. Most people movements to Christ throughout history have taken place among illiterate peoples who repeat the stories, allowing the gospel to flow from friend to friend, family to family, village to village and, in cities, neighborhood to neighborhood. Simple stories with appropriate applications flow readily in illiterate societies, if told in a reproducible way. Use of sophisticated technology or analytical reasoning to teach others is not very reproducible.

Stories touch the heart, when used to communicate rather than merely entertain. Stories motivate and apply the truths of God's Word better than abstract analysis. The Lord told many stories and the Bible is full of them.

Stories enable more people to participate in the teaching, especially when both children and adults participate together in presenting them. Avoid letting people become passive "hearers only." Wise teachers do not always present the stories themselves and ask others to do so.

Role-plays done with humor facilitate the communication of controversial and otherwise incommunicable issues. As an example, traditionally-minded believers often want the mother church to be perfect before allowing her to start daughter churches. They delay church planting and discourage workers from starting churches. They fear that doing so would cost too much, or they make up rigid rules for naming leaders and performing other church activities. Role-playing church planting often corrects such interference. Here are some guidelines to follow:

- Let actors talk about common fears and objections to church planting, arguing humorously on behalf of the most detrimental traditions.

- Have them relate ideas in their own words, without memorizing exactly what to say. Let them argue a point, but then ask anyone in the room to answer them.

- Name such arguers according to their roles "Mr. Legalist," "Dr. Academician," "The Rev. Perfect Church," "Mr. Moneybags" or whatever else. Use your imagination.

What to Do and Not Do in Dramatizing Stories and Using Role-Plays

Let adults tell or dramatize stories together with children. Did you think that stories are mainly for children? Adults also learn, retain and apply truths better when they are conveyed with stories. When children or teenagers act out a Bible story, ask at least one adult also to participate, in order to bring seriousness and respect to the story. Especially include fathers.

Avoid elaborate productions. To teach Bible truths and help people make plans and commitments, do not "act" in a professional sense or memorize lines, but simply discuss the ideas with each other. Focus on points to make rather than on acting performance. Avoid costumes and use only the simplest props, if any. Highly trained actors are not always the best ones to use; few adjust to the simplicity required to communicate spiritual truths. Most want to perform and use their acting ability to the fullest, which distracts from what the Lord wants to communicate.

Keep dramas brief. Normally two or three minutes suffice to make a point. For example, you might name some actors as church planters and others as contacts in a pagan society. Tell them to plant a church. They will usually start by conversing casually with their contacts to build a relationship, which takes too much time to act out. So, when they have begun building a relationship, say something like, "Good! You are building a relationship. Now, two days have passed. What has to happen next?" Ask the participants to suggest what the actors should do next. Keep the skit moving. Inexperienced teachers let role-plays drag on too long thereby weakening their value.

Ask others to help create a scenario. Do not fear that people lack creativity, and do not rob participants of the freedom to portray a truth in an imaginative way by structuring their roles with too much detail. Let them do it their own way, and you will have many happy surprises.

Use stories to teach doctrinal books like Romans, Galatians and Hebrews. New Testament writers assumed that their readers already knew the common Old Testament stories. The book of Romans can prove boring and obscure, if one does not include in its teaching the stories upon which Paul based his doctrines. To teach the apostles' letters without relating the historical events that gave rise to their doctrines can rob learners of a joyful understanding of those doctrines' foundations.

Christianity is unique among religions in that all of its doctrines derive from historical events such as Creation; Adam's Fall; the Flood; the Holy One's promises to Abraham the Believer; slavery in Egypt and the Hebrew's escape; the Law given at Sinai; the founding; division; and fall of the Kingdom of Israel; the exile and restoration. The New Testament adds the birth, baptism, miracles, death, resurrection, and ascension of Jesus and the coming of the Holy Spirit at Pentecost, and many more.

Give preference to Bible stories. Bible stories convey all crucial doctrines and Christian duties. The Holy Spirit uses the historical events of Scripture more readily than fiction, to convince and illuminate men's minds. The spiritual impact of Bible stories makes them easy to recount and to act out. For example:

- To teach original sin, ask someone to play Adam. Instruct that person to speak what Adam says in Genesis 3 and to act out briefly what the person thinks he did.

- Name others as Eve, the serpent, the voice of the Lord, and a narrator who reads sentences that are not dialogue.

- Do not rehearse it too much lest it prove too stiff. Do not expect perfection, for mistakes offer opportunities to laugh.

- Discuss stories afterwards and ask, "What does the Lord want us to do in response to this? Confess our sin? Pray with stronger faith? Show our love for needy people in a more practical way?

Be creative when planning role-plays. Some teachers look for ready-made role-plays that are explained in detail. Others prefer to add details themselves. Do as much as you can to develop role-plays yourself, with the help of other participants. Creative teaching and pleasant surprises stir people's imaginations, so use creative methods to help individuals take active parts in the teaching. Participating and watching others do so inspires many to make commitments and to form action plans. Wise teachers develop, over time, a repertoire of demonstrations. For example, to tell the story of the wise and foolish builders from Matthew 7:24-29, let two men play the builders. When the narrator mentions the rain falling on the foolish man's house, pour a small bit of water over his head and have him fall down.

Aim for total participation. If possible, present role-plays in which everybody present takes part. The more who participate, the better the teaching, and the more animated the setting, the better. Arrange seating in a circle or semicircle, for participants' ability to see one another enhances their participation.

Let demonstrations raise questions. Visualizing how to do God's work on the field stimulates questions about planning for it. During or following a demonstration, let both students and teachers ask their questions.

Keep role-plays short and simple.[45] Some Bible passages are too long to dramatize within the available time, so choose portions that present the main point and quickly summarize the rest. A shortage of volunteer actors may also limit how much of a story they can dramatize.

A role-play should save time. If it takes more time than lecturing, then it may be wiser to lecture briefly. Trainees can get carried away by the acting, waste time, and thereby defeat the purpose of the training. Keep focused on the truth or skill that you aim to impart, and skip time-consuming dialogue by asking the actor who is speaking to simply tell what he thinks should happen next. Simple role-plays give better results if actors ad lib, that is, use their own spontaneous words, keeping in mind only the idea of what to say and do.

Use Bible stories when possible instead of making up stories. The Holy Spirit prefers to apply His own Words to transform lives, so biblical stories usually give better results.

Have fun with this!

---

[45] Download an extensive index of role-plays and skits from <www.mentorandmultiply.com>.

Guideline 35
Build mutually edifying relationships.

Let us see how flocks
cultivate edifying
fellowship...

Show your trainees how flocks must cultivate loving relationships, like the Israelite leaders did. Those leaders brought the people together to celebrate joyful Old Testament feasts (2 Chron 30:21). Christians can strongly edify each other by meeting weekly in small groups that obey the "one another" commands of the New Testament. Other ways of cementing relationships include social events and the celebration of important historical events.

Loving fellowship between members of a ministry task group requires that they agree on objectives and methods in a spirit of submitting one to another in love (Phil 2:1-11; Eph 5:21). This requires respecting other believers' spiritual gifts and helping them express their gifts in ministry.

Solemn celebrations like Advent, Christmas, Epiphany, Lent, Palm Sunday, Good Friday, Easter, and Pentecost often prove more meaningful and edifying for new Christians in a new field than in places where such holidays and seasons have become routine. Some Westerners unwisely ignore sacred and national holidays in their drive to carry on regular programs without interruption. In many societies, people come to Christ more readily during holidays that have a religious significance, if believers plan well for those special events. Fearful Westerners sometimes shun holidays having pagan overtones when, rather, they should rather bring Christ into those events.

Bring Christ into occasions such as births, birthdays, coming of age, engagements, weddings, anniversaries, deaths, dedication of new dwellings, and any other event that people take seriously. To assure that a congregation celebrates these in a culturally-relevant way, ask local believers to write poems, songs or skits for them.

To build better relationships one must often do a little "social engineering," arranging events that bring together people who otherwise would not interact, such as lunches, coffee time, sports events, parties, outings or retreats. Be creative and ask local believers about useful local customs.

Show your trainees how flocks can encourage mutually-edifying relationships. Let the Holy Spirit harmonize several different spiritual gifts in the living Body of Christ (1 Cor 12). The Body in urban areas is often a cluster of congregations or home groups working closely together. The first church in Jerusalem met to worship and break bread as small groups in houses (Acts 2:46).

A church practicing "Body life" must organize differently from program-based churches that group individuals having the same spiritual gifts in specialized programs or departments. Doing so isolates the gifts from each other, often segregating different age groups in the process. Children who are not personally made disciples by older youth or adults often fail to get along well with people of other ages later on.

A true disciple making community brings together in small shepherding groups as many different spiritual gifts as possible, so that each group will have a well-balanced ministry and provide complete pastoral care as its members serve each other reciprocally. So keep groups small enough for strong interaction, normally not more than about fourteen adults. Let each person and family speak if they want to, and minister one to another.

Guideline 36
Boldly affirm the Almighty's forgiveness.

Many pastors and missionaries
do not sin enough to feel the need
that new believers have
for assurance of Heaven's
forgiveness!
They are too sheltered from life!

Proclaim the forgiveness of sins with the authority given by the Lord. Use the "keys" of the Kingdom that assure the forgiveness that Jesus promised first to Peter (Matt 16:19) and later to all his disciples (Matt 18:18; Jn 20:22). Boldly unlock the door of the Kingdom of Heaven by proclaiming, with the Holy Spirit's power, Jesus' death, resurrection, and forgiveness of sins to those who repent (Lk 24:46-48; Acts 1:8).

Witnessing for the Lord includes assuring seekers of forgiveness. Do not be stingy with God's grace! A person's conversion often depends on the faith of those who witness to him as much as on his own faith. Jesus, for example, assured a paralytic of forgiveness, because of the faith of his friends who had lowered him from the roof (Mk 2:1-12).

Evangelists who seek conversions by explaining theology often fumble the keys. Detailed theology should come later. Keys lose their function if they lose their shape, so do not tamper with the original, changeless news of Jesus' death, resurrection, and forgiveness to all who repent and believe.

Shepherds need to affirm forgiveness continually. A pastor who serves daily in the Lord's work is sheltered. He is not subjected to worldly influences as much as his flock is. He may not sin enough to feel the plaguing guilt and the sting of an offended conscience like his parishioners do. He easily forgets how guilty most new believers feel when they begin to worship. They have been hearing profanity for eight hours daily and having to listen to men brag about the woman they visited with the night before. They feel regret for getting angry with their wife or children. They desperately crave assurance of forgiveness but sometimes fail to receive it.

Guideline 37
Connect Jesus' commission with His command.

Let us look at ways in which our Master's servants
flap both wings in harmony.
His two "great" commands resemble my two wings.
If you trimmed the feathers of only one wing,
then I would fly in circles and go nowhere.

The two foundational commands of the New Testament are Jesus' *Great Commission* to make disciples of all peoples, and the *Great Commandment* to love God and people in a practical way. Pastors must equip their flocks to help communities deal with emergencies, poverty and injustice, like Nehemiah did for Jerusalem. In the New Testament, Paul wrote, "Let us do good to all people, especially to those who belong to the family of believers" (Gal 6:10).

Bill Taylor, a former missionary to Central America, once addressed new missionaries and said: "Listen to the cry of the disenfranchised, the poor, the street children and determine how [to] impact this ever-growing sector of pain and hopelessness."[46] How to deal with poverty and desperate community needs without building dependency is a challenge for Western missionaries. One solution includes a thorough integration of mercy ministry with evangelism, church planting, and pastoral work. "Dependency is not just a welfare condition. It becomes an insidious state of mind that can

---

[46] William D. Taylor, "Some Words for Expat Agencies," *Evangelical Missions Quarterly*, July 2003, 309.

debilitate generation after generation once it gains a foothold."[47] Galen Currah reported:

> An example of successful holistic ministry that combines mercy work with church planting comes from Medical Ambassadors[48]. They begin by training national Christians to serve as trainers of local community health workers. The communities where they serve choose and compensate their health workers. As a result, they and the churches have been able to avoid dependency from the start. Most of those workers become believers and start churches in the homes of those whom they teach. This has happened in more than fifty countries in the past ten years.

Too many mission organizations do relief work apart from local churches, while too many others do church work apart from mercy ministries. Both err by separating those gift-based ministries. Short-term outsiders often deal with only symptoms of poverty and injustice, not its causes. Patterson recalled that, in an extremely poor area where he visited, short-term workers helped growers to get better prices by transporting grain and chickens to market in affluent areas. The only farmers who grew enough, however, to make this practical were larger growers who were already doing well and needed no help. The poor residents suffered greater misery as a result of the short-term effort, because the project inflated the local prices of grain and meat.

Believers are to let the Holy Spirit harmonize ministries in the Body (1 Cor 12-13). Some pastors rightly suspect that development programs could compete with the church for resources and personnel. Specialized work should not be isolated from church ministries, lest both grow weaker. An ongoing mercy ministry is far more effective when it sinks deep spiritual roots among the members of a community.

Trainers can help direct their students in the right direction by teaching integrated units that combine different ministries; they

---

[47] Saint Steve, *The Great Omission—Fulfilling Christ's Commission is Possible If...* (Seattle: YWAM Publishing, 2001), 66.
[48] Visit <http://medicalambassadors.org>.

would hinder holistic ministries by teaching them as isolated sub-jects. Mission agency field leaders can also promote or stifle this integration with their organizational strategies and structures.

Who ultimately integrates the ministries of a congregation? It is the Lord Jesus Christ who holds all things together (Col 1:16-18), His indwelling Spirit who coordinates spiritual work with develop-ment efforts within His Body on earth. This is not metaphysical rhetoric, for development work done by godly Christians consis-tently has a greater and longer-lasting effect.

Guideline 38
Keep church body balanced; avoid stressing pet ministries.

Our flock has fantastic Bible teaching.

So, that is our ministry!

Careful! A flock's greatest weakness is its greatest strength taken to excess.

Let us look at ways to balance vital ministries in a healthy, holistic church body.

David Garrison has shown that reproductive congregations, how-ever young they may be, enjoy good church health. However, an inward-oriented congregation or organization that focuses only on the ministry that it does best for its own members will soon become ingrown and less effective.[49]

---

[49] David Garrison, *Church Planting Movements.* (Richmond: International Mission Board, 2000).

How can leaders avoid a subtle and damaging imbalance within a church body, a church planting team, a denomination, a mission agency, or an educational program? How can believers with different ministries work together as a body, keeping a healthy balance? One solution is to harmonize various gift-based ministries. Here are several guidelines for keeping a church body balanced by integrating its vital ministries:

Believers need diversity! Focus on developing various expressions of obedience through a number of ministries. The apostle Paul told Titus to name shepherding elders who would take care of what was lacking in the new congregations in Crete (Ti 1:5). To do so, Titus and the elders had to know what the essential truths and duties of a church are before they could discern what was still lacking. A brief summary of some essential body ministries that have to be harmonized includes the following:

- *Evangelism.* Witness for Jesus, baptize new believers, send workers to needy regions near and far, etc.

- *Prayer.* Intercede, hold family devotions, conduct spiritual warfare, etc.

- *Stewardship.* Show the flock how to give, to use time and property wisely, etc.

- *Pastoral care.* Counsel, correct, encourage, and strengthen marriages and family life, etc.

- *Teaching the Word.* Equip believers to serve, train leaders, correct error, etc.

- *Fellowship.* Cultivate loving interaction within the flock and with other congregations.

- *Organizing and overseeing.* Enable and empower all believers to use their God-given gifts to serve one another.

- *Building virtuous character.* Encourage godly change, holiness, and loving obedience to the Lord.

- *Worship.* Facilitate worship in which all can participate.

Wise leaders launch special ministries that current or local conditions warrant. For example, in a society where suicide is common, a congregation should offer counseling for troubled people.

One's very success can breed eventual failure. Leaders who succeed in a limited, temporary way so often crystallize their methods that they become stubbornly inflexible. Wise shepherds initiate the entire spectrum of essential ministries and not only those ministries in which they excel, equipping their flocks to do all kinds of vital ministries. The outcome of a balance of ministries is that they all are strengthened, including any that previously received too much attention. For example, a church planter who combines church planting with other vital ministries normally plants more congregations than does one who aims only to start them. Diversity also reduces boredom in the field, keeping workers on their toes.

Leaders need diversity, so ministry team leaders should cooperate with leaders of other ministries. Since shepherds normally serve in close harmony with other ministers, a wise leader avoids serving as a lone worker. Many congregations and organizations have discovered the value of having a team of two or more leaders, with one of them serving as their coordinator. The New Testament congregations had multiple shepherding elders, because the church in a city at that time consisted of a cluster of closely-knit, small groups, or what some would call cells or house churches.

An enemy of a healthy ministry balance is excessive specialization of one ministry or of only a few. Ministry leaders should recall how the Lord scolded the tribe of Ephraim when it had become "a flat cake not turned" (Hosea 7:8). Congregations easily become "half-baked" when they focus only on the side of their ministry that they do well. While coaching leaders, mentors often encounter damage where congregations, mission agencies, and church planting teams had overemphasized their strength. The greatest weakness of many teachers is to take one area—for example, teaching—to an excess, neglecting other expressions of obedience that are equally important. Overemphasizing a ministry that believers perform with excellence often leads to neglecting other imperative ministries. Common areas of one-sided emphasis and their remedies include the following:

- *Teaching.* Many congregations become spiritually inert, because their pastors are such eloquent teachers that the body neglects other areas of church life. Members become "hearers only." Leaders fail to counsel believers with marital problems, unruly children, alcohol or drug abusers, and those with other bad habits. To bring balance to ministries, teachers should take a servant's role, working closely with those who give compassionate member care, serving the needy, reaching out to those who need the Lord Jesus Christ, and undertaking any other ministry that might be neglected.

- *Building Relationships.* Some congregation members want to take part in frequent social events, but do little else to serve God or others. To bring balance, a church body should aim to develop leaders of their neglected ministries.

- *Prophetic utterances, interpreting tongues and demonstrations of power.* Some believers so eagerly seek signs that they over-look the greater reality that the signs signify. Those who have these spiritual gifts should make sure that they balance their experiences with practical ministry, bringing the Holy Spirit's power to bear in an edifying, transforming way to people with definite needs, restoring broken family relationships, and bringing friends and relatives to Jesus. They must learn to heal bruised emotions, sickness, and demonic oppression, while serving needy and rejected people.

- *Campaigning for social justice.* Some congregations and mis-sionary teams focus exclusively on Jesus' command to love one's neighbor that they neglect his command to make disciples who obey *all* that He commanded. To assure balance, they must work more closely with evangelists, disciple makers and biblical teachers, as evidenced, for example, through the life and ministry of William Carey. Vishal Mangalwadi, one of India's foremost leaders, an evangelist, political activist, and intellectual, wrote of Carey:

> He did more for the transformation of the Indian subcontinent in the nineteenth and twentieth centuries than any other individual before or since.... He was an Indus-

trialist. An economist. A medical humanitarian. A media pioneer. An educator. A moral reformer. A botanist. And a Christian missionary."[50]

The constant aim is to keep the Great Commission connected with the Great Command.

• *Not too big!* Cell group and home church leaders should keep groups small enough to remain functional. Many congregations have grown very big by staying very small. That is, they multiply cell groups or house churches. A small group enables individuals to interact. Maintaining balance calls for group effort, and remember, the Lord Himself is a part of the group.

The apostle Paul, in 1 Corinthians 12 and 13, compared a healthy church body to the human body. Members are to use their God-given gifts to serve one another in the same way that a body's organs work together. Such harmony is strong evidence of a powerful working of the Holy Spirit. It is He who gives gifts, the power to use them, and the love needed to harmonize one's work with that of others who have different gifts. Without such love from God, a believer merely strives to develop his ministry to a pinnacle of excellence with little regard for others' ministries.

Since only the Lord can turn a group of believers into His true Body, a leader's task is to let Him do so, by helping the members of the Body to use their spiritual gifts freely, serving one another in love. A top-notch leader lets this loving, edifying interaction take place, which easily happens in small groups. It seldom happens well in large gatherings led only by paid staff members.

Gather several flocks at once. Church planters who form multiple flocks as soon as possible in an area enable new congregations to encourage and serve one another. A single flock in an area often becomes defensive, with an unhealthy, ingrown focus. Whereas members of a solitary body begin to feel that the church planters owe all their time and attention to that one congregation, loving inter-

---

[50] Vishal and Ruth Mangelwadi, *The Legacy of William Carey* (Wheaton: Crossway Books, 1993), back cover.

action between several new congregations better enables a healthy balance.

The New Testament shows that an interactive, "one another" church body life is to be practiced, not only within congregations, but between them. Workers who are strong in a particular ministry go and help other groups that are weak in that ministry. This kind of interchange among congregations and cells greatly improves their balance. Pray that the Lord will enable those whom you shepherd, train or coach to build a balanced church body.

Those who teach theology in a relational way with immediate applications bring balance to their training like the apostle Paul did in his pastoral letters. Remind students that the Lord loves balance. All creation demonstrates balance —the stars, atoms, plants, animals and the many systems within nature. Scripture reveals harmonious balance within the eternal God. The Bible calls Jesus both "the Lion" and "the Lamb," both Son of God and Son of Man. The Almighty spans the spectrum between omnipotence and weakness, glory and humility, justice and mercy. Jesus yearns for a balanced body in cell groups, ministry teams, mission agencies, congregations, and alliances of congregations that work together.

Chapter 3

Let Flocks Multiply

Guideline 39
Let God's Spirit play the midwife as flocks reproduce.

Let us examine how our flocks can grow
spiritually strong enough to multiply...

God enables His Kingdom to expand by addition and by multiplication.

Addition appears in the book of Acts where three thousand were added to the church by baptism (Acts 2:41). *Multiplication* begins in Acts chapter 8 where small "core" groups of believers, fleeing persecution, scattered into other countries and there multiplied. Those small groups served as nuclei around which growth by addition could easily occur.

Let congregations grow in the normal, biblical way, from the Word of God sown in the fertile hearts of repentant sinners. Growth does not come from duplicating the external forms of a mother church. Rather, church planters tap a new congregation's God-given power to reproduce itself through its daughter and granddaughter flocks, leading to a movement of spontaneous church reproduction.

Multiplication of churches arises in a situation in which trained nationals—having been entrusted with the reigns of leadership—reproduce themselves and their congregations through chains of indigenous churches in a way that is rapid, efficient and inexpensive.

A mother church passes on its DNA enabling a cluster of believers to become a daughter church, another living, serving, loving body. Flocks often fail to reproduce when daughter churches try to do the Lord's work exactly the same way that the mother church did. The mother church may have evolved a worship style that fits a bigger, more spiritually mature group, and not a smaller, younger flock. Since a daughter church does not have to resemble its mother in external forms, its mother should pass on only essential spiritual elements such as the Spirit-empowered life in Christ, vital truths, and evangelistic fervor. Missiologist Tom Steffen states emphatically that effective church planters must think in terms of multiplication rather than addition.[51] Patterson remembered:

> When I started teaching church multiplication, some thought it rashly irresponsible, even dangerous. One of the few who encouraged me was Donald McGavran who led the School of World Mission in Pasadena, California. When I asked him about the concept of church reproduction, he said, "Give it wings!" I found other missionaries with the same view, but often their mission agency leaders squashed it, fearing whatever they themselves did not initiate and could not control.

> Now that the concept of church multiplication has become accepted in mission circles, is there a danger of its becoming a superficial fad? One must not see it as a ministry by itself or even a motivating strategy. The Bible does not mention the term. What Scripture does reveal is that where the apostles and their trainees made disciples the way Jesus said to do so, congregations would reproduce. So let church planters emphasize the need to obey the commands of Jesus and of His

---

[51] Tom Steffen, *Passing the Baton* (La Habra: Center for Organizational and Ministry Development, 1997), 169-86.

apostles in love with childlike faith. That is about the only thing on this planet that men can never carry too far.

Myths and Facts about Church and Cell Group Reproduction

Myth #1. "To start a church, church planters must leave their mother church."

Fact. In most church planting projects around the world, workers do not leave their home church or cell group.

In the case of Peter and his church planting team in Acts 10, and Paul and Barnabas in Acts 13 and 14, workers did not transfer membership to the new congregations; they retained their relationships with their mother churches. Patterson affirmed, "I cannot recall any church plant in which our workers left their home church. Rather they evangelized the other communities and trained the novice leaders without leaving their own congregation."

Myth #2: "To start a new church or cell group you must *hive off* a substantial number of members (a critical mass) from a mother church to become the core of a new body."

Fact. In urban areas many new churches do start by hiving off enough members to pay a pastor and practice a worship style similar to the mother church's. This method has a number of weaknesses. It works only if a mother church is big enough to send a large number of its members to the new congregation. It does not work for most smaller, poorer, and newer flocks. It works only if the leaders are willing, which in most little congregations is not the case. It also works if transportation is convenient for a large number of people to travel to the location of the new congregation without changing their residence.

Hiving off can take place with little or no evangelism, and the new congregations sometimes do none. Hiving seldom sustains the reproduction in a widespread movement for Christ and, therefore, is seldom seen in pioneer church planting movements.

Myth #3. "The job of an evangelist is not done until new believers are established in an *existing* church or cell group."

Fact. The problem is with the word "existing." Where healthy churches and cell groups reproduce rapidly, workers will bring new families into an existing group only as a last resort. Their first goal is normally to build a new cell group (or church in a pioneer field) around the newly-believing family.

Each new believer, especially if he is the head of a household, opens a potential, new "vein of gold," the existing social network of the new believer or family. The gospel normally flows readily along the same route as does gossip, from friend to friend and from relative to relative.

Most Western church planters' first impulse is to extract a new believer from his social network and help him make new friends in an existing church body. In most church planting movements, the evangelists do their best to keep new believers in loving relationships with others in their current networks, letting the gospel flow along the lines of those natural relationships.

Myth #4. "Where churches and cells multiply rapidly, it is always necessary for new believers to find and make *new* friends quickly within their new congregation."

Fact. The problem is with the word "new." In the church and cell group reproduction that have been observed, new believers have old friends who come with them into the new congregation or cell group.

People certainly need to have close friends in a congregation or most will leave after attending a few times. These friends, however, do not need to be new ones. Workers can build new congregations around new believers from the same vein of gold. Thus, most of their friends in a new congregation will be old friends.

Myth #5: "It takes a lot of money to start churches."

Fact. It takes much money to send and support missionaries that are not tentmakers, but congregations that require no building or paid clergy will be self-supporting from the start.

Usually what costs a lot of money are non-biblical, Western traditions and practices. Where workers and congregations can avoid those traditions or shake themselves loose from such, they normally need no more resources than what is locally available.

Some Western congregations and missions too quickly adopt methods and requirements on mission fields that create financial dependency. The finances often attract unscrupulous, power-hungry schemers who ascend to the head of new congregations and organizations.

Myth #6. "You can only start Christian congregations in a free, democratic society with freedom of religion."

Fact. Throughout history and around the world today, except in traditionally Christian lands, most congregations start under hostile conditions.

Jesus and his Apostles set the example by their radical faith and willingness to suffer persecution to advance the gospel and to start congregations in new culture groups. People groups around the globe suffer all kinds of abuse at the hands of their governments and of local rebel movements. To suffer willingly for righteousness often brings on more of the same kind of abuse, but also an eternal reward.

Myth #7. "You have to have highly educated, trained church planters to start high-quality churches that will remain doctrinally sound and long lasting."

Fact. Experience and research have shown that having church planters with higher education often hinders church growth and reproduction! Patterson remarks:

> Even more important than education is that church planters be culturally similar to new believers and enjoy freedom to gather flocks, unfettered by church traditions that allow only the clergy to perform the activities that Jesus commanded all his followers to do. What is consistently helpful is that existing church planters and leaders empower and coach novice church planters and shepherds who start and lead new flocks and start training other, even newer, leaders in turn.

Myth #8. "The impulse to reproduce weakens as it passes from a mother church to daughter churches, to granddaughters, etc."

Fact. Every strong, healthy flock alive today is a distant descendent of the first church at Jerusalem.

The presence of Christ and the gifts of the Holy Spirit are communicated by the Lord into every new congregation, giving it the vitality and life it needs to remain vibrant. Among the main causes that weaken the impulse are liberal theology, legalism, depending on outside resources, and growing too big before reproducing.

Leader reproduction appears in 2 Timothy 2:2. Paul had brought Timothy from Antioch to Ephesus to train others who included Epaphras from Colosse. These trained more believers in other places, including Hierapolis and Laodicea (Col 4:12-13). Paul knew that mentoring could quite effectively train leaders on four levels in reproducible chains. Congregations reproduce only as fast as current workers will train novice ones. If mentoring is sustained in a pioneer field, then there will not be many new congregations in which the impulse weakens.

Myth #9. "You need a strong *doctrinal* base before a church can be sound enough to reproduce."

Fact. To reproduce, all you need is a congregation that lovingly obeys Jesus by making new disciples.

Reproduction that happens around newly-evangelized families can see churches planted almost as rapidly as evangelism moves from one family, clan or friendship circle to another. Detailed doctrinal instruction normally comes later. What Westerners often mean by a "strong doctrinal base" is a mental assent to their organization's dogmas that neither inspire faith nor require loving action. Such "doctrinally-strong" churches seldom reproduce!

Young flocks do need to grow in their understanding of biblical truth, especially the basic truths taught by Jesus. So let them focus on His claims, promises and commands, supplemented by Bible teaching that emphasizes the main idea of a text along with its immediate application to daily life.

Myth #10.: "You must ensure a strong 'home base' first. That is, churches must be strong, before you can start new ones, extend into new social groups, and penetrate new geographical regions."

Fact. The longer a congregation waits, the harder it will be to reproduce.

When reproduction is part of a new flock's DNA, then its daughter and granddaughter churches will also set reproduction without delay as a priority.

Myth #11. "Only a permanent church planting team that enjoys good relationships among its team members can reproduce healthy churches."

Fact. There are no permanent apostolic teams in the Bible and most new congregations begin without formal teams. The best church planting teams are made up of workers from a nearby congregation of the same culture. Expatriate workers can help form such teams.

Jesus' apostolic band lasted three years. Peter's team that started the Caesarean church included believers from Joppa who did not continue with him any farther. Paul's team continually changed members. Good church planting teams focus on every church planting project as its primary purpose, not on building up the teams.

Myth #12. "There are already too many churches in the area."

Fact. About a third of the world's population has no church of their language and culture, and there is no major society that does not need more churches that are relevant to today's generation.

To discern if more churches are needed, do not count the existing churches. Rather count the lost and suffering souls who still need to have Jesus presented to them in a meaningful way.

Although there are churches within most cities where this third of the world's people live, most of them cater only to the expatriate community, often in a foreign language, and cannot reproduce indigenously among the common people. This huge segment of mankind has little hope of knowing the Lord Jesus Christ until congregations reproduce not only within their country but also within their language and culture group.

Myth #13.: "Church multiplication is a passing fad and a fetish of some missionary agencies."

Fact. Continually starting new flocks is the most effective way to evangelize a society and to make disciples of its population.

Wherever the apostles of Jesus went, congregations multiplied. The same has happened throughout history when workers have made disciples the way Jesus modeled. Most missionary agencies serve already reached populations and have church planting practices that fail to allow congregations to reproduce rapidly, in a truly apostolic way.

Myth #14. "If workers start too many churches, then many of them will only die prematurely."

Fact. Wherever workers start many new congregations rapidly, their rate of survival is higher than where missionaries have, out of caution, kept the pace moving slowly.

Most congregations, even formerly-reproductive ones, will probably die when they become sterile, failing to reproduce and failing to practice the ministries that the New Testament insists upon. What a sad tragedy when a church dies before it has reproduced!

In rapid church planting movements, most congregations thrive and start new, healthy congregations, in turn. It is part of their God-given, spiritual DNA.

Guideline 40
Envision what God will enable his people to do in pioneer fields.

True leaders need eagle-eyed vision
for neglected people groups.
Let us look at ways to sharpen our sight...

"Lift up your eyes and look on the fields, that they are white for harvest" (Jn 4:35). See neglected people groups as the Lord sees them—ready for harvest.[52] Let missionaries share His heartbreak for the lost, love them as He does, and know that He is already preparing them for eternal salvation (2 Pet 4:9). A brief tourist's trek to a neglected field seldom imparts a God-given vision, but it can help prepare to be more receptive to God's call.

The Spirit of God prepares people in a neglected field to receive His Kingdom even before missionaries arrive. Millions are ready now to trust Jesus Christ in fields that have few churches if any. Unfortunately, mission agencies often cluster workers in fields that already have a national church capable of reaching the rest of their people without outside help. Policies for placing missionaries sometimes reflect inaccurate or outdated information.

Let others work in places where God has not yet prepared souls for harvest. Jesus commanded not to cast pearls before swine (Matt 7:6), and he told evangelists to leave those who resist His reign (Lk 10:10-12). So we should evaluate the effectiveness of our ministries by their results, not by how much work has been done. Do not assume that a people group is non-receptive until the gospel has come to them in a culturally-relevant way. Sometimes church plan-

---

[52] Most neglected people groups live between latitudes 10 & 40 in Africa and Asia.

ters blame the people for being "hard" when it is their method of evangelism that is hard for the people to accept or understand.

George Barna explained that "vision comes in the form of a 'mental portrait,' indicating a picture that exists in the mind's eye of the leader."[53] The compiler of this book had in his mind from the Lord a mental image of the new chains of churches in western Honduras that were yet to be started. Following many of the guidelines herein recorded, the Lord blessed the work with the birth of a new movement of churches, bringing life to that mental portrait, or vision, which we held over a number of years. Here are some ways to awaken a missionary vision and to develop a strategy to realize it:

- Pray for neglected people groups. Ask the Lord to lead by giving His vision to the churches for reaching neglected peoples. Visionary workers often receive specific guidance, as Paul did on the way to Troas, when seeking to reach a neglected people.

- Visit or investigate neglected people groups. Study biographies and books that focus on missions.

- Get to know missionaries and only join up with those who have a burden for the unreached. A senior pastor or leading elder can set the pace by his example.

- Teach from God's Word His plan to reach all peoples. Some key Scripture passages relating to mission outreach include the following:

  Show the historical basis of mission: Genesis: 12:1-3 and 22:15-18. The Holy One of Israel from very early times has covenanted to extend the blessings of His Kingdom to all tribes and people groups.

  Show that the channel of blessing is Jesus Christ: Galatians 3:16.

  Show that all tribes and peoples must hear the Gospel before Jesus returns: Matthew 24:14 and Revelation 7:9-17. Jesus will

---

[53] George Barna, ed., *Leaders on Leadership* (Ventura: Regal, 1997), 47.

not return until the Gospel is proclaimed to all nations (people groups). The Body of Christ—His celestial bride—will not be complete until it is populated from all nations.

Show that even before Jesus was born, the Lord was preparing the nations: Psalm 67.

Show that the Lord commands His churches to send missionaries: Matthew 28:18-20; Acts 1:8; 13:3.

As soon as new believers are obeying what Jesus and his Apostles have commanded in the Bible, they are ready to receive training for leadership tasks. The Lord led Paul to Macedonia, not while he waited idly for guidance, but while he was on the road doing what Jesus had commanded (Acts 16:6-10).

A flock should only vote on proposals made by those who can creatively articulate God's will concerning mission.

Careful! God's guidance does not originate in men's imagination nor is it subject to popular vote. Just follow the plain directives of Scripture!
Let us look at some of them...

Confirm God's will for strategic plans and career work by:

- Studying Bible passages and using common sense.
- Asking the Omniscient One for wisdom.
- Consulting with godly advisors, including the writings of those who have gone before.

Some fear that God's will might restrain them, putting them in a cage. Reality is quite opposite. He who truly loves God and others can do whatever he wants, because his desires are pure. He does only what is good, wise and just; his motivation comes from the Holy Spirit. Love liberates and fulfills the Law (Matt 22:37-40; Rom 13:8). Patterson commented:

> A young man, the story goes, asked an experienced pastor, "What is the key to your success?"
>
> "Good decisions."
>
> "How do you make good decisions?"
>
> "Experience."
>
> "How do you get that kind of experience?"
>
> "Bad decisions."

I made some unwise decisions on the field, and now, looking back, I realize that I made them *alone*. I failed to consult with my wife, co-workers, and God. The choices that He blessed had been made together with others. I learned the hard way to pursue New Testament guidelines and prayerful, group discussions to avoid decisions based on culturally-insensitive ideologies, heavy-handed organizational policies, and on fear and human traditions. Jesus and his Apostles consistently worked in cohesive task groups, and so should we.

Guideline 41
Mentor in the background in order to sustain genuine apostolic succession.

Train new leaders in the way Jesus and the Apostles did. They instructed trainees on the job rather than in classrooms. Former missionary to Argentina, Jon Lewis, whom Patterson mentored in northern Honduras during the 1970s, quipped: "Trainee is as trainer does. Trainers must model the kind of character and skills expected of trainees."[54]

---

[54] Jon Lewis, "A Metaphor and a Model for Missionary Training," *Connections*, summer 2005, 15.

Guidelines for Those who Mentor New Leaders

Train new leaders "behind the scenes." In western Honduras, the compiler of this book learned how expatriate missionaries had to become "shadows" working in the background, allowing attention and credit to go to national leaders-in-training. A missionary to the Pacific Rim commented, "The post-colonial missionary must be willing to lead inconspicuously and empower others to take the credit and limelight."[55]

Mentor?

What is so special about mentoring?

Training as Paul did it can generate an explosive chain reaction.

Paul mentored Timothy, who mentored Epaphras and others, who in turn mentored many more, novice leaders.

Multiply churches or home groups by relaying to others the apostolic baton of authority, message and responsibility, as Paul passed it to his apprentice, Timothy, who passed it on to faithful men who, in turn, passed it on to others (2 Tm 2:2). When the church planting movement in western Honduras began to take off, later resulting in many new chains of churches, the author was often asked, "At what point do you hand over the baton of leadership to the new churches?" He would wag his head and reply with a smile, "From day one, of course." When asked, "But how did you start all of those churches?" his reply was always the same, "I did not start those churches. Local men of whom I made disciples and to whom I entrusted the baton of authority and responsibility, it is they who started those churches."

---

[55] Don Dent "Cross-cultural Challenge," *Evangelical Missionary Quarterly*, July 2005, 281.

Keep the baton light. Make the Lord's work easy to pick up and pass on to others. Model a style of ministry that does not require a theological background beyond the newer leaders' present level, and let him grow. Use only methods that he can imitate at once and do not introduce equipment that is unavailable to him. Let him acquire more advanced skills and knowledge later, while serving the flock that the Lord has assigned to him.

It is congregations—not disciples or disciple makers—that reproduce. To disciple a leader, do not focus on him alone but also focus on the flock that he shepherds. When he has proven his ability and meets the New Testament qualifications of a shepherding elder, confirm it with the laying on of hands (1 Tm 3:1-7; 4:14).

Train new leaders by mentoring them without drawing attention to one's self, as Aquila and Priscilla did for Apollos (Acts 18:24-28). Although his doctrine was deficient, instead of criticizing him they graciously instructed him in private, which, the passage shows, improved his ministry. Paul's letters to Titus, Timothy and Philemon are examples of mentoring new leaders behind the scenes by mail. Patterson still mentors via e-mail.

David Miller reports that among the Quechua Christian churches of Bolivia, "The growth is especially strong in congregations where native leaders ... have taken over. Once churches become auto-nomous, the elders are allowed to govern their own congregations, and they make the decisions without depending on anyone from outside."[56] The opposite is revealed by the reflections of an African church leader: "As long as there is one white missionary present in the meeting, we will vote the way he wants us to vote, even if he doesn't say anything. We will watch his eyes and we will know how we are supposed to vote."[57]

Listen first, and then advise. A competent mentor listens to a trainee to learn what the trainee's flock is doing. He listens to learn what it needs and what its opportunities for service are, before

---

[56] David Miller, *World Pulse* 33, Sept 18, 1998, 1.
[57] Glenn Swartz, "How Missionary Attitudes Can Create Dependency," *Mission Frontiers*, Sept 1998, 22.

helping him to plan and assigning reading. On the basis of this report, assign Bible reading and other studies that apply to his plans.

Model pastoral work in a way that an apprentice can imitate and pass on at once to other novice leaders. Even where authorities are hostile, this kind of mentoring effectively trains large numbers of new leaders. Without a caring relationship such mentoring seldom continues long enough to reproduce. Mission leader, Bill Taylor, in his ReMAP[58] project asserted that adequate on-field care and encouragement complemented with regular evaluations are key indicators that can sustain worker enthusiasm and restrict attrition.[59]

Model pastoral skills wisely for new workers. Paul told the Corinthians to imitate him as he imitated Christ (1 Cor 11:1). Modeling avoids equipment, worship styles and preaching methods that trainees cannot imitate. Jesus never insisted that His disciples do anything that they had not seen Him model first, in a way they could easily imitate. Workers stifle church reproduction, if they fail to model vital skills in an imitable way.

Common Errors

Some common errors that keep new workers from taking responsibility include these:

- Failing to pass the baton soon enough, controlling too much and too long.

- Using equipment that is too expensive or sophisticated. This so discourages leaders who lack the equipment or technical know-how, that they fail to take initiative.

- Being so generous with outside funds that believers who depend on them fail to depend on God.

- Using teaching and worship styles that require education that national leaders lack.

---

[58] Reducing Missionary Attrition Project. See *Connections*, June, 2004.
[59] Taylor, William D. and Jon Lewis, ed., *Too Valuable To Lose* (Pasadena: William Carey Library, 1997).

Show your trainees what servant-leadership is, leading by serving. Jesus modeled servant-leadership when he washed His disciples' feet (Jn 13:1-17) and prohibited them from lording leadership over others and manipulating them in His Kingdom (Matt 20:20-28). Peter later told church leaders to be humble servants and not to lord it over their flocks (1 Pet 5:1-4).

In some pioneer fields, new leaders receive no mentoring from servant-leaders, rather, missionaries send them off to theological schools. The few who return often come back with the only style for leading that they have seen modeled—as dictators in a classroom.

Satan tempts leaders who have more education, money and experience to lord over others. Instead, they should trust the Holy Spirit's work in the new leader and keep giving to him more responsibility. Missionaries should ask God to let the work grow out of their control. Such humility opposes the human nature inherited from Adam, and grows from continual prayer to crucify one's appetite to control. A servant-leader indeed has authority and uses it firmly, but without lording over the believers. He leads the sheep without driving them like cattle.

Show your trainees how to be "doers of the Word, not hearers only, deceiving themselves" (Jas 1:22). Jesus taught his followers to obey His Words, not just to analyze them (Matt 7:24). Paul, too, urged obedience to the Word (2 Tm 3:16-17). Evaluate teaching by results seen in students' lives and families, not only by examination marks.

Some pastors think that if they simply teach the Bible accurately, then everything else will work out well for their churches. Such flocks often go into decline, especially after an eloquent preacher retires or moves on; for they prove too weak in evangelism and other ministries that Scripture requires.

New congregations often struggle and fail to grow and multiply because of some common mistakes made by teachers:

• Highly educated teachers confuse knowledge and faith. They erroneously equate belief with thinking correctly about truth.

- Mission organizations require such high academic credentials for overseas ministers that only scholars get appointed who neglect other gift-based ministries.

- Missionaries send immature national leaders to distant training programs, isolated from the churches, thereby fostering an institutional mentality.

- Workers start *preaching points* that neglect baptism, the Lord's Supper and other basic activities.

- Teachers let listeners grow passive by spouting big words and evangelical jargon, convincing hearers that the Bible can be understood best by religious specialists.

Guideline 42
Encourage flocks to follow God's rules rather than man's.

Keep alert!
You never know when
a hungry predator
is eyeing you.

Some, probably most, human traditions are good ones, and churches cannot function without them. Others are like the birds in Jesus' story of four soils that snatched away Heaven's seeds (Mk 4). Shoo them away! They transmit contagious "doctrines of demons" that replace New Testament commands and guidelines with man's customs and doctrines.

Require only what the New Testament requires for getting baptized, becoming a shepherd, being a church, and serving the Lord's Supper. Adding non-biblical requirements for these biblical practices breeds legalism and obstructs the Lord's work, undermining trust in His Word.

Base ministries and teaching solely on the powerful, double-edged sword of God (Heb 4:12). The Holy Spirit uses the inspired Word to transform believers by developing an eternal relationship with the Author of all wisdom, holiness and life.

Teach new shepherds from the start to be doers—not hearers only—of the authoritative Scriptures (Jas 1:22; 2 Tm 3:14-17). To build flocks that are culturally relevant, use this sword ruthlessly to cut off policies and customs that circumvent the New Testament. Some who know and believe Scripture still unwittingly base missionary policies on human traditions rather than on the Word, thereby exporting to the field their own culture.

Some harmful, common traditions include these:

- Man-made requirements for baptism and ordination.

- Extreme individualism and its private approach to faith.

- Program-oriented organization instead of interactive Body life.

- Extraction of converts from their circle of friends and relatives.

- Decision-making rites that bypass repentance and regeneration.

- Worship and music styles that create "hearers only".

- Abstract theology that omits historical foundations and duties.

- An anti-ritual bias that ignores the biblical purpose of the sacraments.

- An anti-informality bias which hinders freedom in Christ and localized creative expressions of worship.

- Segregation by age of young people and family members, which tends to individualize the Christian life experience while doing violence to Third World cultures.[60]

---

[60] "The vast majority of people in our world live in *collectivist* societies where the interest of the group prevails over the interest of the individual." Ruth Knutson, "Discipling Individuals in Collectivist Cultures: A Healthy Biblical Tension" (DMiss diss., Western Seminary, 2001), 1.

Allow believers in a pioneer field freedom to develop customs and methods that fit their culture, just as Westerners have done for theirs, by modifying external forms to fit current field conditions. Do not confuse local, temporary, human methods with general biblical guidelines that endure throughout history and fit all cultures. Narayan Varnan Tilak, known after his death as an apostle to India, was never fully at home in the Westernized systems imposed upon him by expatriates. In the early 1900s he pioneered the adoption of local Hindu forms to expressions of biblical faith in Christ that others were able to adopt without compromising the exclusive lordship of Jesus. [61]

Guideline 43
Make sure mission funds meet real needs.

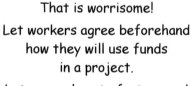

| We gave money to a worker in a neglected field. | That is worrisome! Let workers agree beforehand how they will use funds in a project. |

When he returned, he would not tell us how he spent it.

Let us see how to foster good missionary stewardship...

Practice biblical guidelines for mission stewardship to make wise use of missionary funds by examining a neglected field first to confirm the best way to reach it. Most of the remaining neglected fields need self-supported ministers, for authorities in most of these fields deny residence to traditional, professionally-trained, full-time missionaries. Some missionaries to such fields raise full support and

---

[61] H.L. Richard, *Following Jesus in the Hindu Context* (Pasadena: William Carey Library, 1998).

merely pretend to be self-supported, having a "front" business or other pretense of employment. Such ploys may work for some but cannot provide enough workers.

Obeying Jesus' Great Commission to reach all peoples requires tens of thousands of self-supported, non-professional missionaries that serve like the Apostle Paul did. Cross-cultural workers come increasingly from non-Western churches that cannot afford to work in the expensive way that Western mission agencies do. Western missionaries with big incomes must not stifle the initiative of missionaries from poorer fields by controlling them and by making them dependent upon Western funds.

While many congregations and believers give financially to mission agencies, others practice their stewardship by providing capital for bivocational workers to start small businesses that support tentmakers, as did Paul, Aquila, and Priscilla, in hostile fields. Even so, some workers in poor societies solicit funds from the West, some for good projects and some for self-gain, requiring wise stewards to make very sure how mission funds are spent.

Guideline 44
Lead humbly and firmly.

A leader must make his flock fear him, so they will obey.

I am going to be tough!

Who has been whispering in your ear?

Our Master's leaders are humble servants who lead not by force but by love, setting an example for their flocks.

A servant-leader shepherds God's flock humbly by authority of the Lord Jesus Christ, feeding and leading the flock that the Chief

Shepherd has assigned to him, out of love, as Jesus told Peter to do (Jn 21:15-17). Peter passed this advice on to all shepherds, urging them to deal lovingly and firmly with believers, serving their flocks without lording it over them (1 Pet 5:2-3). Loving authority from God the Father flows eternally through God the Son into the Body of Christ. Christian leaders, like God's Son, submit in love to the Father's authority, shepherding their brothers, not as a profession or a job as the world views the role of clergy. Rather, shepherds are responsible to the Chief Shepherd to care for the flock that He has assigned to them. In return, God's Spirit-filled children obey their shepherding elders who have spiritual rule over them (Heb 13:17).

Many pastors try to shepherd groups that are too big for them to do so well, for one can shepherd effectively only in groups that are small enough for him to listen to each member. Wise shepherds listen to their sheep before trying to help them plan activities and solve problems. He shares pastoral leadership with other elders by mentoring several novice shepherds at once, as his trainees who are of similar background, ministry and spiritual development. Patterson recalled:

> At first we gathered pastoral trainees of different backgrounds to mentor them. Those of humbler estate did not participate well in the presence of their "superiors." They talked little and took no initiative. We soon learned to separate them by social level into separate mentoring sessions. In our case, the sharpest barriers were neither race nor color but economics.

I'm too busy to teach all of my chicks to obey Jesus' commands.

Such neglect defies Jesus' authority and brings confusion. So prepare co-workers to help you.

Jesus said to make disciples by teaching them to obey His commands. When a leader fails to teach believers to obey Jesus, they lose respect for Christ's authority. On the one foundation of obedience to Jesus, wise shepherds build up the flock and equip all the believers for their gift-based ministries (Eph 4:11-16).

Guideline 45
Let a big church form tiny ones within it.

My old hens say our flock has grown too big, because they no longer know everyone.

Few take an active part in ministry; they just perch and listen passively during worship.

To shepherd everyone well, let a big flock form tiny flocks within it.

Let us look at ways some have done it...

The Holy Spirit normally does in small groups more than what can happen in big assemblies. Seekers come to repentance more easily in small groups, and new believers find their place as "living stones" in God's Temple (1 Pet 2:4-5; Eph 2:19-22). Good church organization fits each stone in a useful place, such that each believer is free to serve according to his gifts and is aided to do so by the others. Big flocks can organize for small groups on three levels, sometimes called "three Cs":

Cell groups. Cell groups of 14 or fewer adults are small enough to allow interaction between individuals and families as they serve one another. Intense shepherding can take place at this level, provided that groups remain small enough that members listen to each other, serve each other, and pray for one another. To remain this small, let growing cells reproduce by continually apprenticing new shepherds. Cells may welcome believers of the same neighborhood or those who have some other affinity.

Congregations. Congregations of 100 or fewer adults are small enough for everyone to know each other well yet big enough to enjoy well-prepared social events such as sports and picnics. They might even enjoy spectacular teaching. These may meet weekly, monthly, or whenever they choose, and their large flock may organize a number of such congregations. Leaders may temporarily cancel meetings at this level in order to give cell group time to develop and become the center of gravity of the larger body.

Celebrations. Special gatherings take place less frequently when several congregation gather to celebrate what God is doing as leaders give reports. Celebrations may include only one big church's congregations and cells, or many smaller ones as a regional event. When more than one gather and praise God with joy and reverent awe, believers receive encouragement and God's power proves palpable.

In cities where there is freedom of worship, churches should organize for worship and edifying fellowship through all three "C"s. Large flocks can organize smaller groups in different ways to maintain its corporate personality while multiplying cells in its own way.

In a pioneer field with few or no experienced believers, do not rush into open sharing by urging everyone to talk, for it can quickly grow out of control and the shy may not return. Intensive interaction requires some maturity, and the less-educated, especially those who live in totalitarian societies, are slow to enter in. So let group discussion develop at its own speed without forcing it. First explain that obeying the New Testament's "one another" commands enables believers to serve and build up one another, and help them gradually to learn and practice those commands.

Typical Organizational Patterns

- Big congregations establish home cells with complete pastoral care. Some cells may replace the traditional Sunday school.

- Churches form clusters of small groups from the beginning with no custom of meeting only as a big assembly.

- House churches form fellowships with other house churches, meeting together occasionally and undertaking projects of common interest.

The nature of cell groups is so simple that many churches make a healthy, thorough transition to cells, while others try and fail. When one examines what they did or failed to do, the reason usually becomes obvious. In nearly every case, they fail to prepare the flock adequately with God's Word for the radical change. Observations from many countries reveal these common features of cells:[62]

- Small groups built around seekers, new believers, and recently-converted group leaders easily grow and reproduce, provided that they receive good discipleship and leader training. Small groups of only mature Christians seldom grow and almost never reproduce, for they have few unbelieving friends and have become accustomed to non-reproductive forms of organizing. Also, being mature believers, their spiritual concerns do not include basic issues of repentance and reconciliation that are vital for seekers. Long-time believers are more interested in "deep" Bible study like that in a classroom of passive students. Sometimes mature believers prefer a style of worship more suitable to a big assembly and seems weird to seekers visiting a tiny cell. New believers, however, usually have many unsaved friends and relatives who are willing to listen to them, for they have not yet adopted religious customs that offend ordinary sinners.

- Small groups that grow out of existing, natural relationships and that build on the strengths of those who attend them grow and reproduce readily, regardless of the model they follow. However, importing a model of external forms and organization from other churches and relying on it almost never produces healthy, reproductive cells. It is a mistake for teachers to try and launch small groups through seminars or workshops by following external forms and structures that fit only one social

---

[62] For several international examples, see Mikel Neumann, *Small Groups for Urban Cultures* (Pasadena: William Carey Library, 1999).

group, rather than by applying universal New Testament guidelines. Multiplying small groups requires skills that one gains
through practice, whereas training seminars usually provide only
ideas about models.

- Social factors can create significant differences between any two
  flocks. Those differences will likely be magnified exponentially,
  if an organizational model comes from a different society or
  country. There are, indeed, universal principles that apply everywhere, but these will take on very different external forms and
  structures in each locality.

- Small groups are birthed and reproduce most readily when they
  grow out of members' sincere desire to fellowship together, to
  talk about Jesus Christ, and to serve one another in love. Formal
  classes and seminars, in contrast, rarely enable Christian workers
  and lay people to launch small groups that grow and reproduce.

- Smaller groups can easily maintain the intimacy, honesty and
  spontaneity that most people expect from friends and relatives.
  New leaders, properly prepared, are more apt to allow spiritually
  immature people freedom to relate openly and to serve one
  another, even though in quite imperfect, even rustic, ways. "The
  most obvious benefit to this method is that an inexhaustible
  supply of working personnel is provided."[63]

Western and Non-Western

Non-Western congregations generally have fewer problems in
forming reproductive small groups, for they can perform many
activities that Western churches, because of their non-biblical traditions, find difficult. Missionary to Madagascar, Mikel Neumann,
discovered:

Cell groups grow through family and friendship networks. In
other words, small groups of people grow as the people involved
bring in those people they are close to.... North Americans are

---

[63] W.R. Read, V. M. Monterroso and H.A. Johnson, *Latin American Church Growth*
(Grand Rapids: Eerdmans, 1969), 316.

less in tune with their neighbors and often live in cities far away from family members. However, their networks run along lines of common interests or affinity groups.[64]

Other points of contrast can prove equally instructive:

- Non-Western churches are more willing to allow the poor and less-educated to serve as leaders. In Western society, middle and upper class clergy often want their groups to be "high-quality" and do not consider most of their church members to be "leadership material," because of dress styles, personality traits, educational level, or economic standing. Their laymen are often "not ready", that is, clergy often look for suave, articulate, theologically-minded, respectable types who—they imagine—will be able to attract others of the same kind into their congregations.

- Non-Western pastors are usually more willing for lay people to serve as genuine shepherds. Reed, Monterroso, and Johnson, in their exhaustive, though now aged, study of Latin American evangelical churches, noted that effective leaders, especially among Pentecostal churches, "emerge from among the converts through in-service training at the level of the local congregation."[65] On the other hand, non-Western clergy are often hesitant to "put the cap on" capable lay leaders who might challenge their position. Sometimes such pastors unconsciously sense their own inability to teach, guide, encourage, or control able lay people, and so they often protect their position by hiding behind the tradition of an elite, exclusive, priestly class.

- Non-Western churches have, for the most part, escaped the deadening influence of affluence. Wealth taunts spirituality. Personal pride, cultural or religious arrogance, and satisfaction with material possessions tend to kill faith. The poor are often more willing to change and therefore more willing to listen to the promises that Jesus offers to them. Pearl S. Buck provided an

---

[64] Mikel Neumann, *How to Reach Your City with Cell Groups*. A free download from <www.acquirewisdom.com/cellsign.htm>.

[65] W.R. Read, V. M. Monterroso and H. A. Johnson, *Latin American Church Growth* (Grand Rapids: Eerdmans Publishing Co., 1969), 321.

insightful and helpful perspective on poverty from more than 40 years in China:

> The longer I lived [in China], the more deeply impressed I was, not by the rich, but by the farmers and their families, who lived in the villages outside the city walls. They were the ones who bore the brunt of life, who made the least money and did the most work. They were real, the closest to the earth, to birth and death, to laughter and to weeping. To visit [them] became my search for reality, and among them I found the human being as he most nearly is.[66]

- To see many come to Jesus in new small groups, look on the fields that are ripe for harvest, as Christ commanded; most of them will come from the poor and the immigrant groups around you. Jesus did!

Do drastic surgery!
To reproduce cells and flocks,
follow New Testament guidelines
for selecting and training leaders,
and cut out other traditions.

Laymen in action

Where Christianity is growing rapidly, it is usually due to some kind of small-group ministry, like social action teams, Bible discovery groups, church cells, discussion groups, and so on. Such cell groups are launched and led by ordinary believers who are encouraged and equipped to do so by their leaders. The most effective ones show several common traits:

- Most groups that grow and reproduce are led by new believers and usually meet in the homes of new believers and seekers.

---

[66] Pearl S. Buck, *My Several Worlds* (New York: Pocket Book, Inc., 1954), 164.

- The groups that grow fastest are those that begin smallest. Large growth comes through multiplying many tiny groups that at first appear as too small.

- Most conversions and new churches arise from the poorer, less-developed social groups in a country. Often they are the kinds who embrace more vices and crime. In western Honduras, this compiler has seen that some of the best shepherds in new chains of churches include some who had formerly been addicted to various vices. *Good soil*, it seems, is composed of "bad" people. Paul wrote, "Since the creation of the world God's invisible qualities—his eternal power and divine nature—have been clearly seen, being understood from what has been made, so that men are without excuse" (Rom 5:20).

Checklist of Implications for Cell Groups

The following sections suggest a few guidelines for the preparation of cell-group leaders:

☐ When looking for potential leaders of seekers and new believers, seek them among the culturally-rustic, theologically-naïve in your congregation who are willing to bring together unsaved friends and relatives. While we do not lay hands on neophytes, we do groom those who are "diamonds in the rough."

☐ Provide coaching for the new leaders outside of formal classrooms and other formal groups, such as Aquila and Priscilla did for Apollos (Acts 18:24-28). Coaching means mentoring in the way that Jesus and the apostles did it. They did not approach their training sessions with a prepared outline, rather they observed needs and listened to their trainees (Mk 6:30). A coach learns worker's needs by watching them and listening to them instead of dispensing lofty ideas and well-packaged curricula written originally for other social classes and other cultures. A coach provides insights that answer the current needs of persons and families in his trainees' flocks, helps the new leaders to make short-term plans for what to do with their respective flocks, and prays with them for those whom they are helping and teaching.

☐ Help new leaders to look constantly for a fresh "vein of gold," those friends and relatives of new believers who have not yet been hardened to the gospel by boring sermons, hypocritical believers, and popular media.

☐ Let small group leaders train other novice leaders by apprenticing them within their flocks until they can lead their own groups. When they launch a new group, let all who wish to partner with him from the parent group do so, and maintain cordial relations with them by occasionally providing united celebrations and coaching.

☐ Make sure your small group leaders are shepherds, not merely preachers or teachers. If you do not know the difference, then let others train leaders.

☐ Build strong, edifying ties between groups by arranging for members of one group to coach members of another. Now, a group small enough for spontaneous interaction is too small to have a good balance of spiritual gifts and gift-based ministries. Therefore, it is just as important to practice interactive church body life between groups as within them.

☐ Deal with immediate needs. Pray for healing of the sick.

☐ Prove God's transforming power by having all the believers serve one another as Romans Chapter 12 describes.

☐ Keep participation positive. The enemies of edifying interaction are the leeches that sneak into small groups and suck the life-blood from them. These include opportunists seeking material benefits or personal attention. Help small group leaders to avoid wasting valuable time dealing with chronic problems and individuals who thrive on being the victim of bad circumstances. These parasites on the Body of Christ can easily absorb too much time and attention in meetings. It is better to deal with such in private and to quiet them in groups meetings by saying, "Let us hear from someone who has not yet spoken," and, "Now let us deal with the needs of others who may be too shy to speak." If a parasite like this does not modify his negative behavior, then ask him to stop coming to the group, so that it can survive.

☐ Help your leaders and all the members to see that small groups are normal for churches. The first century churches in Jerusalem and other cities in the book of Acts consisted of clusters of tiny house churches whose elders were their shepherds. Small groups are the backbone of Christian people movements all over the world.

☐ Let groups be different one from another, neither pushing them into one mold nor forcing one curriculum on all of them. Rather, provide them with options that will meet many of their current needs and ministry opportunities. Do not dictate when or where groups must meet, and let leaders with more experience experiment with new ideas. You may find that the Lord is willing to save many more people than you imagined possible, but they may be culturally or economically different from your present congregation and cell groups. You may have to let your new leaders shepherd them in quite separate groups, even in separate congregations. Let Christ's Kingdom grow!

Guideline 46
Let house churches and cells reproduce normally.

Let us look at some ways
to take advantage of
the benefits of small flocks ...

Start flocks in homes or wherever they can meet. No chapels or church buildings are mentioned anywhere in the New Testament, but Philemon, Nympha, Aquila, Lydia and many others hosted flocks (Phlm 1-2; Col 4:15; Rom 16:3-6; Acts 16:14-15, 40). In most neglected fields, a conventional church with building and a full-time pastoral staff would be impractical. So just keep on starting house churches or cells and let them multiply.

To strive for one's congregation to keep growing ever bigger in a building limits the Holy Spirit's work of bringing more and more people to Jesus. Buildings tie congregations to a limited budget and lead to an unhealthy, institutional structure that limits a continual spread of the good news. A house church movement leaves the door open for the Almighty to keep on extending His Kingdom indefinitely.

Big congregations without home groups can mobilize only a tiny percentage of their members to do solid ministry, for few find natural ways to evangelize outside the walls of their meeting place. You can remedy this situation in two ways:

- If your congregation is already large, then multiply cell groups— small flocks—in which the growth potential is much greater.

- If your congregation is new or small, then let it grow by multiplying house churches or cells, keeping them small enough to provide pastoral care on personal and family levels. Small flocks foster more intimate fellowship, more easily serving one another through loving interaction.

To let a group multiply without breaking up relationships, do not simply divide a group surgically down the middle. Rather, send with new leaders only those who want to start a new flock together. Continually train apprentices in each group, letting them take on more responsibility a little at a time while a leader, normally their parent group leader, mentors them along. Keep mentoring them as long as they and their new group need it. Christian Schwarz said, "The true fruit of a church is not a new group, but a new church; the true fruit of a leader is not a follower, but a new leader."[67]

Sometimes a new leader and his family form the core of a new group; at other times two or three leaders may band together to create a nucleus. Let new groups grow out of existing relationships,

---

[67] Christian A. Schwarz, *Natural Church Development* (Carol Stream: ChurchSmart Resources, 1996), 68.

and let organizational structure build on what the Almighty is doing. Avoid organizing by adhering blindly to a detailed, preconceived plan, and never adopt management designs from regions with different field conditions.

Grow not only by addition through conversions but also by multiplication through starting new flocks. Addition growth is illustrated in Acts 2:41 where God added 3,000 converts to the church; multiplication growth characterizes Acts 8 and the rest of the book. Many small nuclei or core groups would spin off from an original body and from each other. Core groups are still small enough to easily attract and add new believers, for sinners come to Jesus readily in a small body where they feel loved and wanted. Philip and others who fled persecution in Jerusalem formed the core of a new congregation in Samaria while Peter and his companions multiplied flocks on the Mediterranean coast, Paul and his band sowed seed that reproduced many-fold in Galatia and beyond, and Aquila and Priscilla hosted new flocks in Rome, Corinth, and Ephesus. To reach a vast region for Christ, aim for both addition and a multiplication of tiny core groups and keep on adding converts to them. To do so entails the continual apprenticing of many new leaders.

In most neglected fields of the world, underground house churches can multiply rapidly in spite of official prohibitions, as long as workers let God multiply flocks in the New Testament way.

Guideline 47
Organize for dynamic body life in the way that Scripture prescribes.

I shall see you later!
I need to go now and organize my flock like my great aunt's big old church downtown.
I visited it last week.

Come back!
That church has been declining for years.
Organize in a way that fits your small, new flock.
Let us look at ways to do so...

Teach your trainees to shepherd one another in small groups, just as Jethro advised Moses in Exodus 18 to shepherd an entire nation in groups of ten. In small groups, shepherds can listen to each person that has needs and treat them on a personal or family level. Ask caring believers, both older and newer ones, to shepherd a small group, by starting with their own family and, when they are confident, to include friends.

Groups of fewer than fifteen adults can easily apply the Bible's "one another" commands, serving one another in many ways, while apprenticing new leaders on the job. This is like pushing a novice swimmer into a pool; start with the shallow end and let him work his way to the deep as he learns to swim. Start with shepherding duties related to the commands of Jesus and his Apostles, and keep adding more pastoral responsibilities until a novice leader reaches his capacity.

Assemblies having hundreds of believers can organize on three levels:

- Small home groups of two to four families.

- Intermediate congregations of 50 to 100.

- An entire body of any size.

The bigger a congregation is, the more it needs small groups. If a large congregation has many leaders willing to take initiative, then build the organization from the ground up, starting with many small groups. Several small groups can gather to form a larger, intermediate congregation for occasional fellowship and social functions that are comfortable in groups of 50 to a 100, which is too big for small group interaction yet small enough for individuals to know one another. These congregations can then gather together from time to time as a united body for big celebrations.

When organizing cells into bigger networks, avoid control by outsiders, letting local elders do their God-given jobs. Some missionaries wrongly use their superior education and resources to control men rather than letting them take initiative and make important decisions, thereby suppressing them as persons and denying the supernatural work of God through them.

Teach your trainees to avoid implementing restrictive church bylaws. Interaction between members and between congregations should enjoy freedom to do as the Holy Spirit leads them. Believers do not serve one another simply because their mission statement or bylaws say to do so. Not even electing or appointing leaders to foster interaction ensures that it will happen. Only total freedom to do ministry using each person's God-given gifts in the power of His Holy Spirit brings about full church body life.

The more bylaws a flock has, the less room there is for the Heavenly Dove to hover in our midst and guide us.

Do not keep your flock in a tiny cage!

Free them to serve spontaneously.

Problems may arise from purely democratic church elections that limit serious work to official positions:

- Those who would serve voluntarily out of love, but whose abilities are not known well enough to win an election, are bypassed.

- Stipulating a specific number of elders overlooks others whom God has gifted for shepherding work.

- When a stipulated term of service has expired, an elected leader coordinating an essential ministry must step aside, even though it is the Holy Spirit who equipped and called him to that work.

Guidelines for Developing a Cell Church

When you consult, mentor, or coach leaders who are transforming a big congregation into a church of small groups, give them clear guidelines. Provide action points similar to these:

Let believers enjoy the spiritual chiropractic that comes from interactive small groups.

It is crucial that members discover the joy of meeting with a group that is small enough to practice the kind of edifying interaction that the Spirit yearns for believers to enjoy. A healthy trend is gaining speed among Western churches, correcting deeply-entrenched traditions that used to limit what believers could do when they gathered; many such churches are now placing New Testament guidelines above conformity to ecclesiastical traditions.

The New Testament commands believers to "bear one another's burdens," "confess faults to one another," and "admonish one another." There are over forty such "one another" commands, and many are repeated several times. As urban populations become more talented, literate, and aware of non-Christian religions and political trends, they grow impatient, even bored, with the typical, one-way, Sunday diet dispensed almost exclusively by a paid, professional staff who may not even apply the New Testament's requirements for dynamic interaction between all members of the body.

Free up believers to obey the Lord Jesus Christ.

"Where the Spirit of the Lord is, there is liberty (2 Cor 3:17). Many believers, especially among the younger generation, seek freedom from the routine of assembling weekly to sit facing a pulpit or worship team, watching singers and musicians perform, and listening to a clergyman lecture and ask for money. That form was adopted in the 18th century, codified in the 19th century, elaborated in the 20th century, and is now dying in the 21st century.

Begin groups with an organizational structure and a curriculum that is entirely new and radically New Testament.

Start cells that are entirely new, for it almost never works to force change upon old structures and small groups that have neither reproduced nor done any evangelism. Pastors who simply add on small group ministry to their existing programs and preach the benefits of "body life" will usually experience disappointment and later become resistant to cellular ministry. Their disappointment often leads to casting blame on the cell concept.

Some Christian leaders voice the complaint that small groups are "effective only for poor, rural, and Third World churches," that "house groups simply pool the ignorance and bitter attitudes of frustrated people," and that "cells that act like little churches will split your congregation and shrink your budget." Although such problems probably do exist, they are exceptions to the rule and are seldom the real roots of the failure of cell churches.

Build new cells around new believers.

Bring new believers into an existing cell group only as a last resort. Try first to start a new cell in new believers' homes, and keep "mining the new vein of gold." As new believers, they still have many non-believing friends and can often bring them easily into their homes. Let new believers host meetings for their family and friends, as did Zacchaeus, Levi, Cornelius and Lydia. Sometimes cells begin simply because a new believer starts shepherding his family, while being mentored by an older believer. Aim to keep entire families together.

Keep groups small enough that every participant has a chance to talk if they want.

Believers, especially of the younger generation, enjoy small groups, cell churches, and even independent house fellowships where they can develop close, edifying relationships. They also seek to encounter Christ in a mystical way as the Holy Spirit activates the different spiritual gifts of the body as members serve one another.

Aware of this trend, even some traditional pastors are now experimenting with forms of small groups that offer more than the home Bible study and prayer group of the 1960s did. Many large congregations have incorporated small groups as an important part of their church life, and often talk about launching a church planting movement like those they have read about happening in developing countries. Keep experimenting until you get it right!

Focus on current concerns in the cells.

Believers and seekers increasingly seek to enter into a mystical experience of Christ along with genuine community, hoping to find timely help with their temptations and the exigencies that they face daily. The only way leaders can know what members' current concerns are is to listen to them.

Allow small groups to take to themselves many of the functions and privileges of traditional pastors.

Pastors must recognize that small groups often do a better job of shepherding than they themselves do. Even professional counselors increasingly use groups to provide the personal and social growth for their clients.

Risk the inevitable failures. Dare to trust the Lord to let you reap the benefits of face-to-face groups, in spite of their problems. Some small groups have become self-centered and unsupportive of the congregational budget and have ignored other programs. Such examples should, however, prove minimal, if biblical guidelines are put to practice unashamedly.

Let new leaders make mistakes. Older pastors, especially more educated ones, almost always expect too much of new leaders, often refusing to let new believers lead a group of their own family and friends. Yet new believers are the very ones that the Lord uses most often to win others to Himself and to give them their first instruction.

Novice leaders should, of course, be mentored behind the scenes by a more experienced believer.

Let new believers lead temporary gathering groups. Normally, new believers make the best leaders of temporary gathering groups such as the group that Cornelius gathered in his house to listen to Peter's message (Acts 10). These gathering groups prove short-lived, for the non-believers who come at first either receive Christ and join a regular group, or they reject Him. Such temporary gathering groups can meet on a playing field, in a coffee shop, on a commuter train, in a home, or anywhere else they find convenient.

Start small groups as a means of making disciples of seekers and new believers rather than simply as a means to numerical growth.

Let cells grow out of prayerful, aggressive evangelism. If a church is not evangelistic, then simply changing the structure of its organization to incorporate small groups will not cause evangelism to happen. Having a tightly-organized structure is not the important issue but evangelism and a passion to disciple new believers biblically, supported with fervent prayer is.

In a number of countries there is a clear, strong relationship between small groups and numerical growth, leading some to an erroneous conclusion that small groups automatically attract non-believers. Groups will do so only when members reach out to their friends and neighbors with courageous love.

Let small group participation remain voluntary.

Keep the entire congregation aware of what the Lord is doing in the small groups. One way to encourage small group workers is to briefly interview them, during the congregational worship time, allowing them to report the spiritual victories they have witnessed in their small groups. Even where group members find some affinity one for one another and make the group part of their busy lives, groups can stagnate if left to their own devices without continual, fresh input and encouragement from their pastors through their small shepherds or hosts.

Organize small-group shepherds to help older believers grow in their practice of church body life, as they receive ongoing guidance from church leaders.

Equipping the members of His Body is the primary task of teachers and pastors. Ephesians 4:11-16 speaks of pastors and teachers who train others for ministry by modeling a mature Christian life. They do this better in congregations with multiple elders or group shepherds who receive regular coaching from experienced pastors.

Listen to those whom you coach before telling them what to do. Pastors who coach small-group shepherds must listen to them often and help them to serve their groups, responding to urgent issues and adding to group activities more of the "one another" activities that the New Testament requires.

Establish ministries according to local needs.

Develop your own forms and methods. Cultural variables disallow a wholesale adopting of forms and methods from another culture. Every shepherd should try different approaches, develop what works, and grow in his own coaching skills and mentoring wisdom.

Start three groups at about the same time, if possible.

Starting several flocks simultaneously has some advantages. Even if one or two disband, there are still one or more groups. A pastor can meet with more than one group shepherd for mentoring, and have time to hear from all of them, give them advice, and make plans with them for their groups. It will quickly become clear faster what kinds of group activities meet needs and lead to the starting of new groups in their society. Furthermore, the group leaders can encourage and counsel one another.

Aim to reproduce! From the very start, let each group shepherd share the vision to lead his group in helping to start other groups. Seldom do groups start another one by splitting, for it is too hard to break up their friendships. Usually group members start new, smaller groups with others, while maintaining ties with their first group. Groups and their shepherds should envision and pray to make that happen continually. Often those who start a new group never leave their original one. They simply visit friends to win them to Christ and train new leaders in their new group, while remaining with their original group. This process resembles what Paul and Barnabas did when they would gather many new flocks and occasionally return to their sending church in Antioch.

Start new groups with new believers.

Let new believers start immediately to establish new groups. Where new believers have no other opportunity than to sit on pews once a week and listen to sermons, they are not likely to bring seekers with them.

Let each new believer serve as a doorway to others who have been neglected. Where every new believer is seen as a member of a family and of a circle of existing friends, they should also be viewed as the door into a potential new cell. So you should coach shepherds in how to encourage new believers to identify those of their acquaintances who might be interested to hear about their new life with the Most High. Shepherds should also coach those new ones to witness and pray for their relatives and friends.

Allow new believers to participate from the start.

Recognize the gift of leadership in local believers when it emerges, for new leaders will often emerge, as Cornelius did, whom the Most High affirmed as a spiritual person even before he knew Jesus. While the New Testament sets standards for ordination as an elder, the Holy Spirit often distributes shepherding gifts even to immature believers. Where these "diamonds in the rough" are able to bring others together, share with them and care for them, shepherds should treat them as apprentice shepherds and coach them in pastoral duties.

Hold up to new workers the hope of becoming elders.

Let them view church leadership as something that they can grow into, while serving with all the love and skill that the Almighty gives to them for their small groups. Although some may eventually leave their shepherding tasks, others will become competent shepherds and, later, elders.

Provide regular, patient coaching, in addition to training seminars.

The mentoring of novice shepherds is a primary pastoral duty. Where a pastor is too insecure or unskilled to mentor others, he should assign the training task to another, and show frequent, public support for that helper's work.

Maintain a balance between mentoring and classroom training. Rapid cell group multiplication demand a continual training of new leaders in the way that Jesus and the apostles did it. Pastors who rely mainly on big-group training classes for small-group leaders will be disappointed, for shepherding is not so much an academic subject as it is a relational skill rising from a God-given desire to see others grow in faith and obedience. This skill is not only to be taught, but to be modeled.

Avoid over-training with too much information. Experienced trainers have found that providing information before workers need it will require training them again later when a need for it becomes apparent to them. Furthermore, learning without implementation often leads to a haughty attitude and unwillingness to listen later.

Keep group leaders focused on the commands of Jesus and of the New Testament.

Focus primarily on obeying and on helping others to obey New Testament directives. Pastors who are educated in systematic theology, management practices, and popular psychology, tend to demonstrate doctrinal precision, smart social skills, and cultivated personality traits. They often like to preach about these ideals and seek them in others. However, Jesus and the New Testament put more emphasis on spiritual power, on loving obedience to His commands, and on showing grace and love to fellow believers, neighbors, and enemies.

Keep coming back to these directives.

There are enough explicit New Testament guidelines to keep every group and its shepherd quite busy growing in faith and obedience for a long time, without demanding that they adopt or demonstrate non-biblical cultural ideals. An obedient peasant or laborer usually proves more useful to the Lord than does a sophisticated "doctrine inspector."

Establish new groups mostly from existing relationships.

Keep new believers in a loving relationship with their relatives and friends. In the book of Acts, throughout history, and as a common pattern across cultures, new groups of believers form mainly by new believers drawing relatives, associates, and friends into their group and to faith in Jesus. Pastors who will let such natural bridges serve as paths for faith will see far more growth than will those who depend only on public evangelistic meetings.

Avoid forcing new believers to meet together with people with whom they normally would not associate. The groups of new believers that are least likely to grow and reproduce are those that have been forced together by a pastor or missionary for his own convenience or have been forced together as a show of interethnic unity. There are better ways to express Christian unity than by forcing new believers to commit cultural suicide in order to become followers of Jesus.

The key here is to build up new believers through small, face-to-face groups while building new cells around them. Let such small groups freely discuss their social and spiritual needs and find answers from the Bible and from each other's testimonies.

Pray for grace simply to serve others.

Where pastors have a vision not merely of growing a bigger congregation but also of serving their city and nation, continually seeking ways to meet the social and spiritual needs of their communities, normally many will repent and come into the churches.

Guideline 48
Create interchurch cooperation and friendship.

The Body of Christ is bigger than any one congregation. Vigorous spiritual health and ministry can result from interaction between flocks as much as from within them. That fact is especially evident in pioneer fields where infant churches are multiplying rapidly. New groups can often strengthen their weak ministries by grasping the hand extended to them from nearby churches and cells that are also very new. Robert Vajko, a church planting missionary in France, found that new churches that were a part of a fellowship of churches reproduced more than independent churches.[68] Patterson recounted:

> Some villages in Honduras needed clean water, but we lacked experience digging wells. Mennonite churches to the east of us had dug wells and came to our aid, voluntarily. We helped them also, in other ways. We taught our leaders to arrange mutual aid projects, in which a number of churches blessed one another.
>
> Some pastors from different denominations tried hard to steal sheep from our flocks. At first I argued with them publicly, which merely cemented the division. I learned to report their unethical activity in friendly terms to their leaders who, in every case, corrected the problem without acrimony or delay. This approach helped in another way, too: when one of our own immature pastors proselytized from another organization, they told us and we corrected the problem.

---

[68] Robert Vajko "Why Do Some Churches Reproduce?" *Evangelical Missionary Quarterly*, July 2005, 299.

Our congregations in a region held meetings two or three times a year in which they worshipped together, feasted and planned projects in which a number of flocks cooperated. Those regional gatherings always proved a blessing. Occasionally our churches met with churches of different denominations for united worship, which also brought blessings. However, we did not ask very young flocks to meet with those that taught very different doctrines, to avoid confusing new believers.

Originally, my way of solving problems in new churches was to rush in and teach what the Bible says about it. Humberto Del Arca, the Honduran who replaced me as director of extension training for pastors, had a better way of treating problems. When churches needed help, he asked experienced workers from other flocks to visit them until the problem dissolved or, if it was a chronic problem, to shift residence to the town where the suffering flock was located.

Another flock now meets in our town, and they worship differently from us.

How can I resist them?

Why resist them? Help them! Serve them! Remember, your flock seems different to them.

Work with all nearby flocks that willingly obey Jesus.

If any do not oblige, then pray for God to bless them anyway!

The New Testament commands about serving one another apply to the entire Body of Christ and the congregations of an area, not just to members of a single flock. The Lord desires us to show such loving interaction, and Scripture advocates for believers exercise their various spiritual gifts in serving one another within His Body (1 Cor 12-13; Eph 4:11-12; Rom 12:3-11).

In New Testament times, the new apostolic congregations, such as those in Jerusalem and Ephesus, were closely-knit, city churches, not big assemblies meeting in one place. They consisted of clusters of tiny house churches and cells that celebrated communion and applied the Word from house to house (Acts 2:46; 20:20). Interaction between those small groups was so intense that the apostles called them "the church" (singular), because they saw the clusters as one body. Church history records no church buildings until nearly 300 years after Christ.

The book of Acts and the apostles' letters reveal that workers often visited or moved to other areas to help other flocks:

- Peter and John traveled to the new church in Samaria to pray that they might receive the Holy Spirit (Acts 8:14-5).

- The Jerusalem church sent Barnabas to encourage believers in Antioch (Acts 11:22-23), and soon after that, Agabus and others came from Jerusalem to instruct that new flock (Acts 11: 27-30).

- Paul and Barnabas, sent by the Antioch church, repeatedly visited Lystra, Iconium and other cities to strengthen new flocks (Acts 14:21-23) as they did in Phoenicia and Samaria (Acts 15:2-3).

- The Jerusalem church sent Paul, Barnabas and others with letters of comfort and assurance to Gentile churches in Antioch, Syria and Cilicia (Acts 15:23-27).

- Churches in Macedonia and Achaia sent contributions with Paul and others to help poor believers in Jerusalem (Rom 15:25-26), as did churches from Galatia and Corinth (1 Cor 1:1-3).

- Paul asked the Roman church to receive Phoebe from the church in Cenchrea (Rom 16:1-2).

- Stephanas, Fortunatus, Achaicus and Titus all traveled at different times to serve the believers in Corinth (1 Cor 16:16-17; 2 Cor 8:16-19).

- Believers in one flock greeted friends on many occasions in other flocks through the apostle's letters (e.g., 3 Jn 14).

Develop practical, working relations between congregations by maintaining frequent communication. Do not limit cooperation to annual, national, or regional meetings. Small, regional fellowships consistently prove to be a source of blessing and strength, for they resemble the annual Israelite festivals that the Lord used to renew and bless His people. Where missionaries or pastors organize on a large scale without members of the different flocks interacting directly in practical ways, controversy and political competition often ensue. Local fellowship and cooperation in evangelism and mercy ministries generally prove to be more edifying than ecumenical and inter-faith meetings that are more political in which only representatives of the churches attend. Patterson recalled:

> Pastor Mike Blondino of Vancouver, Washington, prays weekly during Sunday services for the other churches in Vancouver and for their pastors. A believer once complained to him, "While on vacation I visited a church and nobody spoke to me!"
>
> "Well, shame on you!" replied Blondino.
>
> If no one speaks warmly to you, it is probably because you have not spoken so to them. Take the lead and set the example by the power that the Holy Spirit gives us to reach out, not waiting for others to talk first to you.

To improve communication between flocks in our area, we need another workshop—a seminar on inter-flock relations. Right?

Wrong!
It helps little to send leaders afar to discuss ecumenism! Rather cooperate in a practical, local project in which members of several flocks can serve together, and not just their top leaders.

Leaders seeking to strengthen a ministry sometimes run to seminars to learn another new method, asking, "What should we do?" and "How can we do it?" That is often the wrong question. Ask rather, "Who can help us do it?"

A relational solution usually works better. Those who can give help in nearby congregations are often willing to do so, if leaders will let them know that they need help. Most believers are eager to serve others when they are aware of opportunities. Gaining awareness requires regular opportunities to talk freely to one another.

Avoid interchurch politics that dwell on controversial issues and promote power-grasping cliques. When the distance between congregations is too far for interaction between their members, their focus shifts from practical projects to interchurch politics. Church politics at a national level through newly-formed church associations on mission fields often prove bumpy, because denominational structures often attract those who seek positions of power. In older mainline denominations, some leaders openly deny that salvation comes only from Christ's atoning death and life-giving resurrection. Such churchmen often embrace inter-faith alliances and are ashamed to pray publicly in Jesus' name, lest they offend Buddhist, Hindu or Muslim "brothers."

Guideline 49
When storms rage, stay focused on crucial objectives.

My flock worries too much about minor matters like where to meet and what musical instruments to buy. What can I do?

Help them to look outward! Our Lord says to look at fields ripe and ready for harvest.

Let us consider ways to help them focus on vital purposes...

Show your trainees how to focus on the commands of Jesus and of His Apostles, by giving top priority both to His Great Command to love the needy in a practical way and to His Great Commission to make disciples among all peoples who obey all of His commands. The tempter offers false substitutes for those central aims, whispering to believers to put the good in place of the best, making secondary objectives sound very spiritual. Here are some ways in which to dodge his darts:

- Avoid pouring God's money into buildings. Start humbly and avoid letting anything impede spontaneous church growth, as expensive buildings often do. Throughout history, great movements for Christ have usually taken place through humble house churches.

- Steer away from always meeting in the home of the main leader, for some will say, "It is his church," discouraging other potential leaders.

- Stay away from giving diplomas or certificates to workers, for such recognition implies that they have arrived to full wisdom and need no further studies. Rather, give certificates in recognition of ministry that they have done, which achievement entitles them to study on a more advanced level. Let leaders keep on studying God's Word until they die!

- Avoid "church growth" ideas about letting congregations grow forever bigger rather than reproducing themselves by starting little congregations. True growth in God's Kingdom comes only by sinners coming to Christ, for men cannot *make* Christ's Kingdom grow. However, they can *let* it grow. Paul said, "I planted, Apollos watered, but God gave the increase" (1 Cor 3:6).

Wise shepherds do not convert people by applying human devices, nor do they lure sheep away from other flocks with glitzy, entertaining worship services. God's church grows spontaneously, by the power of the Holy Spirit. Jesus' parables illustrate church growth and multiplication by comparing it to that of plants.

Healthy churches, like all other living things, grow and reproduce after their own kind through their God-given seed. Anticipate the living Body of Christ to grow. If men try to control this growth, they will kill it, for it is a spiritual organism. Men do their part by obeying Jesus' commands. Believers plant, water, weed, and shoo birds away while the Lord of the harvest gives the new life. The Kingdom of Heaven grows on earth by faith, not by force. Christian Schwarz has said, "We should not attempt to 'manufacture' church growth, but rather to release the biotic potential which God has put into every church."[69] If your congregation is not growing well, then do not simply hold more special meetings for evangelism, for evangelism is not something special. It is the ongoing work of every member, as normal as breathing. Help your people to witness to friends and relatives, so that special meetings will not be necessary.

---

[69] Christian A. Schwarz, *Natural Church Development* (Carol Stream: ChurchSmart Resources, 1996), 10.

Guideline 50
Send the right harvesters to the right fields.

We must strive for the highest possible standards of excellence in the Lord's ministry. Therefore, I only let very experienced leaders do evangelism!

Who sets those standards? New believers win more people to the Lord than older ones do! Jesus said to pray to the Lord of the harvest for many workers.

Mobilize many to tell their friends about the Lord Jesus, making it easy for them to do. Just as the Levites rallied as a body to defend the cause of the Lord (Exodus 32:1-29), so should believers act as a body to intercede for their community and to evangelize it.

If your flock is weak in evangelism, then it will do little good to scold them. A better way to kindle fervor may be to find people with the evangelistic gift in nearby congregations and arrange for them to work with your flock and let their zeal rub off onto it.

Help new believers to tell their friends and relatives about Jesus by going with new believers to show them how to do so. Do not wait until they have become "grounded in the Word." By then, they will no longer have close ties with their unsaved friends. So make evangelizing simple so that many can imitate you. Then let them do it while you pray for them. When believers are telling others about Jesus, and when sinners receive Him, tell the congregation about it and praise them, encouraging others to do likewise.

Mobilize an advocate in your flock for foreign missions, whose aim is for your congregation to reproduce itself in daughter churches in neglected fields through those whom it commissions, trains, sends, supports, and holds accountable. An advocate for global outreach usually works with a mission committee or task group to do the following:

- Keep the congregation informed about mission work.

- Help potential missionaries get prepared.

- Provide congregational leaders with brief, regular updates, and encourages him to serve as spokesman for mission outreach. If a church has a senior pastor, then it is he who should be the main spokesman.

- Find individuals in every group of the church—home groups, young people, worship team, classes, prayer groups, etc.—to participate in some way. Provide them each month with brief news reports from mission fields, from periodicals, letters and reports that they can share with their groups. Arrange for skits, dinners, concerts, parties, etc., that promote missions, build awareness, and help potential missionaries to sense their Master's call.

- Organize mission conferences. Instead of having an outsider as the main speaker for a conference on missions, creative local believers can often bring a refreshing emphasis by asking adults, youth and children to make different kinds of presentations. They can depict a neglected people group that they have researched, or they can depict some other aspect of the Great Commission. Such broad participation assures ardent interest.

- Organize various groups to pray regularly for each harvester that the flock has commissioned.

Send workers to foreign fields where they are needed most. The Lord sent the first cross-cultural missionary to Nineveh. However, human wisdom overruled God's assignment, and Jonah fled instead to Tarshish (Jonah 1:1-3). Missionaries sometimes start off in a wrong destination. Although they have a good heart, they need counsel and direction. Paul and his apprentices were on their way to Bithynia when God steered them instead to Macedonia (Acts 16:6-10). Being a man of prayer, Paul let God guide him to a people that He had prepared to receive His Word. How sad it would be to fail to let God's hand turn one's steering wheel!

Today, most missionaries still cluster in fields that already have good churches and capable national leaders, too often staying where they are neither needed nor wanted. Some missionaries persevere in a field or a project, only because it is easy to raise funds for it. Contributors may give to a work in a field that already has strong churches, simply because they are familiar with it and feel good about it. Patterson commented:

National workers have begged me to keep mission agencies from sending more American missionaries where national leaders were doing well. Some missionaries, upon arriving in a field, are surprised to find churches already there, so they begin finding fault with those churches, in order to justify their presence. Such missionaries, instead of evangelizing neglected social segments, often proselytize from existing churches, causing misery for many. Sometimes greedy nationals invite missionaries into their country or region, hoping for material gain from them. Missionary agencies can avoid such evils by sending their workers only to really neglected peoples.

A congregation that has adopted a neglected people should only work with a mission agency that agrees to send the church's workers to that people. Some missionary teams fail to focus on a specific, neglected people group, because, when they arrive in the field, everyone looks alike to them. In order to discover those subcultures that remain neglected and receptive, they must study the field, as Jesus commanded (Jn 4:35). Then they can make strategic plans based on real information.

Send workers to do work for which they are gifted, not merely those tasks assigned by an administrator seeking warm bodies to put into job slots, because some supervisors place workers without regard to their abilities and gifts. A new worker might protest, but few listen to a new worker and may accuse him of insubordination. Therefore his sending church and the mission agency should agree first on what kind of work the missionary will do.

Another common mistake of some agencies is to form teams in whatever way is easiest for their home office to administrate and control. Some administrators set up teams and dictate plans from a distance, rather than letting workers familiar with field conditions decide on their own tactics.

Guideline 51
Apply God's oil to rusty organization.

I flew around a few mission fields and saw shepherds and missionaries with outdated policies that hinder flocks multiplying.

Let us look at some remedies...

Where does the "rust" come from? Well-meaning founders of a congregation or organization, trying to forestall possible problems before they occur, sometimes write prohibitions and rules as bylaws. Overly-eager leaders rush to add rules for members every time trouble surfaces. When a problem occurs, do not simply add another litigious rule to your organization's bylaws or policy manual. Better to just deal with it and move on. If a chronic problem occurs repeatedly over a long time, then a permanent policy may be in order. Patterson commented:

> Pastors asked how they and their people can plant daughter churches when their denomination's policies hinder it. Two of them faced meetings with administrators who had recently belittled their vision for reproducing churches. One hears such complaints often in workshops for church planting. I sympathize with the rogue who once griped, "The last great bulwark against Christianity is the church!"

> Today's churches display vital, normal health, but also abnormal rust. One indicator of normal health is that churches multiply. Wherever the apostles made disciples the way Jesus said to, flocks multiplied, and they still multiply where the same kind of disciple making takes place. No historical denomination in the

USA is currently growing rapidly, and many are declining. Some show growth only among ethnic congregations. Rusty traditions, accumulated over time, keep churches from multiplying in the normal way. Healthy congregations multiply in fields where such restrictions have not yet evolved or bureaucracy is still too weak to enforce them. The Spirit's oil has not yet been diluted with legalism, emotionalism, or rationalism.

Checklist of Rust Removers

☐ Examine your most cherished traditions in the light of the apostles' guidelines for the Lord's work.

Challenge denominational and interchurch leaders, in love, to compare their policies with Scripture, as they relate to evangelism, church planting, and raising up leaders. If possible, arrange for an open forum to pray and discuss this comparison. Doing so works where the core is sound, where leaders embraced encumbering traditions because that was all they knew, not because they were power-hungry and needed such policies to keep themselves in control.

☐ Help missionaries to follow all aspects of Jesus' Great Commission.

Although the Lord clearly commanded to make disciples of all nations by teaching them to obey all of His commands, few missionaries, including those with extensive Bible knowledge, know what Jesus commanded them to do. When asked, they will mention love, and then hesitate. Some ask new believers to do many activities that may have some spiritual value but that are not the foundational activities the Jesus commanded. Although Jesus issued more than 100 commands, many of them can be summarized in the seven basic commands that the first New Testament church began to obey in their most basic form from their beginning. According to Acts 2:37-47, following Pentecost, the 3,000 new believers immediately began obeying Jesus' commands:

They repented in faith and were born of the Holy Spirit.

They confirmed this conversion at once with baptism.

They broke bread in their homes.

They showed love by their fellowship.

They embraced the apostles' teaching.

They prayed.

They gave.

Ignoring Christ's authority in these matters leaves a power vacuum in a new congregation where new believers become confused about just who has the final word. This situation leaves room for egotistical leaders to usurp Jesus' place as King among his people.

☐ Challenge Christian educators and others to restore biblical discipleship.

Teach New Testament disciple making principles in leadership training curricula, including Jesus' basic commands. Few recent seminary or Bible college graduates know how to make disciples in the way Jesus did. Rather they approach it much like a doctrinal study, and then pass that rusty procedure on to others both on the home front and in the mission field. By way of contrast, biblical disciple making builds upon Jesus, the Rock, by teaching how to do his word. Jesus said, "If you love me, obey my commands" (Jn 14:15; compare Jn 15:14; Mt 7:24-29; 28:18-20).

☐ Train national workers in pioneer mission fields to make disciples of new believers in the way Jesus said.

Show new shepherds how to build upon the Rock. The first few weeks of a newborn flock's life in a pioneer field are crucial to laying a sound foundation on which to build loving obedience to the Lord Jesus Christ. Denominational policies, however, often keep new congregations in pioneer fields from baptizing new believers and celebrating the Lord's Supper without the presence of an ordained clergyman. In practice this denies Jesus' deity by ascribing more authority to man-made rules than to His commands. Doing so blurs Jesus' authority for a congregation's activities, opening the door to disobedience towards the Lord and to abusive control by whoever assumes they have the right to rule over them.

☐ Prepare pastoral students to apply the Bible to all ministries.

Too many graduates of evangelical seminaries and colleges use Scripture almost exclusively as content for teaching and preaching, neglecting it as the norm for church practices. They often overlook the guidelines of God's Word as they plan how to evangelize, confirm repentance, organize a congregation, worship and deploy missionaries. Were they, instead, to teach biblical guidelines for these activities, they would enable trainees and their flocks to become doers of the Word and not hearers only.

☐ Affirm biblical authority for church leaders.

Who has the highest authority in a church? Those who have been in the church the longest? Have the most Bible knowledge? Can preach the most eloquently? Have the highest academic degrees? Give the most money? Hold the highest offices? Use the church's bylaws most adeptly to manipulate others?

Scripture recognizes none of those as a qualification for leading a flock. A true leader in the Lord's Kingdom brings his people into direct obedience to the King. One does not lead if he only teaches. He leads only when he enables others to do what Jesus and his Apostles require. If congregations leave most church work to their pastors, then leadership is lacking. Leaders must establish Jesus as the Head and highest authority in the church, so that believers will, in childlike, loving obedience, do what Jesus and his Apostles said to do.

☐ Caution ordination councils and ordination policymakers to respect the biblical requirements for becoming a shepherd.

Paralyzing rust has accumulated on ordination requirements. Shepherds who have received the Lord's pastoral gift and who fulfill biblical requirements for a shepherd are often prohibited to baptize new believers in obedience to the Lord Jesus Christ or serve them communion, because they fail to meet human requirements that have no significant bearing on their competence as shepherds. Such man-made rules have as their main effect to keep an elite clergy in power, and have paralyzed much church planting throughout history. The adding of human requirements for baptism, the Lord's Supper, and pastoral work forces many believers to disobey Christ and to neglect the calling for which God has gifted them.

Encourage modern prophets to remove traditionalist rust by using Scripture in the power of the Holy Spirit to teach examples from Scripture and history of how the Almighty has reformed His people. Welcome prophets as God's gift to the flock, for the Lord promises such spiritual chiropractors in Ephesians 4:11-12. Patterson warned that reformers who apply these Rust Removers will also need Pain Relievers:

Be forewarned... following Jesus with all of your heart will entail suffering. Few missionaries have participated in a church planting movement without painful conflict with colleagues or superiors. Simply do what Jesus says and you will step on some Christians' toes. Receiving painful blows from Christian brothers is devastating. So be forewarned!

☐ Use gentle, positive diplomacy while slaying cherished sacred cows.

Avoid inflammatory rhetoric or any appearance of attacking with a critical spirit, which would solve nothing. If possible, instead of demanding change which threatens traditionalists and persons in power, speak about adding something new, as an experiment. Sometimes reformers avoid rust by quietly disregarding abusive rules. When word gets around later that you failed to conform, just accept men's rebukes graciously. Consider the truism, "It is easier to ask pardon than permission." Once you ask for their consent to obey Christ and they say no, you are in hot water because you have acknowledged their right to veto obedience to Jesus!

Avoid feeling that you must answer every criticism while standing firm in your position on your congregation's biblical heritage. Most denominations have a great history, originating from a historical outpouring of the Holy Spirit and from following sound, biblical guidelines. Remind traditionalists that if they will let shepherds draw nourishment from those roots, then there will be less pain for all concerned.

Honestly confess to the Holy One that many of the charges Jesus made against the religious hypocrites of His day apply to us and our churches today. To our knees! Experienced and respected leaders can bring down top-heavy bureaucratic Goliaths if intercessors back them. The Lord has softened some of the most adamant traditionalists, many of whom have confessed that they had exalted traditions that eclipsed biblical disciple making.

When bringing biblical freedom into church planting movements, a mentor-coach or consultant often faces leaders who strongly embrace denominational traditions. Now, most traditions are useful, enabling congregations to do their work "decently and in order." However, over time, other traditions have proven abusive when leaders used them to bolster their authority at the expense of effective evangelism and church reproduction. Jesus condemned such practices in Mark 7:6-13. There are two main kinds of Christian traditionalists:

1. Those who follow denominational traditions because that is what they learned and is all they know. When these truly desire to win souls and gather congregations, they readily accept what you teach from God's Word.

2. Those who cling to traditions at all costs often do so because they are hungry for power or because they feel insecure with change, which is the bane of a weak leader.

Training workshops for traditional church leaders can prove both entertaining and useful in dealing with inappropriate customs without offense. Have someone wear a funny hat or a sign "MR. TRADITION." While you present guidelines for church planting or other ministries, Mr. Tradition interrupts from time to time to say, "No! No! Not that way!" and proclaims the tradition in an exaggerated way. You, then, can ask the group unashamedly, "Now, is that which Mr. Tradition recommends what Jesus and his Apostles did? Or is it a human tradition?" Participants will usually answer rightly, "Mr. Tradition."

Since it can prove daunting to ask traditional clergymen outright to relinquish their ecclesiastical authority, your task remains two-fold:

- Urge traditional leaders to delegate their authority to those whom they choose, train, and supervise, allowing these co-shepherds to perform pastoral tasks as their assistants. Point out that, according to Ephesians 4:11, the risen Lord gives to every congregation apostles, prophets, evangelists, pastors, and teachers. If leaders do not recognize who they are and fail to let them do their ministry, then they stifle the work of the Holy Spirit. Those gifted people, if kept from doing what Jesus has gifted them to do, become so frustrated that they leave a church, sometimes taking other members with them.

- Help a traditional leader to envision his flock as a mother church which, as a living organism, can reproduce normally by giving birth to daughter churches. Traditionalists often lead big congregations or want their congregations to become bigger and wealthier. A useful analogy is to compare churches to elephants and rabbits (see Figure 10). Elephants are strong and long-lived, but reproduce very slowly. Rabbits, by contrast, are puny but they reproduce rapidly. Wise leaders respect both kinds of congregations. The ideal blend would be to have a few elephant churches that marshal their resources for big tasks, along with many tiny rabbit churches that multiply rapidly throughout their city and region.

Rabbit churches grow and multiply much faster than do elephantine congregations. Believers in an average small congregation win many times more people to Christ than do the same number of believers riding an "elephant." A congregation can be both a rabbit and an elephant, in two ways: (1) an elephant congregation lets cell groups multiply to become tiny rabbit churches within the big one; (2) rabbit churches serve one another and celebrate together occasionally as a temporary elephant. Jesus gave a special promise to rabbit congregations in Matthew 18:20, promising that where even two or three gather in His name, He will be with them.

Figure 10
Elephants and Rabbits

Mature in 18 years	Mature in 4 months
1 baby per pregnancy	Almost always fertile
Fertile 4 times a year	Average 7 babies
22-month gestation	1-month gestation
Family increases from 2 to 3	Family can increase to 476
in three years	million in 3 years

Nine Freedoms Common to Church Planting Movements

When traditional church leaders are willing to experiment with true biblical liberty and permit others to do so, it is important to help them examine their practices and to identify hindrances that keep their flocks from winning the lost and reproducing. Help them to find ways to delegate their authority, so that their elephant churches can also reproduce rabbit churches. To reproduce with the grace of God, congregations must experience the freedoms that Christ bought for them on the cross. Here are some:

Freedom for young flocks to start newer flocks as soon as the Lord makes it possible. This is what Paul and Timothy let Epaphras do in Colosse, Laodicea, and Hierapolis.

What would Mr. Tradition say about this? Perhaps something like this: "Our church policies require that for a church to start another church, it must first apply to our regional headquarters for approval, have a certain number of members, acquire years of maturity, and possess a substantial budget, at least enough for a building and a pastor's salary."

Freedom to obey the commands of Christ and his Apostles above and before all religious rules and traditions. Jesus welcomed sinners and rebuked religious leaders for their traditions that hindered obedience, even though their theology was right.

Mr. Tradition may say something like this: "We must all follow the same policies—those that I approve. Conformity ensures unity."

Freedom to enter the homes of unconverted seekers, to evangelize them lovingly in their own familiar setting, making disciples within their own cultures and family networks. Examples include Peter at Cornelius' house and Jesus' instructions to the Seventy-Two.

Mr. Tradition might argue, "Separate new believers immediately from the bad influence of friends, relatives and culture! And let sinners come to us at church, if they want to be saved!"

Freedom to baptize new believers without undue delay and to celebrate the Lord's Table wherever they meet. Follow the example of the early church in Acts 2:37-47.

Mr. Tradition might insist, "Baptism and the Lord's Supper are performed only by ordained clergy and baptismal candidates must walk on water first."

Freedom to serve one another in the Body of Christ as intimate, loving congregations and cells, using all the gifts that the Holy Spirit has given to them. That was normal church life according to 1 Corinthians 14:24-26.

Mr. Tradition might demand, "Do all things in decency and order. And the order is what I say it is! Only educated clergy should lead public meetings."

Freedom to provide pastoral leadership by those who meet the New Testament qualifications of elders, with or without salaries. Peter focused upon men's motives for service as an elder, not on academic degrees (1 Pet 5:1-5).

Mr. Tradition might contend, "Our church bylaws require ministers to be ordained. Our bylaws list 756 requirements that they must meet first. They must have the specified academic degrees and receive the salary of a professional."

Freedom to apply any New Testament method of preaching and teaching God's Word according to each group's size and its leaders' maturity. This would include freedom to teach and practice the New Testament's "one another" commands.

Mr. Tradition might dispute this. "God has ordained oratorical preaching of the Word for this age. We need top quality and excellence in the pulpit."

Freedom for pastoral trainers to respond to immediate needs of new flocks and their leaders. Biblical models include Jehosaphat, Jesus and Titus.

Mr. Tradition might assert, "My training program has a standard curriculum and every student studies the same topic, starting in the same place and following the same path. What they learn is for some future application."

Freedom to provide regional coordinators who supervise new and immature flocks and also pastoral leaders. That was the role that Paul assigned to Titus.

If Mr. Tradition is from an independent church he might object, "We do not want any godless hierarchy of bishops dictating to churches what to believe and practice. We hold to the autonomy of the local church."

If Mr. Tradition's church is hierarchical he might protest, "I am the Bishop named to supervise this region and I do not want any new coordinators exercising authority in my area of jurisdiction, and I do not have time to coordinate any new programs! So we will continue as we have been doing for a hundred years!"

Guideline 52
Tap others' experience to solve snags with a trouble-shooting chart.

I want my flock to grow in
Christ and to multiply,
but we keep flying into snags!

How can we overcome so many
different problems?

Let us look at what many
experienced workers
have discovered,

to overcome common
problems of new flocks...

Trouble-Shooting Chart

Problem: Evangelism fails to bring people to Christ or to reach families.

Cause #1: Workers lack power for evangelism.

Cures:

- Enlist resolute intercessors and share the vision widely.

- Pray for healing of the sick with childlike faith.

- Proclaim the good news as the apostles did, relating the death and the life-giving resurrection of Jesus.

Cause #2: Workers extract converts from family and friends, overdoing the personal and private aspect of faith.

Cures:

- Find a man of peace in a community and work with his contacts as Jesus instructed in Luke 10.

- Start with heads of families as in Acts 16:31.

- See seekers as the Lord does, as part of a social unit.

Cause #3: Expatriate workers fail to bond properly with the people and their culture, spending time mainly with each other.

Cures:

- Live among the people, allowing them to meet your deepest social needs.

- Keep on learning their language till you speak it well.

- Avoid joining teams that have only short-term missionaries.

Cause #4: Expatriate workers mobilize few nationals for task groups.

Cures:

- Create task groups mainly with nationals or culturally-proximate workers.

- Aim not for permanent teams but form temporary task groups that focus on short-term goals.

Cause #5: Worship style or evangelistic methods do not fit the culture.

Cures:

- Recruit nationals to write and lead music in their style, avoiding Western-style performances.

- Celebrate the Lord's Supper regularly.

- Deal with a seeker's family and social network, and not with him as an isolated individual.

Cause #6: Converts fall back into their old lifestyle.

Cures:

- Call seekers to repent, not simply to make decisions.

- Baptize repentant believers without undue delay.

- Help converts to love their family and friends in practical ways.

Problem: Church or cell group multiplication has lagged.

Cause #1: Leaders encourage work only if they control it, failing to plan for granddaughter churches or cells.

Cures:

- Model servant-leadership for new leaders outside of classrooms. Establish imitable relationships.

- Train and install new leaders fast, at least as quickly as Paul did in Acts 14.

Cause #2: Methods or equipment are too costly, too high-tech, or too Western.

Cure: Limit equipment and methods to those that workers in a 2 Timothy 2:2 training chain can easily obtain.

Cause #3: Leaders fear that false doctrine or bad practices will creep in, if congregations multiply rapidly.

Cures:

- Clarify what history shows: heresy comes from old, stagnant congregations, not new ones. Simply keep on training new leaders in the biblical way.

- Remind workers that where the apostles made disciples, congregations grew and reproduced.

Problem: Organizational policies deter new leaders from obeying Jesus' commands.

Cause: Leaders attribute more authority to human organization than to the Lord Jesus Christ.

Cures:

- Make disciples as Jesus said, by teaching them to obey His commands in love, before all else.

- Base ministries on Jesus' commands, discerning between New Testament commands, mere apostolic practices that were not commanded, and human traditions.

- Discern between the essential purpose of commands and the various external forms that their practice can entail.

Problem: Students fail to carry out their fieldwork or study assignments.

Cause #1: Trainers enroll immature pupils.

Cure: Only enroll leaders that qualify biblically as elders.

Cause #2: Too many attend training sessions.

Cure: Gather no more than you can listen to and help plan during a training session.

Cause #3: Plans require too much field work or prove impractical.

Cure: Plan fieldwork that students can realistically do and agree to do, noting specific persons and places as you record their plans.

Cause #4: Accountability is weak.

Cure: Review each trainee's work, give recognition for good work and note current needs.

Cause #5: Assignments do not fit current needs and opportunities.

Cure: Use a list of optional activities and studies. See the menus of *Paul-Timothy*[70], *Train and Multiply*[71] or *The Shepherd's Storybook*[72], to select activities that fit current needs.

Cause #6: Students find their studies too hard to read.

Cure: Check whether trainees need inexpensive reading glasses.

Cause #7: Students work through books in a linear way, not as they need them to meet current needs.

---

[70] Freely downloadable in several languages from <http://paul-timothy.net>.

[71] *Train & Multiply*® is administered by Project WorldReach (pwr@telus.net). Samples in various languages are available from < http://www. Trainandmultiply. com>.

[72] Freely downloadable in several languages from <http://paul-timothy.net>.

Cure: Explain the concept and need for the menu approach.

Cause #8: Books are too costly or too big to carry around to read conveniently.

Cures:

- Locate other books or those which are smaller in size. *T&M* is an example.

- Do not bind books in larger volumes simply for the convenience of printers and secretaries.

   Problem: Western funding stifles initiative.

   Cause: Leaders work only if paid.

   Cures:

- Halt subsidies that create dependency. Remain firm about this.

- Teach Christian stewardship.

   Problem: Training materials are unavailable.

   Cause: Trainers cannot get a training book when a particular need calls for it.

   Cures:

- Set up book deposits within reach of all your trainers.

- Count the numbers of books on hand regularly to replace low stocks.

Chapter 4

Train Leaders in Jesus' Way

Guideline 53
Train new shepherds to obey Jesus first.

I prepared and preached a great sermon, so I have done all my duties for the week.

I am going fishing. 'Bye.

Wait! The new flock you helped gather is floundering in confusion.

Go help their leaders to build on Jesus' commands.

Let us see what Scripture says about building this foundation...

Obedience-oriented education, as it developed in northern Honduras during the 1960s and 70s, grew out of Theological Education by Extension (TEE) that had its roots in Ralph Winter's work of training pastors in Guatemala[73], along with the writings of Ross Kinsler and James Emery. Wedding pastoral training with

---

[73] Ralph Winter, ed., *Theological Education by Extension* (Pasadena: William Carey Library, 1969).

evangelism, Patterson lengthened the name to Theological Education and Evangelism by Extension (TEEE).

An obedience-oriented curriculum grows out of the foundational commands of the Lord Jesus Christ (Mathew 28:18-20). Systematic theology, church history and other subjects are taught, but not as the foundation for pastoral work. The primary educational objectives are the Lord's orders for His church. Maintaining this priority can revolutionize a seminary or Bible institute, turning it into a dynamic church planting instrument.

TEE takes pastoral studies to the student, where he is. It reaches men who cannot leave their homes or jobs, relating their studies to their local church work in the community without seclusion in a resident seminary. Self-teaching textbooks permit less time spent in the classroom, requiring more private study. TEE aims primarily to educate—not to evangelize or start new congregations.

TEEE integrates evangelism with TEE, aiming primarily to edify and reproduce congregations. Evangelism is not simply "soul-winning," but the birth and growth of congregations, that is, edification of the Body of Christ in the broadest, biblical sense. Combining education and evangelism in one program allows them to reinforce each other powerfully. Pioneer missionaries can use some form of TEEE wherever church planting must be accompanied by pastoral training.

Patterson practiced TEEE through the Honduras Extension Bible Institute. The prior TEE program by itself did not prove an efficient tool for planting new churches and evangelizing the lost. Broadening TEE's scope did not weaken its educational capacity as some predicted, but strengthened it. This happy marriage between education and evangelism blossomed only as student-workers (as Patterson liked to call them) applied their studies as obedience towards Jesus. Workers and churches began to reproduce in a way unknown in the former training program which had been a resident Bible institute.

TEEE's obedience orientation is not just a method but a way of thinking and acting in obedience to Christ, and can be applied to a resident seminary, an extension program, or local churches whose pastors train Timothys in order to multiply ministry. Trainers who start with a commitment of absolute obedience to the Lord and follow through without bending to tradition, soon find that the most effective training requires a student to work with a congregation while studying, in order to apply at once what one learns—hence, the term "student-worker."

What is the difference between a "student" and a "student-worker"?  Let us find out...

In traditional education, a teacher focuses on the material being taught to passive students, seldom looking beyond his students to see what that student does with his learning. The student satisfies his teacher with good papers, exams, and, in the case of a homiletics course, sermons. A traditional teacher's view of a student and the results of his teaching is diagrammed in Figure 11.

Figure 11
A Traditional Education View

An obedience-oriented teacher looks beyond his student and is satisfied only with edifying work done in the field. It is not enough to teach the Bible to students, one must teach it biblically. This kind of biblical education involves the teacher, student and the student's congregation. The objective is not simply to educate a student for subject mastery, but also to edify his flock. The teacher monitors a congregation's progress through the student-worker's reports. The student-worker may be a new pastor, shepherding elder, or an active church member. An obedience-oriented view of a student shepherding his flock is diagrammed in Figure 12.

Figure 12
An Obedience-Oriented View

James 1:22 urges, "Do not merely listen to the Word, and so deceive yourselves. Do what it says." The apostle James would have denounced any educational process which resulted in passive learning. Many traditional pastoral courses do just that. Their students, conditioned by three or four years of passively learning the Word, upon graduating with an institutional mentality, treat their congregations as if they were Bible institutes in which students sit and learn passively. The congregations, instead of becoming the sensitive, creative bodies that the Lord intended them to be, turn into schools—pastor-centered and passive.

Throughout the world, the need to train many more shepherds to care for rapidly multiplying flocks has forced a change. Many institutions now dovetail practical work into the subjects that they teach. Some schools now reinforce doctrine and theory with field assignments carried out within congregations. Although this change is good, for it requires more student obedience, still they teach mainly doctrine-oriented courses. They lay a doctrinal basis first, and practical assignments are added to it. Let us go a step further: why not start with the practical work, and then add necessary doctrinal teaching that will enable students to do their work? Note the reversal: the course is now activity-oriented, but still not necessarily obedience-oriented. The curriculum has become "functionally-ordered" and obedience-oriented. It is functionally-ordered in that it is geared to the needs of in-service training, serving as a crash program to mobilize large numbers of workers in rapidly expanding fields. Develop it further to assure that the activities are done in obedience to the Lord Jesus Christ as a permanent pastoral education program. Students, then, do practical work assignments in obedience to Christ, not to the professor. This usually solves the problem of students who lack motivation.

This approach is not like Bible schools that hand out Christian service assignments for a weekend or merely assign each student to a congregation. Because practical work has been made an integral part of the pastoral course, teachers can develop a course by starting with the commands that Christ issued to His followers. Determine the necessary steps to carry out His Great Commission in your student's areas of responsibility, making Jesus' orders the backbone of the curriculum. The congregational activities necessary to carry out those orders make up the skeleton for the course.

The flesh appears on a skeleton pastoral-training course as activities conducted at specific places, with particular people and identifiable responsibilities. If an educational goal were to train men to start new congregations, then an immediate objective would be to train brother Jagdeep to start a new church in his neighborhood this year. If another educational goal were to prepare men to witness, then an immediate objective would be for Smith to mobilize laymen Sanchez, Johnson, and Ahmed to witness for Christ this weekend to their friends in Westville Colony. An obedience-oriented curriculum always includes specific objectives with names, places, and dates.

The heart of the curriculum remains love for the Lord Jesus Christ. Obedience for any other motive would be a form of legalism. Jesus said, "If you love Me, you will obey what I command" (Jn 14:15). This love has to be cultivated in your trainees, so keep on exhorting, encouraging, and commending the students the work that they have accomplished. The student-worker will respond voluntarily in obedient love for the Lord Jesus Christ and for His work.

In a new congregation, a student may win the first few new believers and work with them to bring them to maturity. In so doing, he learns and grows along with his new congregation. In an established congregation, a student can still win converts and bring them to maturity as a group within the bigger congregation. In either case the student should begin with witnessing, winning to Jesus the group with whom he will work. No one should remain in a pastoral course if he cannot or will not do this. To ensure students' permanent orientation to obedience, secure in advance the active cooperation of the participating congregations.

As part of this overall desire for loving obedience to the Lord, be careful not to demand obedience with a legalistic spirit. Obedience-oriented students serve neither for the professor, nor for grades, nor for a diploma, but because they love the Lord Jesus and seek to edify the Body of Christ.

Believers must first know Jesus' orders for a congregation in order to obey them. However, confusion abounds: one preacher demands to baptize immediately and another pleads to wait several months. Some insist on total abstinence from alcoholic beverages while others call such a demand unbiblical tyranny. Congregations also divide on issues of dress, food, entertainment and methods of evangelism. Clearly, such human opinions can confuse believers. So help them to distinguish between (a) the Lord's commands for His church, (b) apostolic practices that were not commanded (churches may or may not follow them) and (c) human traditions and bylaws (churches may prohibit any that stifle obedience). Discerning these three distinct levels of authority[74] for church activities can provides reasonable basis for determining priorities, and will help to avoid many quarrels.

For example, consider how these three levels apply to celebrating the Lord's Supper which is, of course, a divine command. To celebrate it frequently in homes was an apostolic practice that should be neither required nor prohibited when similar circumstances warrant. To celebrate it only at a fixed hour of a certain day of the week

---

[74] On levels of authority see guideline 16.

in a designated chapel is a human tradition which should be practiced only when agreed upon by a specific congregation.

In summary, obedience-oriented education requires students to perform practical work within a local congregation, in purposeful obedience to the divine commands of the Lord, not merely following human traditions or apostolic practices passed down by men.

Guideline 54
Learn and do God's Word; teach integrated units.

No! Our Lord told teachers to equip believers to build up the flock.

Birds are not hearers only!

Just teach Bible doctrine accurately, and everything else will turn out right

Birds must obey the Word with the Holy Dove's power or your teaching accomplishes nothing!

Let us examine ways in which to teach...

All study courses should lead to obedience, so that a congregation moves forward spiritually, applying each study to its activities. Wise teachers enable each student to fulfill the practical obligations that flow from Bible doctrine. Rather than simply tacking on an "application," approach doctrine with a desire to obey the Lord. Shepherds are to equip all members of their congregation to serve in some ministry, coordinated and empowered by the Holy Spirit (Eph 4: 11-16; 1 Cor 12). Theological truth, when it is properly taught, moves believers to serve together as a body. However, they cannot do so when teachers partition truth into isolated subjects. A wise teacher relates multiple theological truths by focusing them on congregational activities. Systematic theology seeks to relate divine truths in a logical manner, apart from a congregation's application of those truths. The Spirit of God brings those truths into sharper focus as He coordinates the various ministries within an active church body (see Figure 13), integrating many elements of Bible doctrine, history, and Christian education when believers are applying those insights to people's lives and to their struggles in the world. Holistic teaching combines elements from a number of subjects to focus on a current congregational activity (see Figure 14).

Figure 13
Teaching for Congregational Activity

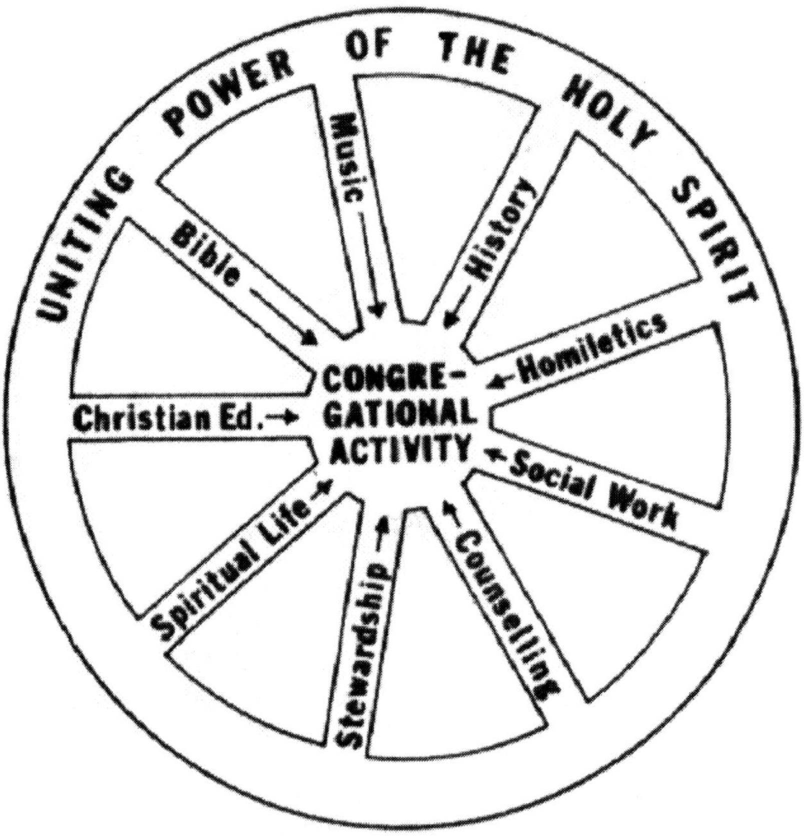

Figure 14
Subjects Meet a Congregation's Need

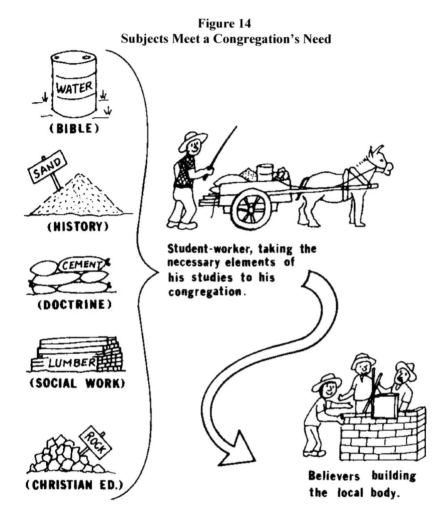

(BIBLE)

(HISTORY)

(DOCTRINE)

(SOCIAL WORK)

(CHRISTIAN ED.)

Student-worker, taking the necessary elements of his studies to his congregation.

Believers building the local body.

How can a pastoral student harmonize opposing interests in his congregation? Within any congregation, one finds believers who have a variety of gifts and interests. One may find an elder with the gift of teaching who is almost exclusively concerned with details of biblical doctrine. Another, with the gift of prophecy, will focus on long-range implications of theological truth for men in today's world, teaching and interpreting church history to show the implications. Another, with the gift of exhortation, will want to see work getting done; so he might seek books on counseling, evangelistic methods and mission strategy. A deacon with the gift of serving may want to give more of the congregation's offering to needy people. A deaconess may want to visit widows regularly or to plant flowers around the place of worship.

A shepherd cannot harmonize these various interests and abilities in a classroom or from a pulpit. Nevertheless, an experienced shepherd governs with wisdom, unifying his congregation to obey the Lord together as a body. When a student-worker observes how God's Spirit harmonizes the efforts of those with different interests within the Body of Christ, he learns to integrate different study topics by focusing on particular activities that Jesus and his Apostles ordered His churches to perform.

A systematic doctrinal study that fails to begin with the Lord and to end with a believer's obedient response falls short of biblical truth and purposes. Divine truth always flows towards loving obedience, except when unwise teachers impede it.

That sounds frightfully metaphysical! How can we teachers hinder truth fulfilling its purpose?

We need to do some theological thinking! Are you ready?

To relate doctrine and duty correctly entails a vertical treatment of doctrine (see Figure 15), so begin with God the Father, the source of all truth and authority. God's attributes originate in the Father's will; God the Son works out the Father's decrees within creation; and the Holy Spirit applies the Son's work to believers who respond in compliant, loving obedience. That is, start with God and end with people. The intermediate steps in this vertical application form the content of a complete doctrinal study. Any systematic study that fails to begin with God and end with an obedient human response remains incomplete, falling short of biblical truth and purpose. Such a study only weakens the Body, unless it specifically contributes to activities that a congregation does. Thus, believers participate in the life and work of the Trinity by their loving obedience to the Father's will, just as their Lord does.

Figure 15
Vertical Treatment of Doctrine

The traditional, horizontal treatment of doctrine (see Figure 16) seldom begins with God and seldom ends with the believer's duty. Academic theology originated with medieval scholasticism and proceeded systematically to cluster doctrinal truths into parallel categories, comparing similar ideas based on a Latin vocabulary. Consequently, much systematic theology fails to connect Heaven and earth. The prophets and apostles demonstrated how to teach biblically, by presenting theological truth that touched men's daily and national lives in compelling, practical ways. They never presented doctrine as outlines of abstract propositions.

Since a resident education program can hardly require every class to have its corresponding practical work, it must provide mentors who can gear each student's studies to his congregation's growth. Teachers of obedience-oriented pastoral courses, however, take responsibility for the weekly progress of their students' congregations. They teach much of the same general content as do traditional seminary and Bible Institute professors, but not in the same order. Rather they teach their students content that fits the immediate, changing needs of their trainees and their respective flocks, as their students take on more pastoral responsibilities.

Figure 16
Horizontal Treatment of Doctrine

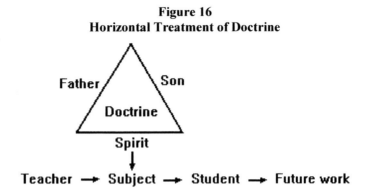

How can a trainer prepare textbooks that focus different areas of study on a given activity? First of all, do not tie one educational objective to one corresponding subject, for church life is not that neatly categorized. Teaching usually fails to produce immediate results in a congregation, if a course or textbook deals with only one subject. Instead, let congregational activities form the core of a study unit, and add to it biblical, doctrinal, and historical truths that support the activity. Teachers can easily develop materials in this way by keeping a paper or electronic filing system (see Figure 17) organized around each of the commands of Jesus and all of the ministries that the New Testament pleads for within congregations.

Figure 17
Verb-Based Filing System.

Each folder can grow without confusion, as the educator adds doctrinal, historical, and practical material, eventually yielding a short textbook. The curriculum evolves as trainers file significant information and insights gleaned from their students' reports. By contrast, in traditional theological education, writers often present subjects in textbooks that state objectives as parallel areas of abstract knowledge, with little relation between these different areas of study.

Another way to show how different subjects relate to congregational activities is to plot the lists of both abstract truths and practical work (congregational activities or "field activities") on a two-axis graph. State the subjects in terms of activities ordered by Christ or His Apostles (see Figure 18), perhaps combining some subjects and activities into integrated units. Patterson commented:

> Originally the word "curriculum" meant a race course or career. It implied action. A good curriculum includes field practice, with no need to add a separate educational category for the practice. A certain seminary curriculum revision committee wanted to help students apply on the field what they learned in class, so they instituted practical to supplement the classroom. The result merely widened the gap between field work and academic studies, for the "practicum" proved quite unrelated to what professors taught in classrooms. Thus the practicum failed to do what a properly integrated curriculum could have achieved. Educators can properly integrate a pastoral training curriculum by balancing classroom instruction with mentoring in the same way that Jesus and the apostles trained new leaders.

  Theological courses are not truly "curriculum" if they only list abstract ideas.

Let us find out why...

Figure 18
An Integrated Curriculum

What one learns (content)		What one does (activities)													
	↘ → ↓	Witness	Baptize	Fellowship	Care of needy	Use spiritual gifts	Oversee	Give	Worship	Break bread	Counsel	Plant churches	Train shepherds	Disciple nations	Apply the Word
	Bible Intro.														x
	Old Test.			x					x						x
	New Test.	x	x	x	x	x	x	x	x	x	x	x	x	x	x
	Doctrines														
	Sin	x							x		x				x
	Salvation	x	x	x										x	
	Holy Spirit, etc.		x	x		x								x	x
	Church life		x	x		x	x	x	x	x	x				
	Missions	x	x									x	x	x	
	Church History														
	Ancient	x					x		x					x	
	Medieval	x					x								
	Spiritual life, etc.					x		x		x	x				

Integrate Truth and Task

While coaching new church leaders, you will meet some who imagine that their task is simply to retain truth and then to pass it on to passively-listening flocks.

Therefore, you will have to explain and demonstrate how truth is to be lived out through loving relationships with God and with one another. Teachers, congregations and small groups can make this experience easy by following biblical guidelines, help disciples to experience the Lord in person and not simply to learn facts about Him. Paul said unequivocally, "I want to know Him" (Phil 3:10).

Is not systematic theology the best approach to teach the great doctrines of the faith?

With some teachers theology is too fragmented to be practical.

Teach in a way that integrates divine truth with Christian work.

Let us challenge some sacred cows...

Billy Sunday, an evangelist of the First World War era, reflected an attitude that is now strong and growing stronger among young Western Christians. Sunday's sweeping rejection of theology was unfortunate, for sincere Christians love to learn about the Lord and that is essentially what theology is about. Rejecting theology may reflect a rebellious spirit, but more often its rejection is due to the approach to theology that unwise educators have inflicted upon earnest believers.

Mr. Sunday, many have come to Jesus through your teaching, but it seems a bit simplistic to us theologians.
What is your theology?

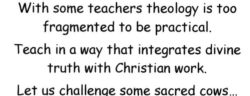

My theology?
Why, if I had a theology, I would sell it to a museum!

Billy Sunday's relationship with God was too dynamic, too life-changing, and too near to his heart for him to dissect the Lord into separate attributes and operations. That would have been as unthinkable as seeking to appreciate the beauty of the Mona Lisa by analyzing the pigments of its paint. Sunday's complaint was with the theological method of breaking down truths about the Lord into neat but useless lists.

Jesus, the Son of God, became human flesh and gave humanity the most complete image of the invisible God (Col 1:15). Believers see the Lord Jesus Christ not by indexing details of His person and work, but by entering into a relationship with Him and with the Father through the work of the Holy Spirit who transforms all aspects of their lives.

In the West, since many "post-moderns" feel alienated from traditional churches, some congregations have tried louder, contemporary music which bridges only one minor aspect of their alienation, side-stepping the heart of the problem. A deeper cause is that many people simply cannot abide preachers' dogmatic, one-way transmission of fragmented facts, so they go elsewhere to pursue a deeper, more relational worship experience.

I want to discover God and His truths together with you guys. I cannot connect with my parents' church and the way in which it presents truth as disconnected dogmas!

Can we know God as a meaningful whole, not a lot of bits and pieces?

Many believers are simply asking for what the New Testament describes as normal church body life. Traditional churches often claim to follow the Bible while straying far from its standards of integration, interaction in teaching, and intimacy of fellowship.

When post-moderns put their faith in Jesus, they seldom attend more than a few traditional worship services—except those who already had a traditional church background and became inured to it—because the formality is too painful for them. To turn their pain into a wholesome experience, a congregation must communicate

God's Word in the same way that Jesus and his Apostles did. Patterson recalled:

> While training pastors in Central America, at first I used the usual fragmented approach to theology, but it did not help sterile church bodies to reproduce. So, we closed the lecture halls and began training on the job. Students had to start and shepherd their own flocks. We then geared our teaching to their flock's needs. We taught doctrine along with its moral duty, along with practical field assignments. We showed how truths about the Almighty relate to church life in the present life and how ministries that grow out of God's works of grace combine with each other, like organs in a human body. Churches became healthier and reproduced.

Let the Holy Spirit integrate different disciplines, ministries and truths in the Body and bring cohesion to Christian teaching, worship, and ministry. This kind of fusion could be called integrated theology. An example of this approach is Demarest's and Lewis' book, *Integrative Theology*.[75] Integrating theological truths with the works of God is no mere mental exertion, for it encompasses purposeful interaction in congregations and in the lives of believers.

For example, trained elders can help believers to grasp the death and resurrection of Jesus as the two sides of one saving work. His death makes forgiveness possible, but does not impart life by itself. Rather eternal, holy life comes by believers' being united with Jesus in His resurrection, just as at the coming resurrection, our mortal bodies will be clothed in His immortality (1 Cor 15). To teach Jesus' crucifixion as His only saving work neglects His resurrection, the event that the apostles emphasized more strongly.

While a properly integrated theology does not oppose having a system, any theology that isolates divine truths risks failing to exalt the Lord Jesus Christ as the Head in whom all things exist and hold together. To isolate theological details is the opposite of a true system. Webster's Dictionary defines system as "an assemblage of

---

[75] Bruce A. Demarest and Gordon R. Lewis, *Integrative Theology* (Grand Rapids: Zondervan, 1996).

objects united by some form of regular interaction or interdependence; an organic or organized whole; as the solar system; a communications system." What some erroneously call systematic theology could technically be called a perversion of the term systematic, for a true system requires integration, such as seen in the human nervous system. The Almighty's whole, beautiful, interactive, interdependent system becomes fragmented in student's minds by the fragmented way in which some theology teachers present it. So do the right kind of analysis:

Traditional systematic theology dissects the Lord. It analyzes separate "ologies" as though each one were an isolated category that one understands by examining it without reference to other theological truths and Christian life.
Fragmented, analytical systemizing is a poor way to experience God and appreciate His work.

Integrative analysis of truths includes the system itself, showing the relationship between the facts, experiences, and moral duties that they entail. Linear analysis chops the body of truth up, isolating interrelated truths without showing their relationships. Its non-system omits a lot of true theology. Of course, teaching unrelated facts is still better than teaching nothing at all about God.

Truth  Experiences

Wise communicators teach about the Lord and mankind by using the system that the Bible displays, showing the logical relationships between truths about God, church, duty, and morality. Unlike the teaching of human religions, biblical truth builds on true stories, such that truth is discovered from the interactions of the real God dealing with real people and real, space-time events. Patterson has admitted:

> I love analytical theology and could enjoy discussing it all day. However, in pastoral and missionary ministries, I have seen that systematically-categorized ideas usually fail to meet the current needs of God's people. Simply teaching the Bible meets their needs better than doctrines listed out analytically. Bible knowledge easily flows from one person to another, for people communicate more effectively when we teach them in the way that we find in Scripture.
>
> When I trained new pastors to think in an analytical way, their teaching failed to touch people's hearts. To correct my error, I pictured for them an army tank on a conveyer belt moving backwards, disassembling into neatly sorted piles of wheels, gears and canon barrels. I explained that good teaching moves towards cohesiveness. The pastors understood this, except one who refused to flex; his ministry proved short-lived.

Oh no!

Stop the conveyer belt!

It is going backwards!

Educators should teach in a way that the average Christian worker can easily imitate and apply at once, passing it on to novice leaders who train still others (2 Tm 2:2). Even though some educators indeed show relationships between two or three areas of theology, they should integrate many more disciplines, just as the Holy Spirit harmonizes many different ministries—if believers will let Him do so (1 Cor 12). Training subjects and disciplines that need to be better integrated include history, prayer, spiritual warfare, serving the needy, social duties, Bible, evangelism, stewardship, relationships, character transformation, worship, disciple making, new congregations, small groups, organizing, missions, family life, and spiritual care. Thus, integrated theology deals with the whole person (often called holistic ministry) and not just his soul. Patterson recalled:

> A development worker I knew of sought to combine mercy ministry with church planting. An agency recruiter assured her, "Our purpose statement requires such holistic ministry." However, when she arrived in Africa, her supervisor said, "Yes, you can plant churches on weekends!" Thus, a fence still separated those two works.

True integration is not made easier by an ecumenical approach to theology, for truth does not fuse the theologies of divergent religions nor enforce uniformity of practice. A church body comes alive when various spiritual gifts and operations interact in love. Plants, people, animals, and landscapes display the Creator's passion for variety, with diversity harmonized in one grand system! Even ethnic groups will retain their distinct identities throughout eternity while worshipping together the Lamb upon his throne (Rev 7:9-10).

Integrated theology differs from right-brained thinking. Since anyone with normal intelligence can think with both sides of their brain, failure to use the right hand sphere of one's brain derives from faulty, rationalistic education. Nor does integration derive from fertile imaginations, for all normal thinkers can easily see relationships between truths, if educators will let them. Unfortunately, even some Christian educators often stifle normal intuition.

Some practical tasks can help believers to integrate truths and experiences in a biblical way:

- Search for all the occurrences of "one another" in your concordance, and then have your flock members teach about them and practice them in small groups. Avoid teaching only by monologue, letting the Holy Spirit harmonize flock members' various gifts in love (1 Cor 12; Rom 12:1-13; Eph 4:11-16).

- Teach how Jesus reigns as the Head of the body, for He is the unifying factor. "In Him you have been made complete, and He is the head over all rule and authority" (Col 2:10). "For by him all things were created: things in Heaven and on earth, visible and invisible, whether thrones or powers or rulers or authorities; all things were created by him and for him. He is before all things, and in him all things hold together" (1:16-17).

- Demonstrate how the Trinity integrates relationships, revelation, and service. God the Father exercises loving authority; God the Son lovingly submits to work out the Father's will on earth within time and space; and the Holy Spirit lovingly and powerfully applies the Son's Work to men's lives and ministries. Each person of the Trinity was and is co-active in every aspect of redemption and Christian service.

- Train leaders on the job in their church body where the Lord harmonizes various ministries.

- Avoid abusing the gift of teaching by letting it eclipse others' ministries. Avoid the arrogant "omniscience" of wanting the last word on every point.

- Teach doctrines by helping people to apply their moral obligations (Eph 4:11-16; 2 Tm 3:16-17). All Scriptural doctrines include duties. For example, the purpose of the Holy Spirit's filling in Scripture is not to grant an "experience" but to enable believers to serve others in practical ways.

- Organize flocks in a way that brings people together who have different ministries, rather than by isolating believers and their ministries in separate programs. A group's greatest weakness is most commonly an overemphasis of its strength, neglecting other vital activities and causing imbalance in a church body or a mission agency. A good way to maintain balance in a congregation is to let small groups practice all the ministries that the New Testament calls for.

- Discern between true theology and merely advertising denominational dogma. Unbalanced theologians defend their denomination's doctrines and the current views of their associates. Loyalty to one's peers is admirable, but does not necessarily promote honest theological study.

- Use a leadership-training curriculum that teaches the Bible in the integrated, biblical way, by applying truth to service.

Guideline 55
Listen to flocks and shepherds before instructing them.

I attended classes
at the Institute,
but very little of what
I learned applies
to my new flock!

The professors lacked time
to answer all my questions!

That is common in classrooms!
Wise trainers, like Paul,
communicate often
with shepherds
of the flocks they serve,
to learn their current needs!

An important difference between an effective instructor who trains new leaders in the biblical way, and a traditional professor, is that the former listens first and then responds, while the latter prepares course without listening to current needs of flocks (see Figure 19). Biblical training integrates teaching content with congregational activity.

Ephesians 1:17-23 reveals an aspect of God's work in theological training: The Lord gives His people a spirit of wisdom and revelation to know Him, more often in the context of a church body. Wise teachers help student-workers to know God and His purposes for their flocks. Conscientious teachers help each student to participate in the divine educational process. Nearly all of what a student studies should correspond to the current activities of the local congregation that he serves. Teachers introduce principle elements of doctrine, Bible, and church history into a student's course when they meet the needs of the people whom they serve. Doctrine and Bible find their rightful place in an integrated, obedience-oriented curriculum. Elements of doctrine take on a surprisingly new importance when related directly to the life and activities of a healthy, reproducing congregation. This means constant communication between trainers and congregations—the nervous system of a pastoral training course.

Figure 19
Education and Training as Communication

TRADITIONAL THEOLOGICAL EDUCATION

An autonomous institution assumes authority by virtue of its professors' intellectual achievements and degrees

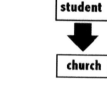

PASTORAL TRAINING WITH TWO-WAY COMMUNICATION

Experienced pastors and church planters in the field should inform pastoral trainers about what each student needs to do next. A student's reports also inform an instructor about his changing needs. A sharp educator designs a broad course of study with its general objectives and unchangeable biblical goals, and then allows flexibility for dealing with the immediate, ever-changing objectives, as the student's disciples progress. With a new flock, the immediate objectives are more obvious, for the congregation should simply begin to do all that Christ ordered, one by one. In an older congregation many new needs normally arise, and its shepherd will find opportunity to apply different studies to it. Eventually, he will have to apply the whole Word of God as well as related important examples from church history.

A seminary that teaches independently of nearby churches can hardly have an obedience-oriented curriculum. Theological institutions must genuinely cooperate with churches, and pastors should collaborate with resident and extension seminaries. Christ gave to His church the task of making disciples, not to autonomous academic institutions (Matt. 16:18-20; 18:18-20; 28:18-20). A seminary working within this sphere of authority will find that congregations provide its most valuable classrooms. Like a lens focusing sunlight on one bright point, the Holy Spirit uses a church body to integrate different streams of study in one program, just as He coordinates various ministries in one body (Eph. 4:1-16).

Some seminary leaders fear being controlled by churches which, in turn, fear being controlled by the seminary. A seminary might defend its independence in the name of academic freedom, scholarship, and intellectual honesty. It may even stand for the authority of Scripture. Yet none of those good concepts is the same as submitting to the authority that the Lord has given to the local church to teach the nations.

Both congregations and trainers should share in the educational process, appreciating each other's contribution to their own ministries. The decisive factor is not control but communication between the two, in order to coordinate the student-worker's service in a local congregation with his studies. Such responsive teaching is so challenging to maintain that trainers are sometimes tempted to revert back to the conventional classroom. Yet through this more challenging approach, the student-worker will be motivated to devour his studies with an eagerness seldom found in a traditional institution, for he knows that he is obeying his beloved Lord and fulfilling his part of the work in a local congregation.

Two-way communication between pastors and educators is as vital as that between a military commander and his trainers. During a military campaign the troops are briefed and oriented. As they pass from one objective to another they are equipped with the additional, appropriate weaponry, according to field reports. A pastoral student may not need to learn how to handle night vision goggles, as would a military solder, but he would need to know how to discipline and restore a disorderly church member. For this he needs certain equipment. His teacher must know what his current task is and relate theoretical studies accordingly.

A commanding general would not send his companies into battle under officers from an autonomous military academy which ignores his orders in the name of intellectual freedom! Would his trainers, set apart from the realities of a modern battlefield, make their own rules and design their own curriculum along traditional lines? No! Military trainers use up-to-the-minute information from the front lines according to directions from their commander. The Christian educator must work like a military strategist at a mapping table, interpreting communications from the field, from spies behind the lines and from the General Himself, in order to mobilize his troops to advance. In any campaign—military or missionary—those on the field should report imperative information continuously to trainers. The educator must depend on his students' reports of progress and urgent needs, to set immediate objectives with students working in obedience to their Supreme Commander's general orders. Immediate educational objectives change from week to week, according to the progress and needs of those whom the student-worker serves. Patterson recalled a time when he learned from his trainee:

> I traveled with a young, uneducated Honduran, Armando, by horse, motorcycle, foot and Jeep to start churches and prepare their shepherds, mentoring Armando in the process. On the way to a distant village he reversed our roles to mentor me, saying, "I have something important to instruct you…" and paused. Curious, I waited. He turned to me and announced, "Brother George, you are dancing with the devil!"

> He paused again to let me consider that announcement. He then explained, "The devil causes a problem in a village, and we rush

to deal with it. Then he stirs up strife somewhere else and we run to it. Then he inflames quarrels in another church and we hurry to correct it, responding always to his attacks. It has not been you who plan our steps but Satan, and we only follow his lead!"

I was stunned. Armando was right! He exhorted me, "Jorge, let us agree to do two things when we travel to help new congregations. Firstly, let us deal with any problem briefly and leave it in the Lord's hands, never letting it take up more than half of our time. Secondly, let us not leave until we have added something positive, have won people to Jesus, organized a new church, enrolled pastoral students, or helped them begin a ministry that is lacking." That was a turning point in our ministry, for I learned the meaning of the word *edify* from an uneducated peasant.

Guideline 56
Keep a useful balance between the classroom and mentoring.

Which is better for learning
to shepherd a flock,
formal classroom teaching
or mentoring?

Both are needed.
Let us learn the conditions
under which each works
better!

Keep a balance of classroom teaching and mentoring. Theological education such as Saul received from Gamaliel (Acts 22:3) is appropriate for some leaders. However, if a shepherd solely studies in an institution separated from the churches, he will later bring to his flock an institutional mentality that dulls its cutting edge. Therefore, wise educators discern under which conditions institutional training is practical and where it is detrimental. Certain conditions favor institutional training:

- When a student's educational level is high enough to absorb intensive studies without failing to retain and apply them.

- When a mature congregation in the area provides opportunities for practical application of what students learn. Otherwise, students become pedantic and invite problems, especially in their first pastoral assignments.

- When the school enrolls as students spiritually-mature elder types who understand what a well-established congregation is like and what an experienced shepherd does, such students can associate the theory they learn with church life. Otherwise, a graduate will follow the only leadership model he knows—the classroom instructor—becoming a benevolent dictator and pulpiteer whose teaching eclipses other vital ministries, weakening the efforts of his co-laborers.

- When men of elder quality and maturity can afford the training while supporting their families. Otherwise, only their unemployed sons go for studies and seldom return to the flocks that need their care.

Although some institutions ask students to serve as apprentices or church planters, successfully gathering flocks through practical internship, denominations have won far more people to Jesus by commissioning non-academic and lay shepherds who meet only the biblical qualifications.

Guideline 57
Give unbiased career guidance.

To learn the options for working as a missionary, should I seek counseling from a mission agency representative at a mission conference?

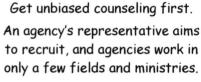

Get unbiased counseling first. An agency's representative aims to recruit, and agencies work in only a few fields and ministries. Let us examine how to get an unbiased view of all options...

Provide career counseling only if you can remain completely objective, having no preferred agenda of your own for a missionary candidate. Allow the Holy Spirit to guide as you present all the options and not just one or two that you favor. James 3:17 reveals that God's wisdom is impartial.

Mission-career counselors should know the different types of fields that remain neglected and how to enter them, including options for bivocational work in fields with restricted access. They should also be aware of the different kinds of people who need to be trained and mobilized for making disciples of the nations, so that the new worker can discern where he fits in best with his spiritual gifts.

As seen under guideline 22, strategic planners plan backwards. Keeping their ultimate objectives and field realities in mind, they can more accurately describe each prior step. Starting with the final objective and working backwards through each prior step, planners discover the categories of people who have to be trained and mobilized. Those personnel usually include:

15. Regional associations of many congregations (final goal).

14. Coordinators (servant-leaders) of these clusters of flocks.

13. Culturally-relevant national churches working in harmony.

12. National pastors and elders (servant-leaders) overseeing flocks.

11. Local leaders mentored by servant-leaders.

10. Believers shepherded by local servant-leaders.

9. New believers whom growing believers teach to obey Jesus.

8. Seekers brought to faith by newer and older believers.

7. Missionary teams which have bonded with the host culture and are trained as servant-leaders.

6. Bivocational workers equipped for restricted-access fields.

5. Mission field supervisors who envision the big picture.

4. Trainers of cross-cultural workers for all of the above.

3. Missionaries trained and aware of all of the above.

2. Sending churches praying, preparing, and planning.

1. Unbiased career counselors who present all options for service.

Backward strategizing casts light on opportunities that a leader might otherwise overlook. For example, there is the need for churches to send Christian businessmen to difficult or hostile fields to gather and host congregations like Aquila did, which traditional congregations seldom do.

Just as Solomon gave sound counsel to young people in the book of Proverbs, so mentors should provide potential Christian workers with objective career counseling. Many potential mission workers receive career advice only from an organization's public relations agent and other biased advocates of some agency, field, or methodology. One can hardly give objective counsel when paid to recruit for a specific agency, school, field, or strategy.

Guideline 58
List optional studies in a training menu.

To train new shepherds in pioneer fields,
let us look at ways that trainers choose —
optional studies that deal with
urgent needs of each trainee's flock...

Let new shepherds choose from a menu, specific studies that fit their flock's current needs and opportunities to serve Christ and others.

Menu-Assisted Mentoring

A distinctive quality of New Testament leader-training is the way in which Jesus and his Apostles gave intensive, guided, and focused attention to their apprentices and their flocks. Paul explicitly stated his training strategy to Timothy, "You then, my son, be strong in the grace that is in Christ Jesus. And the things you have heard me say in the presence of many witnesses entrust to reliable men who will also be qualified to teach others. Endure hardship with us like a good soldier of Christ Jesus" (2 Tm 2:1-3).

Paul was both a source and model of doctrines, skills, guidelines, and insights that he passed on to Timothy, who did the same for others. This approach echoes the advice that Jethro gave to Moses (Exodus 18). Such training chain-reactions find a basis also in Titus 1:5 and Jesus' example of sending out the Twelve and the Seventy-two.

Of inestimable value to a trainer is a menu of training activities, materials, readings, and guidelines arranged so that workers can find them quickly. Jesus approved the use of varied sources for teaching about the Kingdom of Heaven, "Every teacher of the law who has been instructed about the Kingdom of Heaven is like the owner of a house who brings out of his storeroom new treasures as well as old" (Matt 13:52). The purpose of a training menu is to help a novice shepherd to integrate a variety of disciplines and materials, applying them at once to his flock. Experienced pastors and missionaries may not need such a menu, but younger trainers and trainees will benefit greatly from such.

Patterson has prepared several useful menus over the years. Four such menus that are in current use include *Train & Multiply*[®76]: Student Activity Guide (see Table 1), *Paul-Timothy* Menu (see Table 2), *Shepherd's Storybook* Table of Contents (see Table 3), and the *JUMP*[77] home page (see Table 4).

Table 1
Train & Multiply Menu Items

0. Prayer and Devotional Life
1. Evangelism and Church Multiplication
2. Teaching and Disciple making
3. Organization, Leadership, and Spiritual Gift
4. Corporate Worship and Communion
5. Giving and Serving the Needy
6. Fellowship and Church Life
7. Pastoral Care, Relationships, and Counseling
8. Pastoral Training
9. Making Disciples of the Nations
10. Evaluation of Activities

Train & Multiply was developed in Spanish over a span of some twenty years in response to frequent training needs of shepherds in the field, touching on both church planting and community

---

[76] The *T&M* studies were crafted by training specialists at SEAN from Patterson's original, pocket-sized, pastoral training booklets that he wrote in Spanish while serving in Honduras.

[77] JUMP = Just what your flock needs now; User-designed (menu-driven, church-based); Mentoring chains; and Pastoral and missionary level. The JUMP Menu can be accessed and freely downloaded as HTML messages from <http://paul-timothy. net>.

development. Eventually the studies were published by SEAN which reduced the number of booklets and brought them into conformity with a modern educational format. Patterson updated all the booklets in 2001. This version is now translated into many languages and distributed under license by Project WorldReach in Canada. The 65 *T&M* studies are keyed to a "Student Activity Guide" and come in three levels: one for initiating new flocks, another for developing flocks, and a third for flocks as they reproduce. Thus, the intended users include novice shepherds of somewhat-traditional flocks in Christian-background lands, although translated versions make appropriate cultural adjustments.

Some fields, while waiting for *T&M* to appear in their languages, have expressed a need for simpler materials written for non-Christian background populations. Patterson and Currah, while still advocating and training for *T&M*, have produced the *Paul-Timothy* studies. The 72 two-page studies come in pairs, one for novice shepherds of new flocks and another for children's workers. Thus, the intended users include marginally-literate workers in non-traditional church-planting movements.

The *Shepherd's Storybook* reads like a short story about a novice shepherd who lands a new flock while being mentored by a more experienced worker. As the growing flock experiences all that the devil can throw against it, the shepherd learns practical lessons from Bible stories and applies them to his flock. Those who read the *Storybook* do the same. Its table of contents forms a menu of evangelistic lessons, basic commands of Jesus, and New Testament "one another" commands. Thus, the intended users include workers who do not yet have access to *T&M* or *P-T* and prefer storytelling or an oral learning style.

The *JUMP Menu*, written in response to institutional needs, assumes a secondary education and is keyed to Scripture readings, to printed and electronic supplementary materials, and to social research questions. It also refers to the *T&M* "Student activity Guide" and training studies, making it a companion to the series. The menu and study outlines come only in HTML-formatted documents suitable for display with computers and Internet sites. Each of fourteen ministry areas touches on three need-levels: (1) fruitful disciples, (2) church and home group life, and (3) expanded outreach and ongoing ministries.

Table 2
***Paul-Timothy* Menu Items**

0. Introduction to *P-T*: Guidelines for new trainers and trainees.

1. Assurance: Counseling and visiting those who need comfort.

2. Bible: Survey, interpretation, application, and background to God's Word.

3. Church planting: Reproducing congregations and cell groups.

4. Disciple making: Loving obedience to Jesus.

5. Evangelism: Baptism salvation from sin, death, and hell.

6. Giving: Stewardship.

7. Growth in Christ: Transformed character.

8. History: Events of great importance.

9. Love: Family life, serving the needy, fellowship.

10. Missions: Working in different cultures.

11. Organizing and leading: Pastoring churches and networks.

12. Prayer: Faith, healing.

13. Teaching biblically: Communication, storytelling.

14. Training leaders: Mentoring, uniting training with other ministries.

15. Worship: Lord's Table, holidays and special celebrations.

Table 3
Shepherd's Storybook **Menu Items**

Section I: HELP PEOPLE DISCOVER CHRIST

I–1 Find the True Meaning of Life.
I–2 Turn Back to the One God.
I–3 Find Pardon and Life in Jesus.
I–4 Escape the Powers of Evil and Death.
I–5 Discern Important Things in Life.
I–6 Find True Goodness.
I–7 Find Abundant Life in Jesus.
I–8 Become a Follower of Jesus.

Section II: ESTABLISH CONGREGATIONS THAT OBEY CHRIST

II–1. Repent, Believe, and Receive the Holy Spirit.
II–2. Baptize new Believers.
II–3. Make Disciples of Jesus.
II–4. Love.
II–5. Pray.
II–6. Break Bread.
II–7. Give.

Section III: DEVELOP THE BASIC MINISTRIES OF THE CHURCH

III–1 Take the Good News to Others and Baptize New Believers.
III–2 Build up the Body by Using Spiritual Gifts Serving One Another.
III–3 Worship God and Celebrate the Lord's Supper.
III–4 Study, Teach and Apply the Word of God.
III–5 Start New Congregations.
III–6 Train Shepherds and Other Leaders.
III–7 Develop Fellowship Within and Among Congregations.
III–8 Visit and Counsel People with Personal or Family Problems.
III–9 Strengthen Marriages, and the Faith of Entire Families.
III–10 Care for the Sick, Needy, and Mistreated.
III–11 Become Like Christ and Maintain Discipline in the Church.
III–12 Talk with God.
III–13 Be Good Stewards of God's Resources.
III–14 Send Missionaries.

SECTION IV: BIBLE STORIES FROM OLD & NEW TESTAMENTS

Table 4
***JUMP* Menu Items**

0. Orientation (vital for new users).

1. Evangelism & Basic Disciple making.

2. Fellowship.

3. Foreign Missions.

4. Marriage and Family.

5. New Congregations & Home Groups.

6. Overseeing & Planning.

7. Prayer and Spiritual Warfare.

8. Serving the Needy.

9. Shepherding the Flock.

10. Member Care and Counseling.

11. Stewardship.

12. Teaching.

13. Training Leaders.

14. Worship.

Guideline 59
Deal prudently with movements to Christ within other religions.

Some seekers want to hang on to practices of their non-Christian religion.

I studied about their wicked ways.

I shall prepare studies to warn our workers about them.

Wait! The followers of other religions are not our enemies. We are to love them and pray for them. Attacking only brings on needless persecution.

Here is what to do...

Suppose that you have been contacted by someone from a major, non-Christian religion, because God has been working in their life. Or perhaps they learned a little about Jesus from their own scriptures; they may have seen a vision; or they were shown kindness by some Christians who dared to answer their questions when asked, "What would you say and do?"

Movements to Christ occasionally take place within the context of a major, non-Christian religion. Such movements have happened through the centuries and they still happen. The biggest movements towards Christ in the history of Christianity are taking place now. Thousands of flocks are being born and reproducing rapidly in China, India, and in places where authorities prove hostile toward attempts to bring their peoples to faith in the Lord Jesus Christ from a major religion. Most of these flocks are illegal, unregistered house churches.

Sadly, well-intentioned Christian visitors sometimes kill such movements by describing them in the media (including church bulletins). Of course, they want others to rejoice at what God is doing among the unreached people group that they visited. They want intercessors to pray for the believers' safety, growth, and reproduction, but unfortunately, some want the world to know that God has chosen them among thousands of gospel workers to guide this amazing breakthrough.

Indeed, the Lord has chosen many Western believers to facilitate people movements where authorities prove hostile, and He wants them to serve those movements with wisdom in ways that will protect them from enemies of the good news. Many dangers come from unwise publicity about such movements, so leave it to the Lord to choose the right moments and causes for believers in hostile areas to be put to a test of faith.

What should one do in order to serve a movement within other religions that believes in Christ, to help them grow without unneeded hindrances? Here are ten recommended guidelines:

Quietly train leaders in the background as Jesus and his Apostles did. Neither enter into their religious buildings nor try to meet their families, as you would in a friendlier situation. Many new believers do not yet understand how severe can become social pressure and persecution can become, so they may invite you to come where you should not go. Provide teaching that they can pass on to others who will do the same, without having to meet you.

Do not publicize what you do or whom you meet with, lest religious extremists find out the secret believers and dissuade them or destroy them. Also, do not force them to make their faith public, lest their family members threaten them or do worse. When movements for Christ have been given too much attention, nationals who are members of unethical sects have often forced their way into the movement with legalistic teaching.

Make sure that their men remain in leadership from the start. Let them use their social position and spiritual power to influence others towards the good news.

Do not try to get them to join your denominational power structure. Above all, do not put national Christians from another ethnic group in charge of them.

Get advice from those with experience before proposing strategies. There are many wise Kingdom workers who come from a similar background and others who have worked with people like them, making a lot of regrettable mistakes and finding effective methods.

Do not suppose that you know enough, until you have had a few years of experience with such movements that have proven fruitful. Even those who understand principles of contextualization usually cannot predict what forms the Holy Spirit will give to a new Christian movement.

Limit methods and materials to those that others can afford and easily imitate. Let them meet with others at times and places of their choice. Get good advice from the new believers about which forms communicate well and that do not offend.

Do not introduce foreign equipment, or fund complicated schemes. Do not send anyone away for education that might not prove suitable or practical in their culture. Western music, methods, money, and ministries are seldom relevant to the host culture and invariably stigmatize the new movement as being foreign. Nonbelievers who see the foreign influence may avoid the believers, sometimes so much so that it stops the movement. Also, other believers who have not received funds or equipment from the West have often become resentful. In some cases this has stopped the movement, for funds from the West often attract opportunists who temporarily feign faith in Christ for economic advantage.

Practice biblical principles of contextualization. Both you and the new believers will have to learn to discern culturally-sensitive ways to obey the commands of Jesus. Although you cannot make such choices for them, you can ask them a lot of questions about how they will obey the Lord in ways that will win others while trying to avoid unnecessary opposition. Answer questions from the Bible and share stories about how Christians apply the Bible in other places.

Do not presume that cultural and religious forms from other movements in other cultures will prove appropriate for the local one.

Focus on the commands of Jesus. Teach Bible stories and theology that help others to obey Christ before all else. Do not teach abstract Christian theology unless asked for it, since most systematic theology, while true, has been formulated to address questions and controversies of other cultures.

Do not import the common Western emphasis on material blessings. Western prosperity theologies have often proven woefully disillusioning where people are very poor.

Keep the movement a secret as long as you can. If you do send mail and publish articles about the movement, then use pseudonyms for persons and places. Never release a believer's name or address to any outsiders. If there is a big need for relief and development efforts, then try to keep as far in the background as you can, lest your effort be misunderstood as an inducement to convert people.

Do not let outsiders know the identity of secret pastors and evangelists who are very effective. Doing so has often resulted in well-meaning Western leaders offering salaries and personal-advancement opportunities, removing their leaders from the congregations that the Lord has given them to tend, to work in the West or other places where they are not as effective.

Do not tell all of your friends about the wonderful breakthrough, for careless, exuberant testimonials may become known to your enemies. Do not publish articles that your enemies may read.

Do not give secret believers too much attention lest some of them proudly imagine that they be special and deserve such attention, which would lead to failure. Others have become so afraid of exposure by Westerners that they have drawn back and ceased doing effective ministry. Unfriendly civil authorities are quick to notice any attention paid by foreigners and often punish the believers for doing illegal proselytizing.

Realize that believers may suffer for Jesus according to the will of God. Although believers cannot avoid persecution, neither should you seek to be persecuted nor take risks that endanger others. The time will come when the Lord himself will purify and strengthen their movement with some persecution. Teach about persecution and tell stories of martyrs, but do not hasten it. From China, Brother Yun shared, "We have come to understand that the past thirty years of suffering, persecution and torture for the house churches in China were all part of God's training for us."[78] Peter counseled, "Those who suffer according to God's will should commit themselves to their faithful Creator and continue to do good" (1 Pet 4:19).

Practice a deep, spiritual dependence on the Lord of Hosts. Those who practice other religions are often more seriously religious than are evangelical Christians, especially evangelicals from wealthy countries. Many of them imagine that Christians are drunkards and adulterers, as they have seen in Western films. You are perhaps the best model they have of how Christians love God, neighbor, each other, and even enemies.

Do not emphasize any Western evangelical theology or practice that seems irreligious, rationalistic, or even disrespectful towards another religion. Their followers know the weaknesses and injustices of their religion and will find ways to deal with them, correct them, or break with them. Focus upon loving obedience to Jesus.

Let the believers make any public break with their religion on their own initiative. Give time for the movement to spread far within the religious community. Eventually, there will be an internal reaction against the followers of Jesus, perhaps with violence and persecution. Meanwhile, some of their leaders and scholars may become Christians and provide needed leadership, after you have long been expelled from their country.

Do not offer to construct distinctively Western-looking religious buildings, introduce Western clothing-styles, Western evangelical entertainment, or Western theological education.

---

[78] Brother Yun with Paul Hattaway, *The Heavenly Man* (Grand Rapids: Monarch Books, 2002), 286.

Guideline 60
Follow up mission courses with useful action.

Members of my flock finished a course
on missions and want to reach
neglected peoples.
What can I help them do next?

Let us find out ...

After learning about practical mission endeavors through such books as this one and valuable courses like "Perspectives on the World Christian Movement," believers often ask how to apply what they have learned in a practical manner. Sending churches, mission instructors, mission organizations, and field workers can take actions such as the following:

- Sending churches can adopt a neglected people, preferably in partnership with workers who are culturally-similar to that people, planning to take action to reach them based on serious, focused research.

- Mission course coordinators in churches, schools, and mission conferences can create a "launching pad," helping to help launch the real work that alumni are only entering when the course ends. Alumni and other volunteer helpers, while receiving guidance from course coordinators, keep moving and influencing others to fulfill the Lord's Great Commission. Without such guidance, few alumni stay focused on strategic and reproductive mission work.

- Instructors must link theory to action, always. An old horror story is told of a madman who split a policeman's skull with a hatchet. The policeman kept fighting by instinct for several agonizing minutes with the embedded hatchet neatly dividing his brain in two! Do mission instructors split brains? Do they pour data into one part of a student's mind to be stored, without linking it to the part that moves muscles in purposeful activity? Remove the hatchet by helping students to define action plans for every applicable item that they learn. Do not just load the truck; also, start its motor!

• Mission course alumni, missionary trainees, and volunteers can help with mobilization by establishing small, missionary, activity cells. Form (or reform) a small group in a sending church—or among a number of congregations—to pray, plan, and practice skills needed to carry out any of these activities that apply:

Securing and enhancing staff support and zeal, without which little can be done.

Integrating a missions focus into congregational plans, prayers, and budget. Promote the Perspectives class or similar mission courses, among churches.

Providing materials and information to churches, agencies, and field workers.

Providing brief, poignant reports to pastors, to announce to the congregation.

Church planters must proactively prepare themselves before they arrive at their target audience.[79] One of the most valuable pre-missionary learning activities is to start, lead, and reproduce cell groups that are tiny training flocks that do all the ministries that the New Testament requires of a congregation. Practice the skills needed to worship, teach, evangelize, train leaders, and organize in a different culture. New missionaries on the field seldom do what they have read in books and heard in lectures. Rather they mostly practice what they have done before, in their home church. Skills that need practice may include:

---

[79] *"Come, Let Us Disciple the Nation,"* an interactive, software-based by Patterson and Currah, may be downloaded from <www.paul-timothy.net/dn/>.

- Integrate evangelism and church development with mercy ministry.

- Evangelize through families and networks of friends.

- Organize so that believers and congregations serve one another.

- Interact in highly relational small group settings.

- Include children as active participants in worship and teaching.

- Build a foundation of obedience to Jesus' commands.

- Adapt worship, including communion, to tiny cell groups.

- Mentor leaders in the way the apostles did for reproducing churches.

- Acquire the language[80] and bond in love with the people and their culture.

- Promote mentors in congregations and mission agencies who mobilize self-supported tentmakers.

Most of the remaining and neglected people groups (about one-third of the world's population) live where authorities ban or limit the activities of professional missionaries. There the Lord sends workers like Aquila and Priscilla who have vocations that officials permit. Consult with Christian businessmen and other experienced persons who might advise and expedite small businesses or other viable vocations.

Vision Statement

Mission agencies, instructors and field coordinators can help sending-church action groups to agree on a vision that includes the kinds of activities that participants can start practicing now. Consider this portion of a sample vision statement:

---

[80] For helps with learning a language and with bonding to a people group see <www.instantweb.com/l/linguahouse/How-to.html#LAMP>.

Indigenous flocks multiplying within a currently-neglected people group that is receptive and reachable, with local leaders at all levels, obeying the Lord Jesus Christ, and doing the ministries required in the New Testament.

Indigenous churches

Indigenous congregations are neither mere preaching points nor task agencies with specialized personnel, but fellowships of any size rooted in the culture of the local area and sustained by nationals without outside funds and control. Participants' activities might include the following:

- Mission course alumni enlisting and informing prayer partners to intercede for a specific, unreached people group.

- Missionary trainees in big cities seeking to work with people of the same culture if possible, before they go to the field.

- Sending churches and agencies sending short-term workers to gather information about how to prepare for earnest, long-term ministry by teams that include field workers who are culturally-proximate to the adopted people.

- Missionaries practicing and imparting to national workers culturally-relevant methods and appropriate technology that allow flocks to multiply without outside funds and control, teaching biblical stewardship to national believers from the beginning.

- National leaders quickly taking the initiative and responsibility for witnessing, leading their flocks, coordinating regional work, and training novice leaders. If culturally-distant workers present Christ initially or prove too visible in ministry supervision, they can stigmatize the faith as foreign, thereby stifling the work for years.

Multiplying

National flocks reproduce as daughter flocks in a spontaneous movement by the Holy Spirit's power, as Jesus illustrated in Mark 4:1-32. Participants' activities might include the following:

- Assisting with small group reproduction before they go to the field where they will be able to equip new national churches to reproduce rapidly. Thus, participants will carry their mother flock's spiritual DNA to reproduce daughter and granddaughter flocks on the field.

- Sending churches praying fervently for their workers and for those who need Jesus, commissioning workers by the laying on of hands, praying for the Holy Spirit's power.

- Emergency relief and development workers planning to initiate such movements by integrating their mercy ministry with evangelism, church planting, and leader training, planning with national workers to phase out foreign help and control.

Within a people group

By common definition, a people group includes the biggest number of souls among whom the gospel can spread unhindered by barriers of government, economic differences, worldviews, race, mountains, and anything else that might stop the flow. Participants' activities might include the following:

- Looking into working through a mission organization that shares its own vision and biblical objectives. Avoid choosing an agency simply because it is familiar or had a glorious history.

- Recruiting workers who will see the task through to completion.

Neglected, receptive, and reachable

There is currently no known work or movement capable of reaching a people group that has proven receptive and amongst whom a sending flock means to initiate a reproductive work. Participants' activities might include the following:

- Sending churches gathering information to send workers where these conditions exist.

- Field workers shaking the dust from their methodology or their location if people fail to respond to Jesus in a reasonable time. Most workers who do this do not have to change their place of residence, but simply shift to another target audience or subculture. A noteworthy caution here is that lack of bonding by missionaries causes most failures, not rejection of Jesus.

With local Leaders at all levels

Nationals of the local culture lead the work from the start, with outside workers remaining in the background as temporary advisers and trainers. "A modern missionary ... is not intended to be a permanent factor in the life of an alien people. His work is to make Christ the permanent factor, and himself pass away on to other pioneer tasks as quickly as he can."[81] Participants' activities might include the following:

- Training, mentoring and modeling vital skills for new leaders who can easily imitate them as they mentor still newer leaders in their congregations and daughter flocks, as urged in 2 Timothy 2:2. Remember that classroom teaching alone cannot achieve reproductive training.

- Arranging for Bible translation, if needed.

- Demonstrating humble servant-leadership for nationals who will soon serve as regional overseers.

Obeying Christ

Flocks everywhere are to make disciples in the way Jesus said, by teaching them to obey all of His commands (Matt 28:18-20). Participants' activities might include the following:

---

[81] Alexander McLeish, "The Effective Missionary" in *The Indigenous Church* (London: World Dominion Press, 1928), 6.

- Teaching new believers to practice all that the Lord Jesus Christ commands, like the first church in Jerusalem did in Acts 2:37-47. Right away, the first 3,000 converts repented, were baptized, prayed, broke bread, learned and applied the Word, witnessed, gave generously, served the needy, and fellowshipped with fervent love.

- Encouraging flocks to reproduce.

Ministries required by the New Testament

Workers name and equip local elders to tend to what is still lacking in the new congregations, as Paul told Titus to do. Participants' activities might include the following:

- Allowing missionary trainees to practice beforehand all the ministries that the New Testament requires of a congregation.

- Quickly passing on skills to flock shepherds to do indispensable ministries, including those from the following checklist:

Checklist of Essential Christian Ministries

- ☐ Evangelism
- ☐ Prayer
- ☐ Healing
- ☐ Family devotions and spiritual warfare
- ☐ Good stewardship
- ☐ Counseling those who have personal or family problems
- ☐ Strengthening marriages and family life
- ☐ Correcting and restoring offenders
- ☐ Caring for the needy
- ☐ Teaching and applying the Bible
- ☐ Training shepherds by mentoring them
- ☐ Organizing to let all members have gift-based ministries

- ☐ Promoting fellowship within and between church bodies
- ☐ Watching over the flocks and warding off wolves
- ☐ Worshiping
- ☐ Reproducing as daughter churches
- ☐ Training and sending workers to neglected regions

Guideline 61
Mentor workers with proper authority.

Mentors should control every part of a trainee's life and do one-on-one tutoring, right?	Wrong! Mentors should assert Christ's commands and New Testament guidelines, but they must not control other details. Mentoring is not always one-on-one. Jesus mentored twelve, and Paul often mentored several co-workers.

Mentors serve with the authority that the Lord Jesus Christ has given to them. Do assertive mentoring when it is needed to fulfill the basic aim of all Christian training. Jesus, the great lover of our souls and forgiver of our sins, never wavered in his purpose for His followers. He said, "I will build my church" (Matt 16:18). He painted clear visions, gave precise instructions, issued absolute orders, and demonstrated single-hearted devotion to his mission. He wants His followers to evangelize the nations and invite the peoples to repentance and life. The urgency of bringing people to Jesus and of reproducing churches moves Christian mentors to give their time freely to train pastors for church reproduction.

Highly-educated Westerners, in general, find it hard to agree on outcomes and focus on them, because each individual seeks his own interests and personal affluence. Some younger adults, despite their search for spirituality and community, have little sense of purpose aside from enjoying friends and sensory stimulation. As a result, Western mentors fail to press for verifiable outcomes and their trainees doubt their congregations' willingness to plan and take action.

Westerners who mentor non-Westerners may encounter less resistance to the making and following of plans, yet they often err by letting Western concerns sidetrack them. Instead of concentrating on doing what Jesus commanded, they focus on better materials, ensuring workers' financial security, defining Christian maturity, cultural sensitivity to perceived enemies, and advancing their careers and organizational reputations.

To keep congregations reproducing, mentors often must provide highly directive counsel that keeps workers encouraged and motivated. Western mentors, who have found it hard to focus on outcomes, can learn to envision by faith, motivate with love, and plan with spiritual wisdom, by seeking to mentor those who are called and gifted for church planting and by allowing those with other gifts to do what they do well.

Mentors in a pioneer field must appoint shepherding elders, and not have congregations elect them. The democratic process is so highly valued in the West and so widely touted in some parts of the East, that popular elections of congregational elders often replace the Scriptural norm. In the West, it is not unusual for pastoral candidates to give campaign speeches and for there to be more candidates than offices, so that the membership can elect one candidate and reject another. In pioneer fields where new churches are not yet mature, someone who is experienced, like Titus, should appoint their elders (Tit 1:5).

Since shepherding stems from spiritual gifts that the Lord has given, why do some churches stipulate in their bylaws the exact number of elders they must have? The Lord may well give such gifts to more or to fewer shepherding elders than what the bylaws allow.

Since a shepherding elder's gifts do not disappear when his elected term expires, it would be more biblical for all who are gifted and qualified to be appointed as shepherding elders.

Mentors direct shepherding elders; they do not merely inform them. The scriptural task of the apostle who starts new congregations (Tit 1:5-9) is to appoint elders who meet certain qualifications. Where few men or women meet those qualifications, the apostle must teach, counsel, train, and reprimand the believers until some qualify as elders. The teaching ministry in the West has often been more an exercise in precisely defining words than in effectively making disciples of raw human material. Trainers must hold to the biblical standards for new leaders and bring willing trainees up to those standards. Only lay hands on (commission) those that qualify, while continuing to coach those who provide pastoral care while yet to become qualified.

Mentors spur on new shepherding elders and are patient with them. They do not discourage them by demanding perfection. The commands and promises of Jesus and his Apostles remain the most powerful motivators to obedient faith. If trainers continually present both the challenges and rewards of biblical leadership, then students who know and love Jesus Christ will respond enthusiastically. Paul asserted in Ephesians 4:11 that the risen Lord gives pastors and teachers to congregations. He always does, sooner rather than later. Part of the apostolic task is to identify them, to appoint them, and to mentor them, until they are effectively mentoring others, in turn.

Mentors must empower others and do not simply teach them, by delegating authority to them to perform pastoral ministries for their congregations. Merely teaching students risks enabling immature and carnal men to grab power and dominate congregations. That happens when trainers adopt mere cultural standards for leaders, such as advanced education, business acumen, affluence, and political influence. A wise mentor helps leaders to serve Christ and their congregations through personal acts of service, acting as a model to them. Such modeling often initiates mentoring chains; one person empowers another who does the same for others, in turn.

Jesus said to pray to the Lord of the harvest for new workers. When disciples do so, He does so. Most new workers come from the local population, not from some distant land. Jesus walked with his disciples, shared with them his personal authority, sent them to do ministry, listened to them give their reports, and gave new teaching that met their current needs. Should His followers do any less?

Amazingly, at the beginning of the 21st century, in spite of abundant evidence accumulated by mission researchers, too many of us still choose "promising" young men and send them off to Bible school or seminary to become the "future leaders of the flock". Choose for training and leadership only mature men who have already undertaken to lead their families with godliness and purity and witness through their social networks. After a few years of lay pastoral leadership, some of these should, indeed, seek advanced education.

Guideline 62
Write training materials that fit specific fields.

The best materials for training shepherds are those written by famous writers, right?

Not always. Often, local instructors prepare better materials because they know local, current needs. Let us see how to do so...

Sooner or later, nearly every church planting coordinator faces the challenge of writing training materials of some kind. Paul, the coordinator, wrote to the trainer, Timothy, "I urged you upon my departure for Macedonia, remain on at Ephesus so that you may instruct certain men" (1 Tim. 1:3). Patterson recalled:

At first I prepared pastoral training materials the same way I did seminary papers, and our pastoral students did not like them. Later, I learned to prepare studies in a better way, by writing as though it were a letter to a student whose needs I knew from recently visiting him. The sixty-five of my "letters" that were best received evolved into the *Train and Multiply*[82] studies that are now available in many languages.

In a mentoring relationship with novice leaders of new congregations, certain opportunities and challenges come up more frequently than others. These common issues are dealt with and offered as "meals" on the training "menus" of programs like *Train & Multiply*® and *Paul-Timothy* materials. But not always. The culture or religious background where you serve may need something new or better. So, you should not hesitate to write new training materials. In Western Honduras, eighty-six of Patterson's original pocket-sized studies were re-typed, re-formatted, re-edited, and published anew as a nine-volume Preparation and Multiplication series.

The Apostle Paul's letters to Timothy and Titus were training materials. They were so helpful (and inspired) that they have been preserved and continue to be read and followed around the globe to this day. A careful look at how Paul wrote 1 Timothy can provide some guidelines for writing your own materials, making adjustments to the form so as to fit your host culture. Prized-principles gleaned from Paul's teacher-to-student letters include the following:

Keep studies short, preferably in small, pocket-sized booklets, so that less experienced readers can work through them before your next meeting. It is no accident that the biblical pastoral letters are short. Paul may have written scores of such letters. More importantly, less-educated, novice church leaders often cannot read fast and they often cannot absorb a lot of theory. Better to err on the side of brevity than that of boredom.

---

[82] O'Connor adapted *Preparación y Movilización* from others of those early booklets. The nine Spanish-language manuals of *P&M* may be freely downloaded from <www.preparacionymovilizacion.ws>.

Write to a specific person and keep him in mind while writing. Timothy and Titus may have had many issues in common but maybe not at the same time. Their questions were hot issues for them, and Paul dealt with each one's concerns. When you write new materials, write them first for one person and personalize them. Later, when you want to use the same materials with others, you can remove personal references and make each booklet more generally applicable without losing the practical, urgent advice you gave earlier. When educated, theologically-informed types write about a subject with no local application, the result proves theoretical, dry, pedantic, and irrelevant, even if biblically true. Materials that come off the anvil of real church life can more easily provide helpful, timely truth and advice.

Deal with real, current needs of congregations. Paul had correspondence with Timothy and Titus who informed him of their churches' current challenges. When they had questions they could not answer, they would meet with Paul at an arranged location or send to him brief messages carried by travelers going between major centers of the Roman Empire. Once informed of their needs, Paul answered with inspired advice.

When writers try to write handbooks and practical theologies for churches about which they know nothing, the result is often silly. Without knowing the real questions, such writings only deal with one's own speculations or some professor's ideal ecclesiology. Worse is trying to write materials for another culture group, based on experiences from sterile Western churches that have never reproduced in the normal way. Interestingly, publishers churn out such materials in abundance.

Tie every main point to a truth or doctrine about God or Christ. There is as much pure theology in 1 Timothy as in other books of the New Testament. Neither the Lord nor any of the prophets and apostles wrote books of systematic theology. Paul thought theologically about practical issues and salted his pastoral advice with sound doctrine.

Some doctrines taught in 1 Timothy include:

- That the Lord is our King eternal, immortal, invisible, the only true God.

- That the Lord our true Savior, who desires all men to be saved and to come to the knowledge of His truth.

- That there is one God and only one mediator between God and men—the man Christ Jesus who gave Himself as a ransom for all.

- That God has created foods to be gratefully shared in by those who believe and know the truth.

- That one day we shall see the appearing of the Lord Jesus Christ, which will come about at His proper time.

Keep instructions clear with enough action points to make a plan for what congregations will do. Record the practical instructions and action steps that trainees plan to take. In 1 Timothy, most of Paul's verbs are active, purposeful ones related to the actual situation in the congregations at Ephesus.

Likewise, a test to apply to training materials is to ask whether the readers of a study will know what to do. If writers have only supplied concepts, theories, or ideals, then the materials have not prepared anyone to shepherd a flock; they have merely transferred data into students' memory banks or notebooks.

Emphasize the main themes of Christian life. Do not come into a church planting movement with your own agenda. Love directed toward the Lord complemented with practical obedience to His Word is the Most High's agenda. A melanoma cancer patient, now deceased, penned, "God is infinitely creative in the methods He employs to take our wandering eyes and rivet them on Himself."[83] Church planters can facilitate this divine purpose by emphasizing the main themes of Christian life.

---

[83] Dan Roelofs, *A Place Called Surrender* (Minneapolis: One Passion Publishing, 2002), xvi.

Writers frequently have a pet theology that they cling to. Oftentimes, they want all congregations to teach it. Or maybe they have had a certain spiritual experience and want every one else to seek an experience like theirs. Paul, too, had many exciting, spiritual experiences, but he did not mention any of those in 1 Timothy. The main goal of training leaders is to help believers to learn to love the Lord and one another while maintaining a pure heart, a good conscience, and a sound, obedient faith (1 Tm 1:5). All of the writer's advice must have that as its main purpose. Church members must learn to help each other to act as disciples of Jesus who lovingly obey his commands.

A few other guidelines which do not come from 1 Timothy, but are quite helpful, include the following:

- *Keep copies of your letters and lessons* and those of others so that you can edit them later into training materials. Timothy and Titus must have kept their letters from Paul and must have shared them with others, for the Church has preserved them to this day. Since those letters are part of the Scriptures men never edit them into another form. Since our letters to our trainees today will never be Scripture, others can edit them—revising and improving them, as the compiler of this book has done with Patterson's writings.

- *Provide something for every kind of person in the congregation to learn and do:* pastor, elder, deacon, men, women, children, rich, poor—even the cantankerous. While not every training booklet will have advice to deal with every church member, yet, over time, your training and materials will have to deal with many kinds of persons and needs. How can you gain that kind of wisdom? That may take many years of experience in your own church work and in dealing with novice leaders.

- *Get help from training specialists to make your training booklets better.* It helps a great deal to have a mentor with more years of experience than you have to review your writings.

- *Keep it interesting* with a catchy introduction, follow a simple story line, break it up into small learning pieces and provide self-testing questions and practical applications. Your host culture may have its own preferred format.

- *Make your best writing available to others.* You can set up a central office or an internet download site where your writings are available to others.

Guideline 63
Identify servants with a shepherd's heart.

Several workers in my area want to become shepherds.	In pioneer fields, ordination or licensing is proper if it means only what God's Word requires. When men add rules from another culture, they clip our wings.
I will recommend only those who meet the academic requirements for formal ordination!	Let us see how to identify those who should serve as leaders...

Identify new shepherds and appoint them the way Paul said to do it. If your purpose as a church planter is to multiply churches or cells—and it ought to be—then help your church-planting apprentices plan and arrange to turn over new groups to new shepherds as soon as possible (Acts 14:23; Titus 1:5). That is, do not encourage them to settle into a group and shepherd it indefinitely. To facilitate this, implement a 2 Timothy 2:2 leadership training chain reaction from the beginning. Establish new groups through apprentice shepherds, working toward four-level mentoring chains like the one Paul started with Timothy, who trained "reliable men that trained "others also."

Adding man-made requirements to those of Scripture for new leaders sinfully stifles the work of the Holy Spirit and contradicts His placement of gifts. Western clergy sometimes complain, "But there is no one beside myself who is qualified to lead!" It is true that new believers do not meet the qualifications of 1 Timothy 3:1 and should not to be commissioned as a pastor, for they are not yet "proven." But they certainly can gather their unbelieving friends to hear about Jesus the way Cornelius, Zacchaeus, and Levi did in the New Testament. They can shepherd their own families and share Christ with friends, which they normally will do when someone like Aquila and Priscilla mentors them behind the scenes. Recognize them as leaders when they do this, for they are already leading! It is a matter of truth and of sensing the working and gifting of the Holy Spirit.

Informal gatherings with these new leaders often develop into a cell group or church. Keep the perfectionists and legalists off their backs and then you can appoint them as "provisional shepherds." This encourages those who want to shepherd and who show an ability to do so. More than one church leader has expressed diplomatically that they prefer to reserve such positions of leadership for popular, well-dressed leaders who, as they imagine, will attract tithe-payers into their congregations.

In other cultures one seldom sees new cells or churches grow out of groups consisting primarily of mature believers. Groups led by mature Bible teachers almost never spawn a new group in that they reflect a "classroom mentality", as we will see below in the next guideline (#64). Rather new cells and churches normally arise from groups of new believers led by a novice shepherd who is mentored behind the scenes by a pastor, missionary, or a more experienced leader. Think "outside the envelope"! Appreciate the potential in zealous, obedient, and new believers who want teaching and coaching, but in a fresh new context.

So, how can one recognize those who will likely make good shepherds now and, maybe, elders later? Mikel Neumann reported from Madagascar that pastoral giftedness could often be seen in new small groups, just by watching the interplay among the members. When someone showed concern for others of the group by asking them to express their views that person often emerged as the group shepherd. Patterson said that in Honduras the most reliable way to detect a man that would be a good shepherd was to see if he shepherded his family. Galen Currah has seen in India and Southeast

Asia that those who thrived on gathering others around themselves served effectively as men of peace.

New shepherds emerge in three ways. Do not overlook any of them. Find them among converts, apprentices, and self-starters: 1) Help converts to begin shepherding their own families in their own home. Mentor them, and let the new flock grow around them and mature as their unsaved friends join in. 2) Let apprentice leaders practice leading your group, then start their own. 3) Open doors for dormant self-starters who are equipped to lead but have never been offered the opportunity to start. Light a fire under them!

The Lord's promise is clear: "It was he who gave some to be apostles, some to be prophets, some to be evangelists, and some to be pastors and teachers" (Eph 4:11). Scholars say that the word "gave" in the original language is a timeless verb, meaning that the Eternal One still gives such people to churches. Therefore, watch for such people. If they are not there, they soon will be.

When you see a man or woman responding to the Word of God with faith and obedience, approach them about leading a new group consisting of their family and friends, especially unsaved ones. If they are familiar with the traditional church they might object, saying that they are not capable or are unqualified. Offer to coach them from behind the scenes. Assure them that with the Lord's help, they can do it, and that you will be there to meet with them regularly over a number of weeks or months.

Guideline 64
Discern how and how long to mentor.

Is not mentoring
very time-
consuming?

It saves time if done right. Multiply
yourself in other leaders. Let us
discern how mentoring and classroom
teaching differ and when to use
either…

Mentoring has many applications. Choose among them according to a trainee's need, and mentor him as long as he needs it, tapering it off as he gains confidence, knowledge, and skills. The Holy Spirit uses Christian mentors in several powerful ways for the benefit of congregations and communities. Commonly practiced principles of Christian mentoring include these:

- Some Christians mentor others for non-pastoral purposes. Many Christian coaches, teachers, caring neighbors, and business associates let their light shine for Christ by giving loving attention and guidance in non-religious areas of life.

- Others make disciples of new believers and their families, establishing the foundations of obedience and faith.

- Parents train their children by example to pray daily and to feed on God's Word.

- Some counsel persons and families that have problems. This type of mentoring is often called "member care".

- More experienced Christian workers apprentice less experienced ones for church ministries, such as helping believers to do better counseling, to witness for Christ, to train others, and to implement mercy ministries.

- Shepherds and missionaries apprentice novice leaders, including shepherding elders and pastors, church planters, and other types of missionaries. They do so by training them the way Jesus and his Apostles did in the New Testament. For example, a pastor of a mother church may coach a less-experienced pastor in a daughter church.

Mentoring new leaders is perhaps one of the most neglected areas of vital, fruitful ministry among Christian educators today. Mentoring as a method to train new leaders was developed and used widely by God's people long before the man Mentor (from whose name the word derives) counseled Odysseus in Homer's *Iliad*. Today, secular educators and trainers take advantage of mentoring more wisely and widely than do most evangelical Christian training institutions. It is sad that so many Bible colleges and seminaries overlook such a biblical, proven form of education. So, many young people in training are being robbed of one of God's most precious endowments to His church. Patterson said:

> God used mentors to prepare me to receive Christ, lead my wife and me to a mission field, and to follow New Testament guidelines when we got there. Often I now hear someone mention similar fruit from mentoring, including in the secular world. No other educational practice produces as much fruit at the long-range, strategic level, especially when we let the Holy Spirit empower a chain reaction such as Paul told Timothy to start, as in 2 Timothy 2:2.

Mentoring prevailed among God's leaders in the Bible. Scripture shows many instances of mentoring. Some coached "one on one;" more coached a few at once. The size of the group must be small enough for all to listen to each other and to deal with their concerns. Mikel Neumann observed that "people discipled in groups usually have a better track record than those who depend on individual discipleship."[84] Jesus sometimes mentored twelve, other times three or even one. In Scripture, mentoring resulted in generational

---

[84] Mikel Neumann, Evangelical Theological Society (Orlando: November, 1998), photocopy, 4.

"chains" with several "links" of mentors whose apprentices mentored others, and so on.

Mentoring Chains in Scripture

- Jethro mentored Moses.

- Moses mentored Joshua and the elders of Israel. The Almighty originally gave the Ten Commandments for the use of newly-named elders. These included leaders of 10, of 50, of 100 and of 1000. The real shepherding took place in the small groups of ten (Exodus 18–20).

- Joshua mentored the other army leaders.

- Deborah mentored Barak.

- Eli mentored Samuel.

- Samuel mentored Saul and David, who became Israel's greatest king. Ahithophel and Nathan the prophet also mentored David.

- David mentored his army commanders and government officials, to establish the united nation of Israel. David also mentored Solomon.

- Solomon mentored the Queen of Sheba, who returned to her people with his wisdom in the form of Proverbs that applied God's law.

- Elijah mentored Elisha.

- Elisha mentored King Jehoash and others.

- Daniel mentored Nebuchadnezzar, who humbled himself before the Lord.

- Mordecai mentored Esther.

- Esther mentored King Artaxerxes, which resulted in liberation of God's people.

- Jesus mentored the apostles who established the Christian church.

- The Twelve mentored hundreds of other leaders, including Paul.
- Paul mentored Titus, Timothy and many others (2 Tm 2:2).
- Timothy mentored "faithful men" such as Epaphras.
- Epaphras and the other faithful men mentored "others also" which led to a chain reaction that resulted in dozens of new churches in Asia (Col 1:1 & 7; 4:12-13).
- Philip mentored the Ethiopian official who received Christ and was baptized in the desert.
- Priscilla and Aquila mentored Apollos for a much improved ministry.

For most ministries throughout the world, it is far wiser to mentor novice leaders on the job and to meet the needs of new cells and congregations than it is to send them away to a formal Bible school or seminary to learn an analytical, lecture method of education with a lot of theory. Such graduates may consider themselves to be professionals and expect to minister in congregations that can support the life style of a professional.

An exception to this rule is that some mentored lay leaders may benefit from more formal education, especially if they must communicate with more highly educated people in urban communities. But this should only be after months or years of tested practical service. We must consider prayerfully the potential value of various applications of mentoring for the church, keeping in mind that the final purpose for which the Almighty inspired Scripture was not simply to inform His people, but to equip them for every good work (2 Tm 3:16-17).

Mentoring New Shepherds Compared With Classroom Instruction

To train new shepherds in a movement of rapid church reproduction, we must distinguish formalized classroom instruction from mentoring as Jesus and his Apostles did it, remembering that pioneer fields cry for the mentoring of many novice pastors and cell group leaders. The comparison here between mentoring and classroom lecturing shows that we must balance the two as congregations mature. Wise trainers do both.

Physical Factors

Amount of Time Expected

Mentoring. Training new leaders is time-consuming. Paul mentored Timothy and Titus by spending much time with them and giving them fatherly care. When they matured in the faith and outgrew the need for such intensive care Paul left them to train other leaders. Their mentoring tapered off but they kept it up as they passed on what they learned from Paul to newer leaders. Just as newborn babies need much personal attention, new leaders and new congregations need mentoring until they are doing what the New Testament asks of them.

Classroom. Classroom teaching is more time-effective. It works well for more mature leaders who no longer need the intensive care, and whose congregations are doing what the New Testament requires.

Location

Mentoring. Location is not important as long as two-way communication occurs between all present.

Classroom. Lecturers usually prefer a classroom designed for one-way communication.

Seating Arrangement

Mentoring. Trainees form a circle or some other comfortable arrangement that allows easy interaction. When modeling skills, mentors may travel with trainees, or Mt with them sit during informal activities, like Jesus did the Last Supper.

Classroom. Students usually face the same way, seeing mainly the backs of other students' heads.

Frequency of Sessions

Mentoring. Where mentoring is the primary method of training new leaders, sessions are less frequent, with reading and fieldwork done between sessions. Patterson related that he normally held sessions every two weeks with his key national area coordinators in Honduras. He would travel from La Ceiba, Honduras (where he lived) to communities far away.

Mentors meet more often for new congregations and less often for those who live far away or those for whom transportation is difficult.

Classroom. Classes are normally daily for regular students in institutional degree programs. For a particular course, sessions are commonly two or three times a week.

General Acceptance and Enrollment Factors

General Acceptance

Mentoring. Mentoring as a vital part of Western evangelical theological education has limited acceptance. Relatively few educators mentor in a disciplined way or teach the value of it. Observations in movements where congregations reproduce, however, reveal that someone is mentoring new leaders in some way.

Classroom. Especially for more mature leaders, classroom instruction is almost universally accepted as the norm.

Expectations for Enrollment and Field Work

Mentoring. Mentors train potential leaders who meet the biblical qualifications for "elders," who are spiritually mature and, for example, keep their children in order. They normally do not add to the biblical requirements, lest they deny the pastoral vocation to persons whom the Lord has gifted for it. Crucial to understanding mentoring is seeing that trainees are required to work with a flock of some kind or a definite, current ministry. In a pioneer field, the congregation may begin with one's family and grow into a church or cell group. Trainees put into practice immediately what mentors help them plan and prepare for—applying assignments with their family, congregation, or ministry group.

Classroom. When Patterson taught in the original, traditional Honduran Bible Institute (before he modified it drastically to be the Honduras Extension Bible Institute), he and other professors often enrolled single young people who were not proven in service and as a result failed to meet the biblical requirements for an elder. They were not mature enough to gather a flock or lead a group that includes mature heads of families. Graduates who became pastors did so because they studied a certain number of years for a diploma that only demonstrated that they could recapitulate memorized material for examinations.

Size of Group

Mentoring. Mentors seek to keep the group small enough so as to listen and respond to each trainee. They help each one plan what his respective flock will do during the next few weeks. Christ occasionally took three of the Twelve apart for special counsel.

Classroom. Professors often seek larger classes. Floor space sometimes determines class size rather than learning dynamics.

Duration of Training by Instructors

Mentoring. Mentors continue intensive time with trainees until they and their respective congregations no longer need it. The interaction is too time-consuming to continue indefinitely. Jesus phased it out with the Twelve, as Paul did with Titus whom he left in Crete to prepare others (Ti 1:5-9). He also left Timothy in Ephesus to do the same (2 Tm 2:2). Once a leader can carry on ministry without the mentor's help or if a congregation is functioning well, mentors phase out the personal interaction. Ongoing training then takes the form of more conventional lectures or workshops. Mentoring may resume, however, for a special need such as a change in ministry or a personal matter, such as when Paul wrote Philemon, a house church leader, about the matter of slavery. In this sense, mentoring never ends. One missionary put it this way: "Phase out is the farewell period when missionaries overtly and intentionally pass the baton of leadership to national leaders."[85]

Classroom. Degree requirements, class schedules and semester calendars determine the duration of the teaching, often without reference to the maturity of a student's congregation or ministry.

Relationships

Between Instructor and Student

Mentoring. Ideally, mentors show love, care, and interest. Paul shed tears for new leaders in training (Acts 20:31).

Classroom. For leaders who are mature enough to make their own application of the material, the teacher's main concern is normally less personal and focuses on how well students grasp the subject.

Between Students

Mentoring. As among Jesus' disciples and in Paul's apostolic bands, mentors enable interaction between trainees who serve one another and participate together in current ministry. No students worked alone. They traveled by twos or small groups to minister while they learned.

Classroom. Professors generally give only minor attention to students' interaction except for special events or to keep order.

Interaction with Congregations

Mentoring. Mentors train leaders as part of normal church life. After Pentecost, training took place while raising up or shepherding congregations and also as apostolic bands traveled to sow the seed in new areas. Wherever the apostles made disciples, churches or urban cells multiplied. Cells are small churches and may be part of a larger

---

[85] Gailyn Van Rheenen, "Learning... Growing... Collaborating... Phase Out," *Evangelical Missions Quarterly,* January 2000, 44.

one. New Testament congregations met in homes and were part of an interactive, citywide "church" that was a network of tiny house churches or cells.

Classroom. Imbalance in education easily occurs when professors limit teaching exclusively to an institution isolated from the rest of the Body of Christ. Even in a church building, classroom teaching can be quite disconnected from the life of the church members and the community.

Interaction with Society

Mentoring. Mentors keep new leaders in touch with current events that affect their work. John the Baptist's imprisonment and death, for example, profoundly affected Jesus' disciples. Paul's companions were constantly influenced by community events such as the riot in Ephesus. Mentors make sure that their students involve themselves with community matters that relate to their faith and morals.

Classroom. Patterson relates, "Early in my ministry, while teaching in an institution, I purposely shielded students from outside influences. I soon saw that imbalance occurs if teachers have little or no involvement with outside society and who deal with current events only to prepare for ministry in the far future."

View of Students

Mentoring. A perceptive mentor's image of the leaders-in-training includes hands to serve, feet to spread the gospel and heart to obey Jesus in love—a balanced body. Mentors consider them as student-workers or apprentice-pastors who serve in a ministry from the beginning. Mentors help them take on responsibility like Paul did, as they grow in knowledge and skill.

Classroom. Patterson explains, "In our traditional Honduran Bible Institute before we mentored, we gave more attention to scholarship. We expected our trainees to be good students, but not necessarily servant-leaders. Classroom teaching sometimes aims too exclusively at a student's ears and brains, but not toward their hearts and hands."

Formality of the Educational Structure

Mentoring. Mentoring can be informal and spontaneous or totally formal with scheduled sessions and policies as firmly structured as for classroom training. It gives the wrong impression to say it is always "non-formal." Patterson recalls from his time in Central America:

> We began mentoring Honduran pastors for one, two or three years, until their congregations were doing the ministries that the New Testament requires. We used our much-loved menu that offered a variety of modules written for new churches. This made it easy for congregations to do them in the order that they needed them. We found that a good menu monitors both student's progress and his congregation's progress. We gave students certificates when their congregations achieved new levels of development.

It discredits mentoring to assume that it is only for students with a problem or only an occasional unscheduled chat in a teacher's office or hallway. The fact that it often places more emphasis on the immediate implementation of learning content and character development should not lead anyone to assume that its structure must be less formal.

Classroom. Formality is consistent; classrooms and degrees require a formal approach to education. More emphasis is put on cognitive content and standard examinations.

Organizing to Educate

Mentoring. Mentors try to serve in harmony as a team or interactive body, as Scripture requires in 1 Corinthians 12, Romans 12, and Ephesians 4:11-16. A mentor serves those with other spiritual gifts while they serve him with theirs. Normally mentors work closely with a congregation, network of congregations, or an educational arm of a church association or mission agency.

Classroom. Professors organize in departments for the sake of specialization. Imbalance occurs when professors isolate their teaching from other New Testament ministries or, as we have seen, from local churches.

Church Participation in Curriculum Development

Mentoring. Mentors help congregations provide the arena for training leaders. New Testament churches sent out apostles to make disciples in neglected areas and trained new leaders in the process.

Classroom. A congregation's participation in classroom training is nil or perfunctory if professors ask pastors merely to recommend a theological student. It also weakens the students' application of material if professors implement internships too long after regular learning has taken place—or too late for meaningful involvement by the congregation in curriculum development.

Team Ministry

Mentoring. Mentors view team ministry as the New Testament norm, not merely an option. Every passage that describes how to use spiritual gifts requires it. Mentors ask other mentors to help students with special needs while small teams are temporary and task-focused, not permanent; no permanent apostolic teams appear in the New Testament.

Classroom. Professors seldom teach as a team or require team-work between students for most of what they learn.

Recognition of Student's Work

Recognition of Achievement

Mentoring. Mentors recognize pastoral or evangelistic achievement. Assessment of learning depends mainly on results in ministry. Teaching is good only if the students do good ministry. Paul the apostle did not rely on written credentials, though neither did he condemn them.

Classroom. Professors praise students who do well on tests and acknowledge achievement with diplomas, degrees, certificates, or public honors.

Motivation

Mentoring. Mentors help students to aim for effective service for the Lord Jesus Christ and His church and to obey Him in love (Jn 14:15; Heb 13:17).

Classroom. Professors urge students to aim for good grades and, although inadvertently, to compete for honors. Competition, if it leads to rivalry, is listed in Scripture with murder, drunkenness, and adultery as a wicked act of the flesh!

Professional Recognition

Mentoring. Mentors normally are not concerned with professional credentials. Mentoring, even when producing excellent results, usually goes unrecognized by educational institutions. Field practitioners who value results higher than formal credentials recognize skill acquisition.

Classroom. Institutional recognition opens doors for paid positions and offers credentials that are widely accepted.

Objectives and Commitments

Vision and Long Range Purpose

Mentoring. Mentors aim for the same results as the apostles had. Wherever they mentored new leaders, flocks multiplied.

Classroom. Professors often aim with stronger emphasis for such ideals as academic excellence, increased enrollment, growth of the institution, and its positive image.

Students' Commitment

Mentoring. Student-leaders commit to a shepherding ministry from the outset of their training, or at least to shepherding their own families as the core of a new cell group or church. Their education integrates practice of additional pastoral skills as they move forward. Mentors push them into the swimming pool from the very beginning—but into the shallow end, requiring that they do only what their level of training allows. They do no pulpit oratory, for example, while still taking child's steps as new leaders.

Classroom. Students often commit more consciously to completing units of study or degree programs. In some programs, they commit to internships that are quite separate from classroom learning.

Teacher's Commitment

Mentoring. Mentors commit to listen, or in some other way learn, first what the student is doing with his congregation and ministry so as to detect current needs and ministry opportunities. Mentoring includes modeling the corresponding skills. Mentors mix fieldwork with teaching the Word, history, doctrine and any other relevant discipline. A mentor works in cooperation with other instructors or mentors with skills in areas that he lacks. Mentors help students plan activities for their congregations or ministry groups and hold them accountable to follow through.

Classroom. Professors commit more consciously to preparing a presentation well, assigning ample reading that is relevant to the subject and communicating in a way that assures understanding.

Who Benefits

Mentoring. Inexperienced leaders need mentoring. Experienced leaders who are making a career change or are introducing a new ministry/project for which they lack orientation also need mentoring.

Classroom. Institutional education is most effective for those who require mastery of vast amounts of systematic knowledge.

Ability to Resist False Doctrine

Mentoring. Training new leaders by mentoring is more common in newer mission fields where movements of church or cell group reproduction take place spontaneously. A fervent faith in Christ, an awareness of the work of the Holy Spirit in people's lives and a devotion to the Word of God almost universally characterize such movements. Mentoring in this context has an almost universal record of sticking with Christ-centered teaching by people filled with the Holy Spirit. The only false doctrine that appears to be very common is legalism.

Classroom. Through the centuries, it has been observed that traditional, academic, theological institutions have often bred false doctrine and have become excessively rationalistic, as witnessed through many Ivy League schools within the USA and European universities. In some countries it is hard to find a seminary that teaches the authority of the Bible and that focuses on Jesus Christ, as Lord, Savior, and Friend. Especially in older seminaries and Christian colleges, teachers often spend much of their time contributing to or correcting—depending on the circumstances—the errors of the last generation of professors.

View of Leadership for Those Trained

Mentoring. Mentors evaluate leadership from a congregation's view. Mentors consider students to be leaders only if they lead. Teaching is not leading. Mentors move their trainees from one point to another. This movement includes growth in Christ-like character, which requires a corresponding increase in ministry involvement by serving others in a practical way. True leaders initiate and continually improve those ministries that the New Testament requires of a congregation and bring a high percentage of its members into active service.

Classroom. Patterson recalls how he trained new leaders in the original Honduran Bible Institute. "I failed to balance classroom instruction with relational mentoring. As a result, students confused leading with merely teaching and led few people in their congregations into active ministry."

Reproduction

Mentoring. Where the greatest need is to multiply churches or cells, mentors train in a way that new trainees imitate and pass on at once, training others who train still others. Jesus commanded His disciples to do only what they had seen Him do first in a way that they could easily imitate. Paul told the Corinthians to be imitators of him as he imitated Christ (1 Cor 11:1). He trained Timothy and Titus to start a chain reaction. One trained others who immediately began training still others (2 Tm 2:2; Titus 1:5). New leaders begin almost from the beginning to train newer leaders in newer churches or cells. Jethro advised Moses in Exodus 18 along similar lines. For new leaders mentors "lower" pastoral training standards until they are simply biblical standards, to facilitate reproduction.

Classroom. Reproduction is seldom a conscious purpose of the teaching, except when professors expect graduate students to teach the same subject in the same or a similar institution. Institutional pastoral training seldom relates instruction to church multiplication.

Adaptation to Political and Economic Factors

Mentoring. Roughly one third of the world's people, for political reasons, has little or no access to institutional training and must meet in secret. Another large segment of the world's population know mentoring as their dominant learning style, which enables teaching content to be transferable as in 2 Timothy 2:2, for multiplying churches or cells.

Classroom. Institutional theological education adapts better to the following conditions: 1) Sufficient affluence to build campuses and pay salaries and tuition. 2) High enough education level to assimilate intensive input. 3) Enough well-established churches to employ and benefit from professionally trained clergy.

Source of Income

Mentoring. Mentoring new leaders is not normally a viable source of income. Mentors do not view it, by itself, as a professional vocation, but rather as one of a number of duties required by the New Testament of any leader. Pastors trained by mentoring consider that to mentor others is a normal and biblical pastoral duty, the same as preaching, giving member care or serving communion, for which they do not normally charge a special fee.

Classroom. Professors often view teaching being their main duty as salaried Christian leaders. Their profession serves as a viable and legitimate source of income.

Teaching Methods

Criteria for Using Technology to Communicate

Mentoring. When modeling pastoral skills or other activities that new leaders are to imitate and pass on, mentors use only equipment that is available to them—they use a light baton for rapid replication. Especially when training workers for a pioneer field, mentors use only those aids that provide an affordable and reproducible model.

Classroom. For training mature leaders, professors often seek the latest and highest technology that budgets allow. The primary concern for selecting equipment is effective classroom communication, usually without considering if the method is transferable to others in the students' fields.

Teaching Style

Mentoring. Mentors give much emphasis to modeling pastoral skills, discipline, and character on the job. Mentors respond at once to students' ministry needs and opportunities, by observing, listening, encouraging, and demonstrating skills. Such demonstration, if not possible in a church context, often takes the form of role-playing. Jesus did not simply lecture nor did he only teach leaders-in-training what they could learn for themselves. For example, He answered questions with questions such as "Haven't you read in the Law?" Interaction is evident in much of Jesus' teaching, as He responded to questions, comments and assaults. Mentors consider this interaction to be especially important if one's ministry or congregation is to remain "cutting edge."

Classroom. While lecturing, professors do not normally encourage much interaction with or between students. Questions might take place at the end of the class hour.

Teaching Process

Mentoring. Training includes modeling skills and discussion sessions. In the discussion sessions mentors normally do six things. They:

1. Pray for guidance.

2. Listen to each student's report on work done and the condition of the people they are mentoring, pastoring, disciple making, or serving in some other way.

3. Plan. Normally a student's plans flow from his weekly report or update. Mentors then ask students what they plan to do with their people and—often more importantly—what their people will do, too. Plans usually consist of specific activities to be done in the next week or two. Mentors often use a menu that lists ministry options to facilitate planning. Help each trainee to make their own plans.

4. Review studies done.

5. Assign new studies. Normally these correspond to the plans.

6. Pray for power to carry out the specific plans.

Classroom. Research and subject mastery, lesson objectives, organization of material, and choice of learning exercises precede delivery. Professors give more importance to their responsibility to communicate knowledge than to the student's ability to pass it on immediately to others. Patterson recounted:

> A young Honduran pastor had graduated recently from a Bible Institute, in which I had taught. He had neglected the Lord's Supper for several months, so I asked him why. He replied by explaining the doctrine of the Holy Eucharist, its meaning and purpose, citing 1 Corinthians 11. I repeated my question, asking why he had not served communion. Again, he cited by rote what he had memorized about the Lord's Supper in the Bible Institute. I asked a third time and he exclaimed, 'Oh! You mean we should practice it! I thought that teaching it correctly was what mattered.' How inadequately we had taught him!"

When Trainers Prepare What They Impart

Mentoring. Extensive preparation by the instructor often takes place after listening to a student's report on personal issues, a congregation's needs, or ministry opportunities, instead of before a session. That is, mentors use the menu approach to teach in response to current needs of students or their congregations. Mentors listen first as students relate their congregation's progress. Mentors ask questions. Then, normally over the next week or two, mentors prepare studies to deal with the needs and ministry opportunities that students reported. The resulting materials usually prove helpful also for other trainees.

Classroom. Professors normally prepare class material and outlines before entering the classroom.

Application and Order of Teaching Content

How Soon Students Apply What is Taught

Mentoring. Mentors set the stage for immediate application in a new leader's life, family, society, cell group, or church.

Classroom. Professors expect application, but not normally as immediate. Professors seldom apply teaching to immediate ministry opportunities that students currently face. Sometimes professors hope only for some vague future application.

Curriculum Categories

Mentoring. Mentors categorize truths under verbs, titles which plead and push for action. Mentors create teaching content around church, community, or family activities. Teaching modules deal with action balanced with abstraction. Mentors present doctrinal truths together with plans to edify the church body at its current stage of growth. Mentors link abstract content to preparation for immediate tasks, such as when the Lord gave instruction to the Seventy to evangelize Judean villages (Lk 10).

Classroom. Professors generally categorize truth more often under titles that use static, abstract nouns. Professors present material in a logical and analytical order, comparing similar concepts and listing them together. A unit might deal with all of God's attributes, for example, rather than focusing on one of them and using it to define tomorrow's ministry plans, by developing its implication for people's lives.

Scope of Focus

Mentoring. Mentors integrate widely different disciplines and applications, focusing them all on the edification of a person, project, or church body, which is the integrating factor. Each of Paul's Epistles taught a variety of doctrines bundled together but related to the current life of a congregation or individual dealing with others. Mentors verify first what a particular student's congregation or ministry lacks.

Greater flexibility facilitates holistic education tied closely to field ministry. Mentors deal in the same session with whatever disciplines help to edify the students and their congregations or whomever they serve.

Classroom. Professors limit instruction for each class normally to an area that is well-defined in cognitive and analytical terms. Professors relate the subject to other disciplines only when a logical presentation requires it. Focus from an intellectual viewpoint is often sharper because it is limited to one area.

Order of Presentation of Content

Mentoring. Mentors often use a menu. Students select content from different sources as required by current situations. Jesus said a good teacher in the Kingdom of Heaven is like a householder who brings forth treasures from his storehouse, things both new and old (Matt 13:52). As already cited, extensive preparation of material often follows a session, in response to students' reports of needs or ministry opportunities.

Classroom. Professors prepare material ahead of class time and normally limit it to one subject. Professors follow its outline closely.

Materials and Sources

Use of Materials

Mentoring. Mentors use any relevant material. If mentors write, edit, or compile materials, they present it in a menu format so that new leaders can easily select options that edify their people at their current stage of development and need. For example, the pastoral training program *Train & Multiply* uses a menu approach with sixty-five small textbooks, so that students and trainers can easily select material written specifically for current needs, problems or ministry opportunities of a student's new church or cell group.

Classroom. Teaching and reading assignments often follow one or more textbooks written specifically for the subject, with little emphasis on options.

Authority and Foundations

Mentoring. Since mentoring is disciple making on a leader level, mentors base it on the divine authority of the Lord Jesus Christ and His apostles. Jesus commands explicitly in Matthew 28:18-20 to make disciples "by teaching them to obey His specific commands". The first New Testament church in Acts 2 exhibited this obedience by obeying all of Jesus' basic commands. He commanded over forty things, which can be summarized in the seven basic commands that the first disciples obeyed in Acts 2:37-47: repenting of one's sins in faith, being baptized, breaking bread together, loving one another (as seen in their fellowship), giving, praying and making disciples.

Jesus' commandments are the foundation for all ministry; He is the Rock. Building on it means to obey His words (Matt 7:24-27). Bible doctrine, as such, is not the foundation; Christ and the believer's relationship with Him are. Mentors first establish a relationship of loving, childlike obedience to Jesus (Jn 14:15; 15:14). This is foundational—the first floor of the "building". The written Word and doctrine are the second and third stories and on up forever. For all eternity those who know Jesus will learn more and more about God. New Testament curriculum builds upon the verb-oriented commands of Jesus and his Apostles, so that students' congregations soon practice all ministries that God requires.

Classroom. Christian professors normally recognize the authority of Scripture, but give less attention to building ministry on the foundation of obedience to the specific commands of Jesus. Patterson recalls, "When teaching in our original, traditional Honduran Bible Institute I failed to balance abstract doctrine with obedience to Jesus' commands. Students overlooked submission to the living Word, Jesus Christ. They considered the foundation of theological education to be only knowledge of the written Word, expressed in propositions. Their flocks were unhealthy until we corrected that."

Use of Scripture

Mentoring. Mentors use the Bible, especially the New Testament, not only as content for teaching but also as the norm for how to practice evangelism, confirm repentance, organize congregations, conduct worship, relate to other congregations, train leaders, and deploy missionaries.

Classroom. Patterson explains: "At first, while teaching in the original Honduran Bible Institute, I used the Bible almost exclusively as content for my teaching, but not for church practice. As a result, my student's churches seldom used Scripture as the norm for the way they practiced some of the activities taught of within the pages of the New Testament."

Responsibility for Training New Pastors

Mentoring. Mentors aim for pastors and shepherding elders to take the main responsibility and initiative to train the workers for a neglected area. A mission agency or educational program may provide guidelines, tools, and some help with teaching, but should not take the primary responsibility from pastors. In pioneer mission fields, it is essential for normal church multiplication that congregations assume this responsibility. A congregation's apostles (the "sent ones" that Ephesians 4:11-12 promises to churches) start the process in a neglected area, as seen in 2 Timothy 2:2 and Titus 1:5.

Classroom. Faculty of an educational institution tends to assume the main responsibility for preparing mature Christian leaders. Patterson affirms, "If the faculty of a theological institution lacks the pastoral gifts, then they will produce preachers instead of pastors. Students may learn well but will not shepherd their flocks as a result of their professor's teaching. They will merely teach them. They fail to lead them into the gift-based ministries required by the New Testament."

Chapter 5

Pass on a "Light Baton"

Guideline 65
Equip sending churches like the one in Antioch.

A sending congregation is one like the church in Antioch, through which the Holy Spirit sent members whom the risen Lord had gifted to serve as apostles (Acts 13:1-3). They are the "sent ones" who leave behind their earthly possessions and go to neglected regions to make disciples. A sending church embraces the biblical truth that healthy, obedient congregations can reproduce in "chain reactions" of daughter, granddaughter, great granddaughter churches, etc. Reproductive mentoring, as has already been shown from 2 Timothy 2:2, expedites this reproduction: "The things you have heard me say in the presence of many witnesses, entrust to reliable men who will also be qualified to teach others."

Questions a Sending Church Should Ask about Missionary Team Building

Questions are many and while numerous answers exist, none is final. Use the checklists below to spur on churches in building teams and in solving team problems.

Jesus and his Apostles always worked as task groups, except when held in detention by authorities. To work alone often leads to discouragement, burnout, crippling decisions, and even to moral failures. Since many workers keenly desire to serve in a closely-knit community, let them do so in teams.

If possible, form several teams or task groups at the same time, with each team having a majority of nationals lead. Nationals should also serve as team leaders, while experienced expatriates coach them in the background. Sometimes mission agencies throw workers together blindly, expecting them to function together, without regard for their experience, gifts, skills, and interests.

God's work requires a wide variety of coordinated gifts and skill sets. The spiritual DNA that the team carries to reproduce the life of the mother church body on the field, in daughter church bodies, is best carried by a body—a team. Loners usually start weak churches which are deficient from birth, lacking certain vital ministries and spiritual virtues because their genetic code, spiritually speaking, is incomplete. A team, however, can easily model Christian character and unity for new national workers and congregations.

Checklist of Common Traits of Effective Teams

☐ Fewer then six workers.

☐ A balance of gifts and skills that allows a wide variety of ministry efforts.

☐ Continually learning of the local language and culture.

☐ Temporary, like a scaffold. (The national church remains the edifice that the Lord is building. He did not say, "Upon this rock I will build my missionary team.")

☐ Served together to plant and reproduce cell groups or small churches before going to another culture.

☐ Members of less than ten years' difference in age.

☐ Agreement on their vision, goals and general methods.

☐ Restructure as short-lived, task groups at least annually.

☐ If Western, team worship style separate from the emerging church's style.

☐ Specialization of tasks with freedom to make mistakes and some budgetary freedom.

☐ Change of intermediate goals and methods as an adaptation to the culture. (If they do not make at least one radical change during a year, then they are probably stuck in a harmful rut. Think outside the missionary envelope!)

Unfortunately, some mission agencies put so much attention on educational requirements that only academic types with the gift of teaching end up on the team—a devastating mistake!

Checklist of Common Traits of Effective, Mixed Expatriate-National Teams

☐ They maintain a balance of one expatriate to five or so nationals, and expatriates serve mainly in the background as coaches.

☐ They practice needed skills and transfer them without delay to national leaders. If team members lack necessary skills, then they should call in someone temporarily to model them.

☐ They compile a working agreement between a sending church or organization and any national church or organization that receives the team.

☐ They get on-going training to help them understand the host cultures and they adopt local cultural expressions.

Checklist of Common Perils that Effective Teams Avoid

☐ Spending more time maintaining the "scaffold" (missionary team) than building the edifice (the national church).

☐ Creating and maintaining a national scaffold (church planting team) after their own likeness. Nationals can repeat the mistakes and culturally-irrelevant practices of their missionaries.

☐ Making the expatriate team a model for the emerging churches.

☐ Seeking to increase the numbers of expatriates on the team, so that there are more expatriates on the team than nationals.

☐ Pastoring the national church as it emerges, instead of raising up locals for the pastorate.

☐ Allowing agencies to recruit and assign additional personnel to them without regard for field realities and needs.

☐ Settling in for the long term to accomplish short-term ministries.

Should the West Finance Local Ministries?

Why not send Western dollars to national workers who will serve for less pay and who already know the language and culture? This has worked well in some circumstances has also failed miserably in others. Donald K. Smith said:

> Dependency reduces self-respect because of an apparent inability to do anything other than receive. Lacking self-respect, the receiver may reject familiar cultural patterns and imitate the person or group that is the source of help. The consequent change is often not appropriate, creating a need for more help. A downward spiral results that leads to psychological or social dysfunction. The group helped is crippled in their ability to care for their own affairs.[86]

Partnerships works best when missionaries from overseas provide training and resources to "jump start" national mission endeavors. True partnership must ensure that all the partners contribute genuine resources and share decision-making authority.

To send money without proper accounting and accountability at every level of operation inevitably leads to problems and slip-ups:

- *Greed.* The dollars attract money-hungry workers and national organizations whose main motive is wealth—not church reproduction.

- *Fear.* National workers, fearing that the "pie" (the funds from the West) will be cut into smaller portions if they multiply new churches, fail to sustain their church planting movement.

- *Dependency.* National workers, especially pastors, soon come to rely on Western aid and neglect Christian stewardship within

---

[86] Donald K. Smith, "Dependency," unpublished paper, 1997.

their congregations. Herbert Kane surveyed healthy church movements throughout the world and found that the bigger, more effective movements were those that did not rely on foreign funds. Among the positive factors were those of relying on indigenous leadership structures and using culturally familiar forms of worship.[87]

- *Independent spirit.* National agencies with expatriate resources often operate without regard for the national churches that trained and supplied their personnel.

- *Disobedience.* Jesus' Great Commission, to go and disciple the neglected people groups applies to churches of both the East and West—not just to those that are geographically near to them.

- *Disorder.* When new, spiritually immature churches send untrained missionaries, they commit the errors mentioned under the questions listed above. Instead, new workers from a newly-developed field need to partner with experienced workers who mentor them, so they can follow the positive guidelines listed above.

- *Division.* If some workers receive pay from the outside and others do not, deep-rooted resentment and division almost always occurs.

Wayne Allen, professor of missions in Jamaica, reported from research on pastoral subsidies in the Caribbean that "the use of subsidy ... did not further the cause of Christ. In all three districts where it was used, church growth ceased. In the district where it was not used, growth continued. Clearly, there is something wrong with providing money for national pastors."[88] Allen provided these suggestions for subsidy use in those cases where it does take place:

- Foreign monies, if given, should be limited to nationals who are missionaries and evangelists.

---

[87] Herbert Kane, *A Concise History of the Christian World Mission* (Grand Rapids: Baker, 1982), 149.

[88] Wayne Allen, "When the Mission Pays the Pastor," *Evangelical Missions Quarterly*, April 1998, 181.

- Indigenous churches should assume responsibility for pastoral support as soon as possible.

- The indigenous missionaries who start churches are to follow the model of turning over the church to the locals in terms of supporting their own pastor.[89]

How long should missionaries stay?

Effective cross-cultural church planting includes not only knowing when and how to start, but also when and how to leave the field. Successful missions not only pioneer and parent new ministries, but they also pass that new work on to national leaders in the field. Harold Fuller[90] spoke of four "P's" in mission work: Pioneering, Parenting, Partnering and Participating. To these one can add a final P, Phasing out. Sending churches should ask their missionaries to answer these questions:

- Are the disciples baptized?

- Are they gathered into reproducing flocks?

- Are they obeying the commands of the Lord Jesus Christ?

- Are the essential elements of worship in place?

- Are national leaders reproducing themselves through sound biblical teaching?

Expatriate missionaries in the field should ask the same questions about their temporary scaffold.[91] Detlef Blocher warned, "Missionaries can stay far too long and then hinder the development of the local leadership."[92] The lasting edifice that Jesus Christ builds is the national church (Matt 16:18; Eph 2:19-22). Paul and his

---

[89] Ibid, 180-81.

[90] Harold Fuller, *Mission Church Dynamics* (Pasadena: William Carey Library, 1980), 287.

[91] More on scaffolding: Melvin L. Hodges, *The Indigenous Church* (Springfield: Gospel Publishing House, 1996).

[92] Detlef Blocher, "Good Agency Practices: Lessons from ReMAP II," *Connections*, June, 2004, 25.

companions served as a temporary scaffold that the put up and took down repeatedly (Acts 13–21). They would plant the seed, water the new growth, and then leave the new congregations in the hands of newly-appointed elders and move on to other ripe fields.

This scaffold mentality opposes the deadening permanence of many mission institutions and projects where the Lord's work is kept under foreign control, inevitably hindering an indigenous congregation's normal growth and reproduction. The scaffold approach detects the abilities of nationals, raises them up, trains them, and commissions them, so that they will, in turn, pass on the baton to others. Thus, missionaries soon work themselves out of a job and move on to new endeavors, rejoicing over the nationals whom Christ been raised up not only to replace them but also to reach out cross-culturally to other peoples. Indeed, healthy new congregations normally look beyond their own cultural borders. "As a lighthouse gives guidance to a ship, so vision helps us along the way to keep our eyes fixed on the goal."[93]—

Of the many thousands of distinct cultures that make up our world, several thousand (about 1/3 of the world's population) still lack churches that can reproduce within their culture. These include the "tribes" of Genesis 12 and the "nations" of Matthew 24 and 28 among which Jesus commanded His followers to make disciples. In the modern world, many from "unreached" people groups have migrated to other parts of the world. For example, Hindus of most castes may be found not only in India but also in Madagascar, West Africa and the Americas.

A people group can be defined as the largest number of people in an area among whom the gospel can spread to without being stopped by barriers of any kind. Barriers to the spread of the gospel might be political, economic, or physical such as a mountain range or the open sea. At the start of the 21st century, about 95% of neglected people groups were found North Africa, South Asia, and Indonesia. The world's non-Christian cultures can be grouped in several general

---

[93] The Alliance for Saturation Church Planting, *Essential Vision* (Crete, IL: The Bible League, 2000), 41.

categories that include Islamic, Hindu, Buddhist, Shinto, Taoist, Confucian, and secular-materialist.

Guideline 66
Decide wisely who should mentor new leaders.

Only old, white-haired workers with years of experience should serve as mentors of new leaders.

Not so! Often new shepherds are the best coaches for other new shepherds. They share the same concerns. However, an experienced worker should monitor their work.
Let's see who should mentor...

"The things you have heard me say in the presence of many witnesses, entrust to reliable men who will also be qualified to teach others" (2 Tm 2:2). When the time comes to coach new church leaders, three inescapable questions arise.

Question One: "Who should mentor new leaders?"

This question can take several forms:

- A perfectionist might ask, "Who should not be allowed to mentor new leaders?"
- A busy executive, "Whom can I delegate the mentoring to?"
- A controller, "Who is loyal to my position?"
- An insecure type, "Who else can mentor instead of me?"

- A well-balanced worker asks, "Whom do I know that is capable and available to mentor new church leaders in the way that Paul did?"

Wise missionaries seek whoever is available to mentor others. In pioneer fields, that may be a novice learner who is only a week ahead of his cousin, often with excellent results.

Question Two: "What if a trainee asks for help with something for which I lack experience?"

You do not have to know all the answers at once. Rather you can consult with your own mentor or other more experienced workers before you answer. Often the best help comes from someone who has failed, fallen on their face, their back, and both sides, and discovered what to do in the process. It also helps to have some good books on mentoring, like the present one. Take it with you when you go.

Many potential mentors lack experience and confidence, yet want to help newer leaders to grow. These need the right tools in their toolbox, like a menu that lists the basic commands of Jesus, as well as the main doctrines and ministries taught in the New Testament. Create your own lists or copy from those found in this book.

Question Three: "Who would pay any attention to me?"

Some potential mentors may say, "I am ugly and have little education. And my tribe used to be slaves. Why would a novice leader listen to me?"

A deep sense of insecurity plagues many people. This apparently was the case with Timothy whom Paul mentored to coach others. Paul's advice to Timothy was to be strong with help from the Lord, and to let no one despise his youth. Even people who do not want to be friends socially will seek out a mentor's advice, if he lets the Holy Spirit guide them when he mentors them.

These people need the strong assurance of their commission and gifting, just as Paul reminded Timothy of the gift he had received when the elders laid hands on him. Such trainers need constant encouragement, just as Paul encouraged Timothy, until they have grown confident in the Lord.

The same problem appears in disciple making on any level, when Satan attacks a believer's confidence. During worship, a shepherd asked older men to disciple the younger, but the older men felt incapable. Some said that that the younger men would not want them to interfere with their spiritual lives. The pastor asked the younger men to raise their hands if they wanted an older man to disciple them. Every one eagerly raised his hand without hesitation!

When women in a new church in Cucamonga, California, asked Denny Patterson to disciple them, she agreed on the condition that they would disciple a newer believer, in turn. Some were shocked at the suggestion! They felt incapable even though they had been believers for many years and had absorbed great amounts of good Bible teaching! So Denny would meet with them together, some-times over lunch and help them plan what they would do next.

Whom did the Apostle Paul recognize as potential trainers? In 2 Timothy 2:2 he called them "reliable … qualified to teach others". At Jerusalem some of the church leaders might have scoffed at the Galileans because of their country accent, but Jesus chose all of the original twelve from among simple men and personally mentored them.

Guideline 67
Commission and send out workers.

 Let us look at ways to help churches send missionaries on their way to neglected regions…

Find those whom the Holy Spirit has gifted to become "sent ones." When you find in your congregation someone like Barnabas, your next task is to train and send them to a neglected people or community (Acts 13:1-3). If you cannot train them yourself, then get help. It is an apostolic gif that moves believes to go do mission work to neglected populations where they use other spiritual gifts such as evangelism, helps, compassion, or teaching. A pastoral giftedness, on the other hand, normally ties a minister to a congregation, often permanently so. Workers with the pastoral gift yearn to shepherd a new flock and may find it hard to pass on this responsibility to local leaders.

Barnabas and Paul displayed the apostolic gift. Paul wrote repeatedly about his vision for many nations, and he could not even remember whom he had baptized in Corinth, for his heart was not tied only to that one congregation. Someone whose primary gifting was pastoral, however, would have remembered whom he baptized and probably would still have been in Corinth! If a congregation births a daughter church, someone with an apostolic gift would go away to work with it, whereas someone with pastoral gifting would stay with their mother church and help it reproduce by training and sending others.

The Lord promises to give apostles to churches (Eph 4:11). Unless a congregation is new and small, it can be sure that it has such gifted people, so it should detect them, train them, send them, and hold them accountable for starting daughter and granddaughter churches. However, a congregation is likely to fail to detect its modern apostles if it looks only for the traditional missionary stereotype.

Prepare harvesters for other cultures. The Lord prepared Jonah in a rather unpleasant classroom, but he needed a jolt! Workers need training in church planting, in making disciples of novice leaders, and in evangelism that does not extract converts from their families. Those sent out need a foundation in basic biblical doctrine and experience in regular, fervent prayer, in small group worship, in teamwork, and in mining the Word of God. Provide them with tools for bonding with another people and culture, learning a language without a disagreeable accent, and forming task groups with a healthy balance of spiritual gifts. Some workers, being too inexperienced to know their own spiritual gifts, imprudently take on ministries that do not correspond to their gifts or calling. If they do not correct this they will burn out within a few years. Thus, their mentors and supervisions need holy discernment.

Authorize workers formally. Lay hands on new workers to set them apart for specific ministries, that they may receive power and anointing from the Spirit of God for the task He has assigned to them. The leaders in Antioch did so for Paul and Barnabas in Acts 13:1-3. The Lord also gave Timothy a spiritual gift for his pastoral and training ministry through the laying on of hands by the elders (1 Tm 4:14). Such a commissioning should be made a solemn occasion and, as in the case of Paul and Barnabas, the congregation prayed and fasted first. Probably, there were many parting tears.

Write a letter of intention. It can prove wise for a congregation that has commissioned a worker for a specific ministry to give to him a letter stating in general terms for what gift-based ministry he has been commissioned and among what people he is to work. These stipulations should be spelled out by the congregation with any cooperating agency, before a new worker goes to the field. This action often saves both new and experienced ministers much grief. Do not leave it up to new workers to explain their intentions, for their wishes may too easily be overridden by a field director who wants to place them somewhere else, rather than where the team has been commissioned to work.

Take commissioning seriously. Some say the ritual of laying on hands is merely a symbol and therefore of minor importance. Such a view lacks faith, for the Almighty, by His grace, makes every symbol as strong as the reality it signifies, just as He does for the bread and cup of communion, the water of baptism, the written words of Scripture, and the spoken word of prayer. If those who lay hands on a new worker have this faith, then the Holy Spirit does in fact empower him. New workers often feel insecure in their ministry and find that their commissioning strengthens their confidence and their effectiveness.

Although Scripture mentions only the laying on of hands for those doing formal ministry, two common kinds of commissioning have evolved:

- *Formal ordination.* Formal ordination assumes that a council of pastors and elders from a number of congregations in the region has examined and recommended the candidate for ministry. This ordination is expected to be permanent and is usually recognized by congregations of other denominations with similar doctrine and practice. Ordination normally requires a candidate to have formal theological training or its functional equivalent in field experience.

- *Commissioning or licensing.* Often this is called a lay pastor's license. In most churches, such a license entitles one to carry out the same pastoral functions as an ordained pastor, but their position is generally not considered to be permanent. When a particular ministry is completed, one may need to be commissioned again for another term of service. Since it does not require a general ordination council, it is not accepted by all other congregations and denominations. When one goes to another church or mission agency, he may have to be commissioned again.

While these two forms of recognition have become our custom, we must be wary of non-biblical requirements for passing on authority to new leaders. Ordain and commission the new workers while avoiding needless traditions that may distract from their task. If a bad tradition hinders a congregation from obeying Christ's command to make obedient disciples, then diplomatically ask its leaders to choose between obeying God and obeying men. If they choose not to obey God, then consider shaking their dust from your feet.

Send out workers. Send out from mother churches those workers who have the apostolic gift, as the Antioch church did. They prayed with fasting and laid hands on Paul and Barnabas as a carefully chosen, experienced nucleus of a new team. Mark accompanied them as their helper (Acts 13:1-5). These men formed the core of a cross-cultural, church-planting team that was joined by others in the field. They went only to neglected fields that had no churches as later reported in Romans 15:20-21.

The apostles later returned to their sending church and reported what God had done (Acts 14:26-28). Regular communication with one's home church and supporting churches is essential. A mother church should recognize that its missionaries' ministries are an extension of their home church, such that new flocks are daughters of the home church. Commissioned this way by sending churches, workers go out fully authorized and empowered by the Lord to reproduce disciple making communities.

Evaluate their effectiveness. A potent sending church looks at ripe but neglected fields and prepares some of its members for the task of harvesting, and it may share this responsibility with a mission agency. Becoming a sending church does not mean it replaces the mission agency, although for some churches and fields doing so has proven viable. A sending church will recognize those who have a cross-cultural call, and will work hard to prepare them, authorize them, and send them in the power of the Holy Spirit to go and do what the Lord has commanded for unevangelized peoples. It supports them with prayer, finances and accountability.

If a sending church does not have enough people called to a specific field to form a task-group nucleus, it can ask sister churches to work together with it. They should gather additional task-group members when possible, who are culturally nearer to the people to be made disciples, as the apostle Paul did with Timothy (Acts 16:1-3). Wise field supervisors help them do so by cooperating closely with their sending churches and other organizations. The fieldwork is usually overseen by a mission agency, but the primary responsibility remains with the sending church to see that all neglected people groups are made disciples, as Jesus commanded. The task group from Antioch, for example, returned to the congregation to which they were accountable and gave their report (Acts 14:25-28).

Guideline 68
Uphold a high view of the flocks.

View the church through Jesus' eyes. The Lord loves his people so much that He gave His life for them. So let its leaders love and esteem their flocks with the same high view!

Like Joshua, prudent leaders hold a high view of the potential of the people they lead, as they work together as a body. Successful shepherds and missionaries believe in the power that God works through the church, the living Body of Christ. Those who rely too heavily on institutions such as seminaries, Christian organizations, and mission agencies neglect Christ's church as God's primary vehicle to do His work. Leaders who hold a low view of the church's ability to do God's work can become dictators and fail to motivate believers for ministry. Their congregations become program-oriented and institutional, lacking a vibrant, Spirit-filled life.

I think I finally see what church multiplication really is!

It is the devil who wants us to multiply programs, mission bases and institutions —not our flocks!

Right! Let us view our flocks as our Master sees them!

Do not listen to Satan who whispers the lie, "Your flock lacks power to extend Jesus' Kingdom. So why try?"

Conclusions

Missionaries holding a high view of a church know that it can do God's work, so they help churches raise up their own leaders, relying on the gifts that the Lord gives the flock to do its ministry. Such leaders stimulate churches to win the lost and to reproduce with its God-given power. Jesus' parables reveal that, like every other part of creation, the church—His Body and His Bride—has within her the seed to reproduce after her kind. As in Antioch, a Spirit-filled congregation sends its God-given apostles to carry its DNA to reproduce flocks in neglected areas.

Missionaries holding a low view of the church—and of their disciples—pass their doubts on to the emerging church which also fails to reproduce as it should. Such missionaries put their energies into strengthening the scaffold while weakening the building!

Following biblical guidelines, missionaries are to build the congregation and purposely to tear down the scaffold, gracefully stepping out of the way as Paul did. Steffen, in his book, *Passing the Baton*, recommended that an entry strategy should include an exit strategy from the start,[94] while Sharp warned, "A missionary that hangs around too long is equivalent to a wheat farmer who stays in the wheat field from May through September, digging around the tender plants ... telling the seeds how to adjust to the potassium in the soil."[95]

While our suffering world desperately needs hundreds of thousands of Christ-centered congregations, interestingly, at this time in history it is in the less democratic societies of the world where faith in Jesus is spreading most rapidly with hundreds of cell groups and new congregations—underground or otherwise—being formed every day of the year. It is in the democratic nations that the Christian movement has stagnated most. Consequently, to start new congregations in a wider scale, we must move past hoping for tolerant political leaders by adopting a more biblical doctrine and empowering thousands of local, lay leaders who will know how to do the same.

Our task, as the end of the age approaches, is to multiply obedient, Christ-centered churches in spontaneous movements of new flocks led by local shepherds, trained quickly and inexpensively and released for service. We must devote our prayers and energies to empower novice, home-grown leaders who will continually birth new congregations of new disciples. May the Spirit of Jesus Christ enable you to build up the His Body among the nations, quickly and joyfully turning the work over to those whom the Lord raises up to lead his people in joyful, loving obedience to Him!

---

[94] Tom Steffen, *Passing the Baton* (La Habra: Center for Organizational and Ministry Development, 1997).
[95] Larry W. Sharp, "Are We Really about Church Planting?" *Evangelical Missions Quarterly*, July 2005, 281.

Appendix

Two Training Curricula

Patterson spent roughly twenty years on the rural north coast of Honduras.[96] Churches were planted easily through his simple, imitable methods, for which he later earned an honorary doctorate from his alma mater, Western Seminary in Portland, Oregon. In this setting he penned and mimeographed more than 200 pocket-sized, pastoral training booklets, designed for poorly educated, novice pastors. Those original booklets (see Figure 20) were a work of art and of genius. Each one presented biblical doctrine, often with humor, designed to speak to the hearts of student-workers for practical Kingdom results.

Two later series of publications based on those original booklets include Patterson's *Train and Multiply*[R] and *Preparación y Movilización*. The *T&M* provides an entry level leadership preparation program geared primarily for helping those who train shepherds who reproduce flocks, especially in pioneer fields. Some have also used it effectively in urban areas to reproduce churches and cell groups. It emphasizes the starting of new churches and cells where none exist, by training novice leaders rapidly on the job in 2 Timothy 2:2 chain-reactions.

The *T&M* material consists of 65 small booklets keyed to a "menu" called the "Student Activity Guide." Trainers are to listen to their trainees first to find what their respective congregations need.

---

[96] On Patterson's ministry in Honduras, see Patrick O'Connor, *White unto Harvest: Triumph and Tragedy in Central America* (Portland: Enable! Media, 2001).

The trainer then refers to the *T&M* menu, a list of ministry activities with biblical and doctrinal content with recommended study booklets that apply to the trainees' flocks' immediate needs and ministry opportunities.

Figure 20
Original TEEE Pastoral Training Booklet, c. 1972

Although these simple-looking lessons appear elementary at first glance, they contain biblical doctrines for personal growth and ministry, following a "know, be, do" approach. Several experienced church planters commended that they learned more from *T&M* about pastoral ministry than they had in three or more years of seminary. About a third of the lessons deal with *knowing* and applying biblical doctrine, another third with *being*, that is Christian character as the foundation for service, and the other third with *doing* practical pastoral ministry. *T&M*'s user-friendly, uncommon menu approach to leadership development seems to have touched a live need among missionaries in many fields.

In Honduras, consistent use of *T&M* materials in mentored leader training results in continual outreach and new church plants without neglecting pastoral care. Its secret lies in raising up, training, and setting free for the harvest, men and women who are ready to work and need coaching, direction and sharpening. As a complement to Patterson's *T&M*, the author compiled in Spanish the *Preparación y Movilización* (*P&M*) manuals (see Figure 21). Both evolved from those early TEEE materials.

The nine *P&M*[97] manuals are currently available only in Spanish. With their 8½ by 11-inch workbook format the series is geared to shepherds and lay leaders in congregations that are already established. Reader-friendly throughout, each of its chapters recommends practical homework and offers self-examinations, along with a liberal number of graphics scattered through more than 100 pages per manual.

The *P&M* series adapts well to the disciple making networks created by *T&M* users while also proving useful to students and trainers who are not used to the menu approach. *P&M*'s 86 chapters can also serve as a kind of menu, much like *T&M*'s menu. *P&M* manuals also go more in depth and are intended for more advanced students than are the *T&M* booklets.

---

[97] *P&M* is freely downloadable from <www.preparacionymovilizacion.ws>.

Figure 21
Book One of *P&M* Pastoral Manuals

Bibliography

Allen, Roland. *Missionary Methods: St. Paul's or Ours?* Grand Rapids: Eerdmans, 1977.

Anderson, Neal T. *The Bondage Breaker.* Eugene, OR: Harvest House, 1990.

_____. and Timothy M. Warner. *The Beginner's Guide to Spiritual Warfare.* Ann Arbor: Servants Publications, 2000.

Barrett, David B., George T. Kurian and Todd M. Johnson, eds. World Christian Encyclopedia, Vol. 1 and 2. Oxford: University Press, 2001.

Bharati, Dayanand. *Living Water and Indian Bowl.* Delhi, India: Indian Society for Promoting Christian Knowledge, 1997.

Borren, Jean. *Mentoring Beginning Teachers.* York, ME: Stenhouse Publishers, 2000.

Brewster, Tom and Elizabeth. *Bonding and the Missionary Task.* Pasadena, CA: William Carey Library, 1982.

Brother Yun with Paul Hattaway. *The Heavenly Man.* Grand Rapids: Monarch Books. 2002.

Bubeck, Mark I. *The Adversary.* Chicago: Moody Press, 1978.

_____. *Overcoming the Adversary.* Chicago: Moody Press, 1984.

Burton, Sam Westman. *Disciple Mentoring.* Pasadena: William Carey Library, 2000.

Bush, Troy L. "Effective Church Planting: A Qualitative Analysis of Selected Church Planting Models." Ph.D. Southern Baptist Theological Seminary, 1999.

Covell, Ralph R. and C. Peter Wagner. *An Extension Seminary Primer.* South Pasadena: William Carey Library, 1971.

_____. *The Liberating Gospel in China.* Grand Rapids: Baker Books, 1995.

_____. *Pentecost of the Hills in Taiwan.* Pasadena, CA: Hope Publishing House, 1998.

Dayton Edward R. and David A. Fraser. *Planning Strategies for World Evangelization.* Grand Rapids: Eerdmans, 1980.

Demarest, Bruce A. and Gordon R. Lewis. *Integrative Theology.* Grand Rapids: Zondervan, 1996.

Elliston, Edgar J., ed. *Teaching Them Obedience in All Things— Equipping for the 21st Century.* Pasadena: William Carey Library, 1999.

Fitch, David. *The Great Giveaway: Reclaiming the mission of the church from big business, parachurch organizations, psychology, consumer capitalism, and other modern maladies.* Grand Rapids: Baker Books, 2005.

Fleming, Bruce. *Contextualization of Theology: An Evangelical Assessment.* Pasadena: William Carey Library, 1980.

Frangipane, Francis. *The Three Battlegrounds.* Cedar Rapids, IA: Arrow Publications, 2002.

Fuller, Harold. *Mission Church Dynamics.* Pasadena, CA: William Carey Library, 1980.

Galbraith, Michael. *Mentoring: New Strategies and Challenges.* San Francisco, CA: Jossey-Bass, 1995.

Garrison, David. *Church Planting Movements.* Richmond, VA: International Mission Board of the Southern Baptist Convention, 2000.

Hadidian, Allen. *Successful Discipling.* Chicago: Moody Press, 1979.

Harley, David. *Preparing to Serve.* Pasadena, CA: William Carey Library, 1995.

Hendrichson, Walter A. *Disciples are Made—Not Born*. Wheaton: Victor Books, 1983.

Hesselgrave, David J. *Communicating Christ Cross-Culturally*. Grand Rapids: Zondervan, 1980.

_____. *Planting Churches Cross-Culturally—A Guide for Home and Foreign Missions*. Grand Rapids: Zondervan, 1980.

Hiebert, Paul G. *Anthropological Insights for Missionaries*. Grand Rapids, MI.: Baker Book House, 1985.

_____ and Eloise Hiebert Meneses. *Incarnational Ministry – Planting Churches in Band, Tribal, Peasant, and Urban Societies*. Grand Rapids: Baker Books, 1995.

Hodges, Melvin L. *The Indigenous Church*. Springfield, Missouri: Gospel Publishing House, 1996.

Hoke, Steve and Bill Taylor. *Send Me!* Pasadena, CA: William Carey Library, 1999.

Holy Bible: New International Version. Colorado Springs: International Bible Society, 1973.

Johnstone, Patrick and Jason Mandryk. *Operation World*. Grand Rapids: Zondervan Publishing House, 1993.

Kane, Herbert J. *A Concise History of the Christian World Mission*. Grand Rapids: Baker Book House, 1982.

Knutson, Ruth. "Discipling Individuals in Collectivist Cultures: A Healthy Biblical Tension" D.Miss., Western Seminary, 2001.

Kraft, Charles H. *Anthropology for Christian Witness*. Maryknoll, New York: Orbis Books, 1996.

Kuhne, Gary W. *The Dynamics of Personal Follow-up*. Grand Rapids, MI Zondervan, 1976.

Lewis, Jonathan, ed. *Training for Cross-Cultural Ministries*, Number 2 (May, 2000).

_____. *Working Your Way to the Nations—A Guide to Effective Tentmaking,* 2nd Edition. Downers Grove: InterVarsity Press, 1996.

Lingenfelter, Sherwood and Marvin Mayers. *Agents of Transformation.* MI: Baker Book House, 1996.

_____. *Ministering Cross-culturally.* Grand Rapids: Baker Book House, 1986.

_____. *Transforming Culture.* Grand Rapids: Baker Book House, 1992.

Luzbetek, Louis J. *The Church and Cultures.* Maryknoll, New York: Orbis Books, 1995.

Mangelwadi, Vishal and Ruth. *The Legacy of William Carey.* Wheaton: Crossway Books, 1993.

Martin, Robert W. *Mentoring Guidelines for Church Planters*, 2nd Ed. Budapest, Hungary: The Alliance for Saturation Church Planting, 1998.

Mayers, Marvin K. *Christianity Confronts Culture.* Grand Rapids: Zondervan, 1987.

Maxwell, John C. *Developing the Leaders Around You.* Nashville, TN: Thomas Nelson, Inc. 1995.

McLeish, Alexander. "The Effective Missionary" in Sidney J.W. Clark. *The Indigenous Church.* London: World Dominion Press, 1928.

Montoya, Alex D. *Hispanic Ministry in North America.* Grand Rapids: Zondervan, 1987.

Moore, Waylon B. *Multiplying Disciples: The NT Method for Church Growth.* Colorado Springs, CO: Nav Press, 1981.

Moreau, A. Scott, ed. *Evangelical Dictionary of World Missions.* Grand Rapids: Baker Book House, 2000.

Murray, Andrew. *Humility.* Minneapolis: Bethany House, 2001.

Neumann, Mikel. *How to Reach Your City with Cell Groups.* Pasadena: William Carey Library, 1999.

Nida, Eugene A. *Customs and Cultures.* Pasadena: William Carey Library, 1975.

_____. "The Indigenous Church in Latin America." *Practical Anthropology* 8 (May-June 1961).

_____. *Understanding Latin Americans.* Pasadena: William Carey Library, 1974.

Nuñez C., Emilio A. and William D. Taylor. *Crisis in Latin America—An Evangelical Perspective.* Chicago: Moody Press, 1989.

O'Connor, Patrick. *Crossing The Line—A "Know, Be, Do" Approach to Ministry in Latin America.* Guatemala City: Impresos Cristianos, 2002.

_____, ed. *Preparación y Movilizació,* Vol. 1 - 9. Guatemala City: Impresos Cristianos, 2000.

_____. *White Unto Harvest—Triumph and Tragedy in Central America.* Portland, OR: Enable! Media, 2001.

Ott, Craig. "Matching the Church Planter's Role with the Church Planting Model." *Evangelical Missions Quarterly*, July 2001.

Parks, Sharon. *Big Questions, Worthy Dreams.* San Francisco, CA: Jossey-Bass, 2000.

Paton, David MacDonald. *Christian Missions & The Judgment of God.* Grand Rapids: Eerdmans. 2nd Edition, 1996.

Patterson, George and Galen Currah. "Come, Let Us Disciple the Nations." An interactive missionary training course downloaded from www.AcquireWisdom.com.

Patterson, George. *Obedience-oriented Education.* Cucamonga: Church Planting International, 1976.

_____. *Train and Multiply.* Viña del Mar, Chile: SEAN, 1990.

_____ and Richard Scoggins. *Church Multiplication Guide: Helping Churches to Reproduce Locally and Abroad.* Pasadena: William Carey Library, 1993.

Reed, Lyman E. *Preparing Missionaries for Intercultural Communication.* Pasadena: William Carey Library, 1985.

Richard, H. L. *Following Jesus in the Hindu Context.* Pasadena: William Carey Library, 1998.

Roelofs, Dan. *A Place Called Surrender.* Minneapolis: One Passions Publishing, 2002.

Saint, Steve. *The Great Omission—Fulfilling Christ's Commission is Possible If....* Seattle: YWAM Publishing, 2001.

Schwarz, Christian A. *Natural Church Development: A Guide to Eight Essential Qualities of Healthy Churches.* Carol Stream: Church Smart Resources, 1996.

Sinetar, Marsha. *The Mentor's Spirit.* New York: St. Martin's Press, 1998.

Smalley, William A., ed. *Readings in Missionary Anthropology.* Tarrytown: Practical Anthropology, 1967.

Smith, Donald K. *Creating Understanding, A Handbook for Christian Communication Across Cultural Landscapes.* Grand Rapids: Zondervan Publishing House, 1992.

_____. *Make Haste Slowly.* Portland, CA: Institute for International Christian Communication, 1984.

Steffen, Tom. *Passing the Baton.* La Habra, CA: Center for Organizational and Ministry Development, 1997.

Subbamma, B.V. *New Patterns for Discipling Hindus.* Pasadena: William Carey Library, 1970).

Swartz, Glenn. "How Missionary Attitudes Can Create Dependency." *Mission Frontiers,* Sept 1998.

Taylor, William D. and Jon Lewis, eds. *Too Valuable To Lose.* Pasadena: William Carey Library, 1997.

The Alliance for Saturation Church Planting. *Essential Vision.* Crete: The Bible League, 2000.

Trent, John. *Go the Distance.* Colorado Springs, CO: Focus on the Family Publishing, 1996.

Welliver, Dotsey and Minnette Northcutt, eds. *Mission Handbook— U.S. and Canadian Protestant Ministries Overseas 2004-*

2006 (19th Edition). Wheaten: Evangelism and Missions Information Service, 2004.

Winter, Ralph, ed. *Theological Education by Extension.* Pasadena: William Carey Library, 1969.

_____ and Steven C. Hawthorne, eds. *Perspectives on the World Christian Movement—A Reader.* Pasadena: William Carey Library, 1981.

About the Author

O'Connor and Patterson in New Delhi, March 2005

George Patterson and his wife, Denny, have ministered cross-culturally since the early 1960s. For more than 20 years they served in northern Honduras, sparking into life a movement of new churches through what Patterson coined theological education and evangelism by extension (TEEE). Since the mid-1980s Patterson has mentored missionaries internationally and consulted with church planting movements. He is the author of *Church Multiplication Guide*, *Train & Multiply*®, and *Obedience-Oriented Education*. He also co-authors the *Paul-Timothy* studies and the *MentorNet.ws* newsletter. The Pattersons presently reside in Sebring, Florida.

Patrick O'Connor and his wife, Deborah, pursuing their passion for mobilizing others, have served as missionaries since 1989 and currently serve in Honduras. O'Connor came to Christ at the University of Houston, graduated from Moody Bible Institute, completed Denver Seminary's MDiv degree in church planting, and earned his DMiss degree at Western Seminary. He is the author of *White Unto Harvest* and *Crossing the Line*. He also compiled and edited the nine-volumes of *Preparación y Movilización*, pastoral training manuals freely available from <http://preparacionymovili-zacion.ws>. Write to oconnor77056@yahoo.com.